THE PEACE
OF PARIS
1763

THE PEACE OF PARIS

1763

by

ZENAB ESMAT RASHED, B.A., Ph.D.

Lecturer in Modern History
Ibrahim Pasha University, Cairo

WITH A FOREWORD

by

MARK A. THOMSON

Professor of Modern History
The University of Liverpool

LIVERPOOL

AT THE UNIVERSITY PRESS

1951

*Printed in Monotype Perpetua 12 point by C Tinling and Co Ltd
of Liverpool London and Prescot for the University Press of Liverpool
and published 1951 by the University Press of Liverpool*

PREFACE

THIS investigation was undertaken because it appeared that historians generally had neglected the narration of the last stage of the negotiations: that of 1762 carried on through the channel of the two Sardinian Envoys in London and Paris, Viry and Solar, which finally led to the peace. The negotiations of 1761 had been treated in detail in some of the biographies of W. Pitt, Earl of Chatham. However these historians depended mostly on the English sources. There is only Waddington's book *La Guerre de Sept Ans* which could be considered as a valuable and authentic source of this negotiation as well as of the discussions at The Hague which are treated in chapter II and III of the present work. Although this historian used the English as well as the French sources, yet he does not relate the role which Spain played in these negotiations in spite of its importance. It is therefore the aim of this research to give a complete account of these events, particularly regarding the role played by Spain in these negotiations for peace and to throw some new light on different questions on which the writer differs from this historian as well as from others. It was therefore necessary to start this investigation right from the beginning of the negotiations and not only at their latest stage, that of 1762.

The writing of this study was greatly facilitated by the valuable assistance of several persons and organisations and libraries. The writer wishes to acknowledge her indebtedness to Professor Mark A. Thomson, Professor of Modern History at the University of Liverpool, who helped her in the choice of subject and gave most generously of his time in guiding her; his advice and criticism were of the utmost value. She is also particularly grateful for the assistance of Mr. F. J. Routledge of the Modern History Department and Miss M. V. de Lara of the Spanish Department of the University of Liverpool, and of Dr. M. Mahdi Allam of the Semitic Department at the University of Manchester, now Professor of Arabic Literature,

Ibrahim Pasha University, Cairo, and for the useful suggestions
of Professor R. Pares, Professor G. J. Renier, and Dr. R.
Hatton. The writer also wishes to acknowledge her indebtedness to the Egyptian Ministry of Education and particularly
to Professor M. Shafik Bey Gorbal, now Under-Secretary
to this Ministry, as well as Dr. Hosam El Din, the
Director of the Egyptian Education Bureau, London, for
providing funds for studies in England, and visits to the French
archives, and the acquisition of photostats of the valuable copy
of the Viri-Solar Correspondence from the Clements Library
at Ann Arbor, Michigan, and other photostats from the
National Historical Archives of Madrid. She would also like to
express her sincere appreciation of the help of the staff of the
different libraries and organisations: of the Cohen Library,
Liverpool; The British Museum; the Public Record Office and
the Institute of Historical Research, London; as well as the
"Bibliothèque des Archives du Ministère des Affaires
Etrangères," the "Archives Nationales," and the "Bibliothèque
Nationale," Paris.

FOREWORD

viii FOREWORD

D R. RASHED's book is the first attempt to tell in detail the story of the making of the Peace of Paris. The Peace of Paris was a major event in the history of both Europe and North America. Like the other great peaces of the eighteenth century it was a negotiated, not a dictated, peace, and the story of the negotiations is well worth telling. That it has not been fully told before may seem strange. Those English historians, however, who have most concerned themselves with the Peace have tended to discuss it in connection either with the career of the elder Pitt or with the policy of George III. But neither a biography of the Great Commoner nor a study of the constitutional position of George III can be a history of the Peace of Paris. French historians have contributed much to our knowledge of various stages and aspects of the negotiations. One of them, indeed, intended to have told the full story. Had Waddington completed his great work, it would not soon have been superseded. But he was unable to complete it, and none of his compatriots has attempted to do what he left undone. Nor has the gap been filled by a Spaniard. Spanish historians have written on the part their country played in the Seven Years War, but though they have told us much that needs to be known, their object has been rather to vindicate the policy of Charles III—sometimes in a rather curious manner—than to give a full account of the peace negotiations.

The task that no European has yet done has now been attempted by an Egyptian scholar. Dr. Rashed, after graduating in her own country, came to Europe to pursue research, and, like many of her compatriots, became an advanced student at the University of Liverpool. The results of her researches are embodied in this book, which is a study, not of an episode in the life of a particular statesman, be he French, Spanish, or English, but of the making of the Peace

of Paris.   In order to explain the genesis of the final settlement she has very rightly given some account of earlier peace
negotiations and of a subject closely connected with them—
the making of the Family Compact.   These matters have already
been discussed by other writers, and Dr. Rashed's debt to
them, particularly to Waddington, is great, as she herself
clearly states.   What she has to say, however, in this part of
her work is not merely a necessary prelude to what follows,
but also offers some interpretations of her own.   I would
especially draw attention to her account of the policy of
Charles III, in the writing of which she has made use of a
document previously wholly or partly neglected, the instructions to Grimaldi.   It is indeed one of the characteristics
of Dr. Rashed's book that she is ready to draw conclusions
from the evidence she has collected.   Her readers will notice
that she always gives reasons for, as well as references in support
of, her opinions, and that her opinions do explain the events
she describes, even though it be granted that alternative
explanations are sometimes possible.   Moreover, Dr. Rashed
has been exempt from a temptation to which some European
historians have partly succumbed.   She has not identified the
interests of Britain or France or Spain with the dictates of
the moral law.   She does not think either France or Spain
was moved to conclude the Family Compact by disinterested
motives.   What she says about Choiseul's duplicity in 1761
is notable; the interaction of the two concurrent negotiations,
that between France and Spain and that between France and
Britain, is for the first time made clear.   British readers may
be rather surprised at her treatment of Pitt's policy, which,
she argues, not only inspired Spain with a not irrational fear
of British aggression, but also was such as to make peace with
France impossible.   Had Pitt been reasonable, Dr. Rashed
contends, peace could have been made in 1761.   This con-
tention, I would add, has a bearing on a subject with which
she is not directly concerned. Much has been written about
the constitutional propriety of George III's behaviour.   It
is certain that in 1761 he adopted a course of action that,
given Pitt's character, compelled Pitt to resign.   What is

not always realised is that Pitt wanted Britain to stick to a policy that would have made peace almost impossible. Had George backed him, he might have been able to remain in office, but some of his colleagues would probably have resigned, either forthwith or very soon. The King had to come down in favour of Pitt's policy, or of a more moderate policy. In the then circumstances he could not remain neutral. But whichever policy he backed he was pretty certain to be criticized by the supporters of the other.

On these and many other interesting points Dr. Rashed has shed new light. But her book is far more than a discussion of isolated points of interest. It is a narrative and discussion of a complicated series of events as a whole, and it is just because she sees her subject as a whole that her treatment of the several parts is illuminating.

MARK A. THOMSON.

TABLE OF CONTENTS

CHAPTER I

THE EVOLUTION OF WAR AIMS

THE Seven Years' War was an episode in the struggle between England and France for supremacy in the two worlds during the eighteenth century, throughout which the rivalry between the two countries, though occasionally suspended, was never abandoned. They both aimed at gaining supremacy in America, and in the West Indies, and at obtaining the biggest share in commercial relations with the Spanish Empire.

In its origin the Seven Years' War was not a European war; it was a war between England and France on colonial questions with which the rest of Europe had nothing to do; but the alliances and enmities of England and France in Europe, joined to the fact that the King of England was also Elector of Hanover, made it almost certain that a war between England and France must spread to the Continent.[1] The origin of the war was the struggle between the two countries for America. Only an acquaintance with the position of the two belligerent countries in the disputed colonies could enable us to understand the circumstances and the causes which gave rise to the war. At that time, France held Canada, with Isle Royale, or Cape Breton Island, and Louisiana. The strength of these wide dominions lay in a small number of military stations: Louisburg on Cape Breton, Quebec, Montreal, Fort Ticonderoga, Fort Niagara, New Orleans. Outside of these there was no real occupation. England, with a far more numerous body of colonists, held the New England colonies. Moreover, she had obtained by the Treaty of Utrecht the entire possession of the disputed Newfoundland, and the cession of Acadia or Nova Scotia "according to its ancient limits." [2] These limits had never

[1] It was Frederick the Great, by his unexpected attack on Saxony in the last days of August 1756, that started the Seven Year's War in Europe, Waddington, *Louis XV et le Renversement des Alliances*, 498.

[2] Ropes, "The Causes of the Seven Years' War", *R.H.S.T.*, New Series, IV, 148.

been defined by common consent, and their determination was left to commissaries appointed by the two countries, who conferred in Paris from 1750,[1] but did not succeed in reaching any agreement. The French and English propositions, on the American boundary, were in fact incompatible. In the view of the English Government, the "ancient limits" of Acadia included not only the peninsula of Nova Scotia but also twenty leagues of the coast on the mainland. Further, the St. Lawrence and the great lakes were to be regarded as the Southern frontier of Canada. As to the French views on the subject, they were summed up in Rouillé's letter to Mirepoix, the French ambassador in London, of April 13th 1755. In this letter, which was a sort of ultimatum, France declared that Acadia did not include even all the peninsula, the northern part being necessary for communication between Quebec and Louisberg; that the St. Lawrence was in the heart of Canada, not on its border. The strategic position on the East coast was extremely dangerous, since Nova Scotia threatened Louisburg and was in its turn hemmed in by two French settlements.[2]

However, the crisis was in fact brought about by the contest of the Ohio Valley and not by the Acadian boundary which gave rise only to intermittent fightings. In that region, as the distance between the two countries' colonial settlements diminished, the occasions of conflict multiplied.[3] Having made themselves masters of the Canadian colonies on the St. Lawrence, and of Louisiana on the Mississippi, the two Northern and Southern colonies of America, the French aimed at connecting them by a chain of forts along Lake Champlain, the Ohio, and the Mississippi. This procedure by the French presented a menace to the English colonists, who, with that encircling chain, would not be able to extend their possessions beyond it. It was quite natural, therefore, that they aimed at hindering that attempt and confining the French to the sea with

[1] Waddington, *op. cit.*, 52.

[2] Ropes, "The Causes of the Seven Years' War", *R.H.S.T.*, New Series, IV 149-150.

[3] Ruville, 11, 17; "two nations were encamped against one another in North America. There was room for one only." Hotblack, "The Peace of Paris 1763", *R.H.S.T.*, Series 3, II, 238.

the Alleghenies as boundaries.[1] Since the Peace of Aix-la-Chapelle, owing to the unity of the French colonies under the capable Governors General La Galissonière, La Jonquière, and Duquesne successively,[2] the French were more successful in pursuing their object, for these energetic governors made excellent use of their time, and succeeded in building several forts stretching from the St. Lawrence along the shores of Erie and Ontario to Chicago.[3] Their enterprises were facilitated by the extreme ignorance in which the English Cabinet had kept herself of the affairs of America.[4] Meanwhile the British Colonists separated in small units "long injured, long neglected, long forgotten"[5] by their government at home, were not able to oppose seriously the French in their designs; whereas the French settlers received encouragement and protection from their Government, the British settlers could only rely for the protection of their interests on private companies, of which the Ohio Company provided at that time the chief opposition to French ambitions for the exploitation of the interior of the continent.[6]

It must be also added that the one great English gain, during the war of the Austrian succession, the capture of Louisburg, chiefly the work of the New-Englanders themselves, was restored again to France as a compensation for the French conquests in the Netherlands.[7] Thus there was everything to give rise to a fresh conflict.

Such then was the situation in America between the British and the French colonists which the unsuccessful negotiations, in Paris, for the settlement of the boundaries had failed to rectify,[8] when Braddock with his two regiments, on their

[1] See Williams, 1, 251.

[2] La Galissonière died in 1749, was succeeded by La Jonquière till 1752; Duquesne succeeded him. It was under the latter's governorship that war broke out, Ruville, II, 17.

[3] Ruville, 11, 15.

[4] *Memoirs of George II*, 1, 396, "it would not be credited what reams of papers, representations, memorials, petitions, from that quarter of the world lay mouldering and unopened in . . . office." *Ibid.*, 1, 396.

[5] *Ibid.*, 11, 56.   [6] Williams, 1, 252.   [7] Corbett, 1, 18.

[8] These negotiations were going on till the rupture of the relations in July 1755, Waddington, *Louis XV et le Renversement des Alliances*, 52.

march to drive the French from Fort Duquesne was defeated
and killed,[1] and when later on the news of Boscawen's capture
of the two French ships the *Alcide* and the *Lys* in the Newfoundland waters was announced in London.[2] On this hostile
action, Mirepoix, the French ambassador left London without
taking leave,[3] and thus "broke off diplomatic relations," but a
declaration of war was not made for another year.[4] It would
therefore appear that the real causes of the war had been
accumulating for a considerable time round the dispute about
the undefined boundaries, and culminated in the contest of
the Ohio, while the immediate cause which set the war going
was the seizure of the *Alcide* and the *Lys*. England, realising
the danger of the increasing power of France in America, which
danger threatened her colonies,[5] fought the war for "the
succour and preservation of America." [6] In other words, it was
the English Government's aim to make the British settlers
position in America secure. This security necessitated the
definition of the lines of frontiers between the two countries'
possessions in America.

From all the evidence available, it appears that neither
England nor France was either ready or eager to go to war.[7]
On the one hand, the English showed their pacific spirit by
their failure to resist the series of aggressive acts in which the
French Governors in America engaged after the peace of
Aix-la-Chapelle,[8] and by their indifference to the numerous
representations, petitions from that part of the world which
were not even sometimes opened.[9] However, even when the

---

[1] For details on this fight, see Williams, 1, 261.

[2] They reached London July 15th 1755, *Memoirs of George II*, 11, 27.

[3] *Ibid.*, 11, 28.   [4] Williams, 1, 261.

[5] *Ibid.*, 1, 289, King's Speech of December 2nd 1756, with which Pitt inaugurated
his first ministry.

[6] *Parliamentary History of England*, XV, 772. See King's speech on opening the
session on December 2nd 1756.

[7] *Memoirs of George II*, 11, 22-23; Robertson, 52: "Neither in London nor in
Versailles did the governments want another war"; for France's desire to avoid war
see Waddington, *Louis XV et le Renversement des Alliances*, 97.

[8] See Williams, 1, 251-252.

[9] *Memoirs of George II*, 1, 396, see *supra*, p. 3, footnote 4.

moment came and it was quite impossible, for the protection of the New Englanders, not to interfere, and Boscawen was dispatched to America, the English did not think then that their endeavours to push the French back from what they considered their rightful territory, would necessarily involve them in a war against France,[1] and thus the Duke of Newcastle recommended his ambassador in Paris

"to give such a turn to these defensive measures as may make the French Ministers ashamed to complain of them".[2]

On the other hand, the French ministers, uncertain of what they wanted, encouraged the hostile enterprises of their Governors of Canada, not suspecting that they were, by such a conduct, compromising the peace of Europe.[3] Neither of the two countries was then ready to go to war, and thus in spite of Boscawen's seizure of the French ships in June 1755, the two countries for the time being remained at peace. In April 1755 indeed, Frederick the Great described the French Ministers, in their weak attitude towards the English, as "men made of cotton." [4] But as the relations between the two countries worsened, their attitude towards war changed until there came a time when France, whilst only a few months before was avoiding going to war with England, sent her "requisitoire"[5] (January 17th 1756), which was in effect an ultimatum. This, after protesting against the offensive measures of Braddock and Boscawen, and referring to the seizure of several French ships as acts of "piracy," demanded a restoration of these prizes as a preliminary step to a reconciliation between the two countries.

"Mais si, contre toute esperance, le roi d'Angleterre se refuse à la requisition que le Roi lui fait, Sa Majesté regardera ce deni de justice comme la déclaration de guerre la plus authentique".[6]

---

[1] Corbett, I, 26.   [2] Ibid., I, 27.

[3] Jobez, IV, 458; see also Memoirs of George II, II, 22.

[4] Pol. Corr., XI, 119, Frederick to Knyphausen (the Prussian Ambassador in London), April 12th 1755; see also his remarks to the same, on August 9th 1755, Ibid., 240-241.

[5] A copy of this declaration is in Memoires du Duc de Luynes, XIV, 393-394.

[6] Ibid., XIV, 394.

It was now plain that war was inevitable. The English would not grant France any concessions in her claims, neither were the French prepared to yield to England on any point. Having received no satisfaction on her demands,[1] France attacked Minorca at the end of April,[2] and consequently England declared war against France on May 18th 1756.[3] The French declaration of war on England followed on June 9th.[4] These declarations give the reasons of each country for going to war: England blamed France for her usurpations and attacks in the West Indies and in America, since the peace of Aix-la-Chapelle, attacks which were planned by France without taking into consideration "the most solemn treaties and engagements." These attacks of the French in America compelled the English to take "just and necessary" measures for the security of their kingdoms. Thus the seizure by the French of the English fortress on the Ohio was the only reason for which England sent reinforcements for the defence of her subjects and colonies. It was only when the French attacked Minorca, that England realised that they must go to war with France with "the utmost violence." [5] In her declaration of war, France on her part, accused England of having committed aggressions against her possessions in America in 1754, and of violating the terms of the treaties and seizing the French ships. She also accused England of giving France false hopes of an accommodation between the two Courts on American disputes. It was, furthermore, pointed out that France had already stated that a refusal by England to accept the conditions of the "requisitoire" would be considered a declaration of war.[6]

Thus we see that each of the two countries accused the other

[1] See *Memoirs of George II*, 11, 151.

[2] See Williams, 1, 279.

[3] Riker, 1, 431.

[4] See *Mémoires du Duc de Luynes*, XV, 123-125.

[5] For England's declaration of war, see *Gentleman's Magazine*, 1756, XXVI, 237-238.

[6] The French King's Declaration of war is in the *Gentleman's Magazine*, 1756, XXVI, 268-269.

of being the aggressor in America, which aggression each used as a pretext for the dispatch of their respective reinforcements to America.

> "Both nations", said Dr. Johnson, "clamour with great vehemence about infractions of limits, violation of treaties, open usurpation, insidious aritifices, and breach of faith".[1]

It is very difficult to judge which of the two was right; however Johnson's views on this point are very sound:

> "The *English* and *French* may have relative rights, and do injustice to each other, while both are injuring the *Indians*. And such, indeed, is the present contest: they have parted the northern continent of *America* between them, and are now disputing about their boundaries, and each is endeavouring the destruction of the other by the help of the *Indians,* whose interest it is that both should be destroyed". [2]

The West Indies was another region where the English and the French were rivals, and where their rivalry was purely commercial.[3] The West Indian colonies of France were richer than those of England: whereas the latter possessed Barbadoes and some of the north western smaller islands, the former owned the important possessions of Martinique and the western part of St. Domingo, as well as Grenada, Guadeloupe and Marie Galante. Besides, the French founded, without any serious opposition from the English colonists, many settlements in the various neutral islands: Dominica, St. Lucia, Tobago, and St. Vincent.[4] The reason why England did not pay much heed to French rivalry in this domain, not even by expanding her own possessions in the Islands, was that the English sugar planters, who feared that sugar prices could be decreased, were against any colonial expansion in the West Indies.[5]

[1] Johnson, *Works*, 11, 340.

[2] *Ibid.*, 11, 340.

[3] The French Colonists had there substantial advantages over their rivals, see Hotblack, *Chatham's Colonial Policy*, 55-56.

[4] Ruville, 11, 18-19; there is a good map showing these various places in the West Indies at the end of Pares' *Colonial Blockade and Neutral Rights.*

[5] There was another party who did not hold the same opinion, see Hotblack, *Chatham's Colonial Policy*, 18-19; see also Pares, *War and Trade in the West Indies*, 77-85.

As to the East Indies their rivalry was less keen,[1] and the French and the English interests were left to companies.[2]

The question of settling the frontiers between the British and the French possessions in America, which was the "limited object" of the war,[3] was soon to be "forgotten in the vision of much larger acquisitions."[4] In other words, this limited aim lost, as time went on, its limitations and expanded into more ambitious aims which translated themselves into further conquests in America, in the West Indies, and even in Africa. We shall follow now this development of the aim of the war, and see how the English appetite for conquests was growing as long as their victories continued. It cannot be said that the prospects of the war, during its earliest stages, were particularly promising for England. Indeed it started with a considerable disaster, namely the loss of Minorca.[5] The magnitude of this disaster can easily be assessed from the words of the Duke of Newcastle to the Chancellor, the Earl of Hardwicke, "till there can be some Prospect of Peace; Some Scheme, or Measure of *Offence and Attack*, . . . we shall be absolutely ruined."[6] No improvement in the situation took place in the following year. The outlook was very gloomy,[7] and public opinion [8] in England was more despondent, because of the many disasters which were reported within a short space of time.[9] At the same time "in the West Indies and America the French were superior at sea."[10] The position of England was so desperate that Pitt sought an alliance with Spain, and to obtain

[1] Ruville, 11, 20.

[2] For more details on the position of France and England in the East Indies see *ibid.*, 11, 20-25.

[3] See Corbett, 1, 28.

[4] Alvord, 1, 49.

[5] Ruville, 11, 27.

[6] B.M., Add. MSS., 32866, f210v, Newcastle to Hardwicke, July 19th 1756; an account of the disaster of Minorca reached London, on July 14th 1756, Thackeray, 1, 259.

[7] "a gloomy scene for this distressed, disgraced country", is Pitt's phrase, describing the state of affairs, in June 1757, Williams, 1, 337.

[8] The expression "public opinion" is used in this book with reference solely to the opinion of the politically conscious minority which read newspapers and pamphlets.

[9] Ruville, 11, 159.

[10] Williams, 1, 337.

it, he offered not only concessions for the disputes on the logwood cutting in the Honduras, but even Gibraltar in exchange for Minorca, which was to be recovered with the help of Spain.[1] But Ferdinand VI of Spain, who believed that neutrality was the best policy for Spain to follow in the struggle between France and England, refused Pitt's offers.[2]

No one could have ventured to predict that within two years, the position of England would be so completely altered; that the genius of one man could so utterly change the situation and gain for England so many victories in such a limited time. Yet such was the work of Pitt, which was crowned by several victories. Fort Duquesne, the dangerous spear point, which threatened the frontiers of the Southern British colonies, fell into General Forbes' hands on November 26th 1758.[3] By the recovery of this fort "the ostensible cause of the war" was removed; thus the French aim to exclude the English from the Ohio failed.[4] But naturally Pitt was not to be satisfied with the fulfilment of this very limited object. Even prior to that when Louisburg was captured (on July 28th 1758), and when as a result of this victory and owing to financial difficulties (which were usually exaggerated by Newcastle), the latter suggested making peace and the exchange of Louisburg for Minorca, Pitt, aiming already at expelling the French from North America and on the look-out for other conquests to be offered later, as a compensation for Minorca, declared to the Duke of Newcastle:

"The only way to have peace is to prepare for war"[5]

Thus by the end of 1758, England's aims for the continuation of war revealed themselves in the words of King George II:

"We must keep Cape Breton, take Canada, drive the French out of America . . . we must conquer Martinique as a set-off to Minorca".[6]

---

[1] *Ibid*, 1, 248-249, Pitt to Keene (the English Ambassador in Madrid), August 23rd 1757 (most secret and confidential dispatch).

[2] See Collado, 11, 102-105; see also *Chatham's Correspondence*, 1, 274, Keene to Pitt, September 26th 1757.

[3] See Williams, 1, 374-375.

[4] *Ibid.*, 1, 376.   [5] Williams, 1, 379.   [6] *Ibid.*, 1, 379-380.

Her position was strengthened by more victories: Goree was captured by the end of 1758, Guadeloupe and Marie-Galante surrendered in the summer of 1759.[1] As the campaign for the conquest of Martinique failed, Guadeloupe had to take its place in the intended exchange for Minorca. Notwithstanding its economic assets Guadeloupe was to Pitt more valuable as a bargaining counter for Minorca by means of which he could avoid giving up the conquests made in Canada.[2] It should be pointed out, here, that the conquest of Canada in 1759 and 1760 put an end to the colonial phase of the war by deciding the territorial question between the two countries, and that, accordingly, there should be no reason for further postponing the efforts to bring about peace.[3] In fact the war which had started with a limited objective, the Anglo-French issue in North America, had changed its character, and become, as big wars always do, a war with unlimited objectives.[4] The English appetite was growing every day, and rendering the task of making peace more and more difficult. In 1760, there still seemed to be some moderation in the intended demands of England from France,[5] when Pitt declared in the House of Commons that

"Some are for keeping Canada; some Guadaloupe, who will tell me which I shall be hanged for not keeping?"[6]

In the following year, 1761, owing to the most advantageous position of England and her victories in all parts of the world, this moderation gave way to a stiffening attitude and making peace became a most difficult task. It was not easy to make a sufficiently brilliant peace to meet the ambitions of the supporters of imperial expansion.[7] Two years before, when the news of British victories started to follow in rapid succession,

[1] Ibid., 11, 1-2.

[2] Ibid., 11, 2.

[3] Alvord, 1, 47.

[4] Robertson, 97.

[5] Beer, 133, states that Pitt recognised then that he could not retain all the English conquests.

[6] Memoirs of George III, 1, 26.

[7] Alvord, 1, 48.

Pitt had already foreseen this difficulty when he wrote to Hardwicke: "Peace will be as hard to make as war."[1] Pitt was anxious to turn that unusually advantageous position of his country to the utmost advantage and to secure for England "all territorial acquisitions now in military occupation." [2] Thus during his negotiations for peace with France in 1761, he conquered Belleisle, in order that it might serve as a compensation for Minorca, instead of Guadeloupe which he now considered to be as valuable to England as Martinique and St. Lucia (which were conquered in the following year), as he pointed out in his speech on the preliminary articles of peace.[3] All these islands, he considered as necessary for the security of the English colonies both in the West Indies and the mainland of America; as they are important for the prosperity of the English commerce, as well as a great blow to the commercial and naval strength of the enemy.[4] This last consideration in the importance of these islands leads to the most important aim in Pitt's policy of peace or war with France and consequently to the important place which the fisheries had occupied in his negotiations of peace with France in 1761.[5] It must be noted here that Pitt's views on the nature of peace which England should have with France were not the only ones. Although Pitt's views were in conformity with the public opinion then,[6] yet none of his colleagues, save Temple, in the English Cabinet, shared Pitt's uncompromising views as regards the peace with France. Bedford held fundamentally different views from Pitt about the question of the fisheries as well as on the colonial possessions, and was reported to desire peace at any price. Bute and Newcastle were also anxious to restore peace to England, even if it meant

[1] Williams, 11, 74.

[2] Ruville, 11, 365.

[3] See *Parliamentary History of England*, XV, 1264-1266.

[4] *Ibid.*, 1265-1266.

[5] Pitt's policy of peace with France and the question of fisheries is fully discussed in Chapter III.

[6] For views of public opinion in England on the question of peace, see Chapter III, pp. 68-69.

making certain sacrifices to secure it.[1] In 1761, while in office, Newcastle differed from Pitt even more than Bute or any other member of the Council with the exception of Bedford. Professor Namier was right when he stated that "Newcastle's pacifism went the length of *defaitisme*", when the latter wrote in his "Memorandums" on August 20th:

"The victories hurt us as they make the peace more difficult"

However he soon forgot these sentiments on the capture of Havannah, when he was no longer in office.[2]

While there are numerous sources on the English aims of the war, information on the French side is remarkably scanty, the only available source being a document entitled "Projet de Conduite dans la Situation Presente des Affaires relativement à l'Angleterre", dated March 23rd 1755.[3] But what is lacking in quantity is compensated for by quality, as it is a clear and lucid document. Its importance lies not only in its clarity but also in the fact that it shows how France, even before the commencement of the war, predicted not only England's declared aims but, significantly enough, those aims which we call in this chapter the developed aims which England conceived and at any rate declared at a later stage of the struggle. This document points out that England intended to obtain a supremacy at sea and to destroy France completely by seizing her colonies and depriving her of her commerce. The French, therefore, realised from the outset that they were to fight that war, not only in order to defend their possessions in America, but also for a more vital aim, which was to save their country from the dangerous designs of England, and their colonies and commerce from being taken away from them. Moreover, it is remarkable to observe that at that time France should so realistically assess her weak maritime position in a war against England and predict her losses in that field of war, and even plan the way of restoring them. The maritime war would inevitably lead to war on land. The English successes on sea

[1] For more details on the different views, see Chapter III, pp. 65-68.
[2] Namier, 339, 342.
[3] A.E., M.D., Angleterre, 41, ff. 1-12.

would be compensated by the successes which France could procure on land. In the event of war the French had to be prepared that, as soon as English hostilities broke against their navy or overseas settlements, they should attack her in her most sensitive spot: to seize the Netherlands[1]; to subjugate Holland which should no longer be considered an English province, and whose occupation would be very detrimental to the interests of England; to make preparations for a landing in England, which in view of the fear of the Pretender, would keep the English troops at home; to send an expedition to Hanover.[2] This document appears to have been in the nature of a definite plan, yet owing to the important alterations in the European relations, known as the "Diplomatic Revolution", and the treaty of Versailles between France and Austria in May of the next year, this plan was not wholly put into effect; in the stipulations of the alliance between France and Austria, the former country was, naturally, to abstain from all attacks on the Netherlands or other territories of Maria Theresa.[3] Neither was France successful in her war plans: her only military acquisition during this war was Minorca, which was conquered at the very beginning of the war, and which island Pitt considered a sufficient equivalent to the English conquest of Belleisle. Her desperate military and financial position, which did not change much throughout the war, made the leader of her foreign policy, the Duke of Choiseul,[4] resign himself to seeking an honourable peace for his humiliated country; yet this aim was very hard to achieve because, while the British had been victorious in practically all the fields of war, France was succumbing under the weight of her disasters during the war. Nevertheless the Duke of Choiseul continued his efforts to stave off a greater disaster by bringing about the peace he desired and also by a new alliance.

[1] The diplomatic Revolution and the Franco-Austrian alliance in May of the next year made the seizure of the Netherlands impossible.

[2] *Ibid.*, Angleterre, 41, ff. 4v.-5r.

[3] Lodge, 86-87.

[4] He assumed the office of foreign minister in December 1758. Williams, 1, 386.

How far the aims of England and France were realised by the definitive treaty of peace is stated in the conclusion.

By the summer of 1755, war between England and France was inevitable, and its outbreak was only delayed by the unpreparedness of both countries. War was certain but few doubted that it would spread to the Continent. England, superior at sea, was vulnerable through her continental allies and still more through the Electorate of Hanover. France, therefore, could use her great superiority on land to gain advantages which, as in 1748, might be exchanged for colonial possessions. She would again reconquer Louisburg in the Netherlands or in Hanover. In this danger, England relied on the co-operation of Austria, Holland and a subsidised Russian Army.[1] It was, therefore, very natural that England sought a revival of her alliances with Austria and Holland (of the so called "system").[2] The negotiations with Austria which was "the cornerstone"[3] of the old system, did not achieve any results till the end of July 1755.[4] Although the immediate reason of the failure of these negotiations was the rejection of the required subsidies for this alliance by the English Parliament,[5] yet the principal reasons lay in the change in the policy of the Empress Queen of Austria and of her Chancellor, Kaunitz, who, not wishing to offer a direct refusal to the English Government, evaded the demand by attaching to their consent such burdensome conditions that the maritime powers could not possibly accept. As to the change in the Austrian policy,[6] it was due to the fact that both the Empress-Queen and her Chancellor came to the momentous conclusions that Prussia was a more formidable enemy to Austria than France, and that Prussia could not be reduced to harmlessness

[1] Ropes, "The Causes of the Seven Years' War", R.H.S.T., New Series, IV, 152.

[2] For the reasons why this system seemed to be the natural and necessary balance of Europe, see Lodge, 75.

[3] Ibid., 82.

[4] Waddington, "Le Renversement des Alliances en 1756", R.H., LVII, 2.

[5] Ibid., 4.

[6] Kaunitz thought that it was a necessary change in the Austrian policy, Boutaric, I, 71-72.

THE EVOLUTION OF WAR AIMS

unless Austria could obtain the assistance of France. They realised that, if in the present circumstances, they supplied Great Britain with the desired backing in the Netherlands, they must abandon all their dreams of gaining the alliance of France, and this they were not prepared to do; thus "the corner-stone of the old system had fallen away." England also sought an alliance with Russia, who could be as dangerous to east Prussia as the latter country was to Hanover, and could thus prevent Frederick the Great from concentrating his forces against Hanover. H. Williams, the English ambassador to Russia, succeeded in concluding with Russia the treaty of September 30th 1755. England resorted, at the same time, to a third expedient which was the renewal of the subsidy treaties with the German Princes, in order to enable her to ask for an army, wherever she should need it.[1] On June 18th, she concluded a treaty with Hess-Cassel for 8,000 men.[2]

The English statesmen, completely defeated in their efforts to employ the old "system" against France, were in perplexity in the autumn of 1755. They were very pre-occupied by the difficulty of reconciling the necessity of defending the Electoral States of their King with the growing opposition of public opinion against war on the Continent and the expenses which it required.[3] The Hessians might be useful, but they could hardly be regarded as an army. Besides they might be needed for the defence of Britain. Furthermore the Russian Treaty was not yet ratified. Consequently, it was obvious that Hanover could not be protected as things then stood. This difficulty with which the English statesmen were confronted, explains their satisfaction with the friendly and accommodating disposition of the King of Prussia.[4] If the neutrality of Frederick could be guaranteed, it would be an economic and popular means for the protecting of the Electorate and would be considered as a diplomatic success of the English government, and would also serve her by restoring her shaken

[1] See Lodge, 80-82.
[2] Eldon, 16.
[3] Waddington, "Le Renversement des Alliances en 1756", R.H., LVIII, 8.
[4] Lodge, 83.

prestige.[1] On the other hand, Frederick, receiving the unexpected overtures from Great Britain,[2] was exultant to find himself "the arbiter courted by both sides" (England and France) in their vital struggle.[3] There was no real hesitation on the side of Frederick in preferring an alliance with England to that with France. In 1755 he realised that France wanted his help in a war whose results were doubtful, whereas England wanted his assistance in excluding the war from Germany and could offer him, so he thought, security on the side of Russia, his most menacing enemy.[4] Negotiations between the two Courts went on for nearly six months,[5] till the Westminster treaty was signed on January 16th 1756. Both England and Prussia declared their resolution to keep peace in Germany, and to oppose the entrance or the passage of all foreign troops in the Empire. A reciprocal guarantee of their mutual possessions was renewed. A secret article excluded the Austrian Netherlands from the stipulated neutrality.[6] However, by his sudden attack on Saxony in the Autumn of 1756, Frederick broke his obligation to Britain, for this attack rendered inevitable the intrusion of French and Russian troops into Germany, and therefore exposed Hanover to the certainty of a French attack. The protection of his central territories against the enemies which he had provoked, made him unable to give efficient assistance for the defence of Hanover and he had even to withdraw his garrison from the fortress of Wesel, the "key of Hanover." The British ministers dared not quarrel with the King of Prussia, who, if he involved them in danger, seemed, at the time, to be the only power which could extricate them.[7] Their failure in forming a

[1] Waddington, "Le Renversement des Alliances en 1756", R.H., LVIII, 8.

[2] Newcastle wrote to Munckhausen, July 23rd 1755, asking for the neutrality of Frederick the Great. Waddington, "Le Renversement des Alliances en 1756", R.H., LVIII, 8.

[3] Lodge, 83, (for his alliance with France did not expire till the next year, ibid., 83).

[4] Lodge, 84 (the reasons for which his decision was different in 1741 are indicated in ibid., 83-84).

[5] For details of these negotiations, see Waddington, op. cit., 9-13.

[6] Ibid., 13.

[7] See Lodge, 94-96.

large league round the Westminster treaty against France,[1]
persuaded them to render their country's alliance with
Frederick more solid by succouring him with military and
financial aid, measures which did not become effective till the
end of 1757.[2]

The news of the Westminster Treaty met with great
dissatisfaction at the Russian Court. It was difficult to reconcile
the Westminster Treaty and the Convention of September
between England and Russia, and particularly the secret
article of this Convention.[3] In January 1757, Russia finally
joined the alliance between Austria and France.[4]

Meanwhile France, isolated by the loss of Spain's alliance
during the reign of Ferdinand VI, and frustrated in her
attempts to gain Russia on her side, was compelled to cling to
the Prussian alliance, in spite of Frederick's infidelities.[5] Just
four days before the Westminster Treaty was signed Nivernais
reached Berlin [6] in order to renew the French treaty with
Prussia which was about to expire. After several conferences
with the Prussian government, he was acquainted on January
27th with the Westminster treaty,[7] but the Court of Versailles
rejected the Prussian offer of a renewal of the alliance between
the two Courts. Thus France became completely isolated, and
had no alternative, if she wanted to come out of her isolation,
but to terminate her traditional quarrel with Austria and to
accept her proposals for a rapprochement between the two
countries.[8] Kaunitz, the Chancellor of the Court of Vienna,
was then the only statesman in Europe who knew exactly what
he wanted. For the reasons already mentioned,[9] his aim was to

[1] The English ministers aimed at forming a large league against France of Prussia,
Austria, Russia, Holland and the Empire, see Waddington, "Le Renversement des
Alliances en 1756", R.H., LVIII, 18.

[2] Ibid., 20.

[3] Waddington explains this point clearly, ibid., 14-15.

[4] Lodge, 85.

[5] Ibid., 75.

[6] Perey, 360. He arrived in Berlin on January 12th 1756.

[7] Waddington, Louis XV et le Renversement des Alliances, 249, 255; for full details
about Nivernais' mission in Prussia, see ibid., 249-264, and also Perey, 353-401.

[8] Lodge, 86.

[9] See supra, pp. 14-15.

create an alliance between his country and France. Already in 1750, in order to serve that purpose, he was appointed ambassador to the Court of Paris. However, he was not able to obtain any appreciable results for the two years he spent in Paris.[1] In the autumn of 1755, the Austrian overtures were renewed and tempting offers regarding the Netherlands were submitted by Starhemberg, the Austrian ambassador. But nothing came of these negotiations, because France still considered herself the ally of Frederick of Prussia, and Prussian co-operation more valuable to her than that of Austria. The treaty of Westminster altered the whole situation. Prussia by her alliance with England, the immortal enemy of France, made the latter country readier to negotiate with Austria.[2] Nevertheless these negotiations did not come to a conclusion till May 1st 1756, when the first of the successive treaties of Versailles was signed by Starhemberg for Austria, and by Rouillé and Bernis on behalf of France. Austria was to remain neutral in the Franco-British war, and France was to abstain from all attacks on the Netherlands or other territories of Austria. Each of the two countries, in case of an attack on her possessions, was to assist the other with 24,000 men. By the Treaty of Versailles the final stage of the diplomatic revolution was completed.[3] These terms indicated that, of the two countries, the Court of Vienna was the power which benefited most. By converting a dangerous enemy into an ally, Austria extricated herself from every fear for the safety of her possessions in the Netherlands; she also recovered her liberty in dealing with the King of Prussia, in whom she not only saw the conqueror of Silesia, but also the future pretender to the imperial crown.[4] By the treaty, France, as regards her war with England, received no advantages. She had to renounce any attempt to occupy the Netherlands, a plan which she always considered valuable when Austria was England's ally as a compensation for the latter's maritime

[1] Waddington, *op. cit.*, 287; Lodge, 80.
[2] Lodge, 86.
[3] See Lodge, 86-87.
[4] Waddington, *op. cit.*, 365.

successes.[1] Furthermore, France, so tied by the stipulations of
her defensive treaty with Austria, had been driven into the
continental conflict, for the very avoidance of which she had
mainly entered into this alliance.[2] Summing up his comments
on the treaty of Versailles, R. Waddington wrote:

"le traité de Versailles, fort avantageux pour le governement de Marie-
Thérèse, fait honneur à la tenacité et à la clairvoyance de Kaunitz aussi
bien qu'aux talents diplomatiques de Starhemberg. Pour la France, il eut
des résultats funestes".[3]

In order to complete the picture of the factors which
determined, at that time, British and French policy, it is
important to indicate their relations with Spain. Their rivalry
in trading with that country and her Empire,[4] complicated by
the prohibitions imposed by the laws of the Indies forbidding
foreigners to trade with the Spanish colonies, started at the
beginning of the seventeenth century. Each of the two
countries then faced a dual task. They had not only to secure
their own participation in the trade of the Spanish Empire, but
each had also to ensure that that trade should not be mono-
polized by the other.[5] England, owing to different reasons[6]
(which do not concern us here), had enjoyed many privileges
in the Spanish markets, which privileges had been offered to
her, being the more industrialised state, by the needs of Spain
as an agricultural and imperial power. Several treaties concluded between the two countries, in the seventeenth century,
provided for England a dominating position in the commercial
life of Spain. Of these treaties the most important was the
treaty of Madrid of 1667 by whose favourable terms freedom
of commerce between the two nations was restored after the
Cromwellian war, and the benefits of the "most favoured
nation" terms were accorded. After the war of the Spanish

[1] Ibid., 368.   [2] Ibid., 369.   [3] Ibid., 371.

[4] In trading with Spain and her Empire, the emphasis from the point of view of
England and France was on gold and silver, Christelow, "Economic Background of the
Anglo-Spanish War of 1762", J.M.H., XVIII, 23.

[5] Christelow, "French Interest in the Spanish Empire during the Ministry of the
Duc de Choiseul 1759-1771", H.A.H.R., XXI, 517.

[6] See McLachlan, Trade and Peace with Old Spain 1667-1750, 6-17; see also Christelow,
"Economic Background of the Anglo-Spanish War of 1762", J.M.H., XVIII, 23.

Succession, whereas the English desired to return to the
conditions existing in the reign of Charles II, the Spaniards
(under Philip V, a prince of the House of Bourbon), backed by
their French ally, insisted on new arrangements. A new treaty
of commerce between England and Spain, made at Utrecht at
the beginning of 1714, represented a triumph for Spanish
diplomacy. However, this treaty did not last long. The Treaty
of Madrid of December 14th 1715, returned to the English
merchants their previous privileged position. In spite of the
Spanish dissatisfaction with this arrangement, it remained the
recognised basis of the Anglo-Spanish Commercial treaties in
Europe, until the outbreak of the war between the two
countries in 1739. The treaty of Aix-la-Chapelle, which
restored peace again, confirmed in its third article the Treaty
of Utrecht but did not mention the arrangement of December
14th 1715. Spain was soon maintaining that the latter agreement was not included and that the commercial relations then
between the two powers rested on that of Utrecht of 1714.
The ensuing discussion between the two countries continued
until the conclusion of the Commercial Treaty of 1750. The
English merchants returned to their privileged position, they
were to pay no other import nor export duties than those paid
in the time of Charles II and the system of valuation, then
existing, was to be left unchanged.[1] Thus, in spite of the
accession of Philip V, a prince of the House of Bourbon, to the
Spanish throne, at the beginning of the eighteenth century,
England, for about a hundred years, covering the second half
of the seventeenth and the first half of the eighteenth century,
enjoyed intermittently a more advantageous position than
France in her trade relations with Spain. The French, however,
claimed most of the rights given by the above mentioned
treaties between England and Spain, on the ground that they

---

[1] Brown, *Studies in the History of Spain in the second half of the Eighteenth Century*,
(Smith College Studies in History, XV), 40-42. In his letter of January 9th 1750 to
Bedford, Keene pointed to the importance of the commercial treaty of 1750 to
England. McLachlan, *Trade and Peace with Old Spain 1667-1750*, 139; H. Temperley in
his foreword to the same book, XI, stated that: "The new treaty gave back to England
the status of 1667 and restored to her all the trade with Old Spain which she had lost
in the War of the Spanish Succession".

were entitled to most-favoured-nation treatment. The Spaniards, however, never admitted the claim, and the meaning attached to most-favoured-nation treatment in the eighteenth century was indeed vague.[1] From the Treaty of Utrecht to the Seven Years' War, France endeavoured to gain privileges for her commercial interests within the Hispanic area; her plan was to strengthen Spain in order that the British and the Dutch would be driven from American waters and that the monopoly of the colonial market should be restored to Spain, who would control it, while France would supply it.[2] It would be out of place here to deal in detail with the Spanish reaction to the attempts of these two rivals to maintain and extend their various rights; nevertheless the picture of this rivalry could scarcely be complete without at least a reference to the Spaniards' desire to abolish rather than to extend these privileges.[3]

Between 1748 and 1756, during the reign of Ferdinand VI, friendship with England was one of the main springs of the Spanish policy, and the period is aptly called by Miss McLachlan "The Seven Years' Peace."[4] At that time, the policy of Carvajal, the Spanish Prime Minister, was based on the fact that Spain was a colonial power and had also a part to play in Europe.[5] He aimed at making her independent and strong through various internal reforms, which necessitated the development of her colonial resources; he realised also that if she was to play an important part in European affairs before his reforms could take effect, she should conclude judicious alliances, and he considered England a valuable ally.[6]

[1] Christelow, "Economic Background of the Anglo-Spanish War of 1762", *J.M.H.*, XVIII, 24.

[2] Christelow, "French Interest in the Spanish Empire during the Ministry of Duc de Choiseul 1759-1771", *H.A.H.R.*, XXI, 519.

[3] Christelow, "Economic Background of the Anglo-Spanish War of 1762", *J.M.H.*, XVIII, 24.

[4] Ferdinand VI assured Keene of his friendship to England by saying to him, "*Con todos pueblos guerra y paz con la Inglaterra*" : "*War with all the world and peace with England*", Guillon, 364, Keene to Bedford, December 8th 1750.

[5] McLachlan, "The Seven Years' Peace and the West Indian Policy of Carvajal and Wall", *E.H.R.*, LIII, 458.

[6] *Ibid.*, 461.

C

Wall succeeded Carvajal in 1754 as Prime Minister; and having been Spanish ambassador in London during the years 1748-1752,[1] he did not differ in his policy from that of his predecessor. He believed that his country should maintain friendly relations with England, that any war could only end in disaster for Spain.[2] In spite of these friendly relations between England and Spain three causes of difference at that time existed between the two countries. These disputes were in connection with the restitution of the Spanish prizes, a question however which was the least important of these disputes. The privilege claimed by the Spaniards of fishing upon the banks of Newfoundland, a claim first advanced in 1758, was one, as Pitt made it clear in his instructions to Bristol (who succeeded Keene at Madrid in 1758), to which England would never yield. The third and the most important question was that of logwood-cutting. This question had long been an issue between the two nations. Under the Treaty of Utrecht, the English had certain rights of logwood-cutting in the Bay of Honduras, but had gradually encroached by settlements in Yucatan and Campeachy Bay in violation of Spanish territory. The point of issue being that whereas the English were prepared to quit their illicit settlements provided Spain would define their rights of logwood-cutting, Spain requested the English to leave these settlements without having defined these rights.[3]

---

[1] *Dictionary of National Biography*, XX, 553.

[2] Christelow, "Economic Background of the Anglo-Spanish War of 1762", *J.M.H.*, XVIII, 22.

[3] See Williams, 11, 104-105. "The controversies of Newfoundland and Honduras played a much larger part in the estrangement of England and Spain, especially after Charles III came to the throne", Pares, *Colonial Blockade and Neutral Rights*, 289.

CHAPTER II

THE HAGUE CONVERSATIONS

In order to appreciate the initiation, the development, and even the failure of the Hague Conversations, it is necessary to survey, if only briefly, the internal situation of the two belligerent countries in addition to their military position.

When in December 1758, Cardinal Bernis retired, and the Duke of Choiseul took over the conduct of Foreign Affairs, France still seemed "the greatest Power in Europe." In the Mediterranean she had Minorca, in America Canada, Louisiana and some of the richest islands of the West Indies, in addition to her prosperous company in India. But with all this imposing aspect, France was in truth very weak.[1] Within about a year, however, she was humbled by several military disasters, lost nearly all her fleet and became financially exhausted.[2] Since the beginning of the war, with the exception of her conquest of Minorca France had been unsuccessful in her military and naval operations: in 1758 she lost Louisburg, Fort Duquesne and Goree. In August 1759, the French fleet commanded by La Clue was beaten near Lagos, and on November 20th the failure of Conflans dissipated any hope of a descent on Scotland.[3] In the same year Guadeloupe and Quebec surrendered to the enemy as well as their settlements in Senegal.

Of all the anxieties of the cabinet of Louis XV, the most serious was the bad state of the finances of the kingdom.[4] The interruption of her commerce, caused by the loss of her colonies, destroyed her credit and led France near to

---

[1] Williams, I, 386, 387.

[2] "France sees Her Ruin at hand, Her Finances drained, Her Armies beaten, Her Fleets diminished", Yorke to Holderness, November 23rd 1759, P.R.O., S.P., F., Holland, 486.

[3] For details of Choiseul's plan of invasion of England, see Williams, I, 407-408.

[4] Waddington, *La Guerre de Sept Ans*, III, 455; a good account of the French finances then, in *ibid.*, III, 456-458; see also Williams, I, 387.

bankruptcy. In his letter to Count of Choiseul (then French ambassador at the Court of Vienna), the Duke of Choiseul confessed the critical financial position of France:

> "Notre crédit qui faisait la grande branche de notre puissance est anéanti, . . . l'on est donc réduit aujourd'hui à agiter dans le conseil, pour payer les troupes au mois de novembre, d'envoyer la vaisselle du Roi et des particuliers à la Monnaie". [1]

In order to save France from this critical situation, the Duke of Choiseul asked Ossun, his ambassador in Spain, to try and impress upon Charles III, the king of Spain, the distress in which France stood so that Spain would lend her twenty millions. [2] Indeed, the Duke of Choiseul placed all his hopes of extricating France from her difficulties in Charles III, as will be indicated later. Such was the financial position of France that even after the several edicts, which Silhouette, the French minister of finance, issued in order to relieve it, there was a danger of lack of funds for the coming campaign. [3] Francis Thackeray did not exaggerate, when he summed up the situation of France towards the conclusion of the year 1759 as "a vanquished army, a ruined navy, a bankrupt nation!" [4]

When the Duke of Choiseul assumed the office of foreign minister, he was aware of the critical military and financial situation of his country, as he often repeated to the Court of Vienna and to his friend Bernstorff, the Danish foreign minister. His career in the service of his country was but a struggle to extricate her from her difficulties, at times by military plans and by diplomacy and alliances at others. He was confronted with many difficulties: England, by her victories,

---

[1] Duke of Choiseul to Count of Choiseul, October 29th 1759, Waddington, *op. cit.*, 111, 457-458.

[2] A.E., M.D., Espagne, 574, f.7r, Duke of Choiseul to Ossun, October 29th 1759. The document does not indicate the denomination of the money. However most likely écus, for in a letter four days earlier, the Duke wrote to Ossun, "l'Etat est au moment de périr faute de vingt millions d'écus qui sont absolument nécessaires pour soutenir la guerre", Soulange-Bodin, 118.

[3] "It is not yet clear, whether all this (imposition of a Third Vigntième, increase in the Capitation Tax, other Taxes on farms) will produce the Money, requisite for the approaching Campaign", Yorke to Holderness, March 11th 1760, P.R.O., S.P., F., Holland, 437.

[4] Thackeray, 1, 453.

had already laid the foundation of her future colonial supremacy; in addition to that, France's alliance with Austria was not only a source of great expenditure to the former, but often a serious hindrance to her policy.[1] "The hopeless incapacity of the government of Louis XV"[2] made it still more difficult for the Duke of Choiseul to set right the confusion in French domestic and foreign policy.[3] Notwithstanding all these difficulties, Choiseul's courage did not fail him at the beginning of his ministry, for he had a great belief in the capacity of France for a speedy recovery and thought that all her misfortunes were caused by her need of a strong and courageous man, that once directed by the talents of such a leader, she could quickly recover her losses.[4] At the beginning of 1759, he assured Kaunitz, the Austrian Chancellor, of the prospects of this year and of the sincerity of the French Government in her alliance with Austria:

> "avec de l'économie, de la fermeté et de la patience tout reviendra, et nous nous flattons que la Cour de Vienne qui a vu notre faiblesse, rendra justice à la vigueur et à la suite de nos opérations, et surtout à notre fidélité à l'alliance. Monsieur le Comte, je vous en réponds sur ma parole d'honneur, le Roi ne fera jamais la paix sans ses alliés".

He even foresaw the impossibility of finishing the war in 1759 and predicted the coming campaign "jusqu'à la destruction de nos enemis."[5] Yet after having been in office for a short time, during which he bore responsibility, which gave him a closer insight into the hopeless confusion, and the boundless corruption in which the French administration was involved, the Duke of Choiseul realised that, only by peace could he deliver France from her predicament and save what was left of her colonies in America and in the West Indies. However he would neither submit to be the first to propose it nor sign a

[1] "the Court of Versailles had been enticed into an alliance that was foreign to its interests and ruinous to its fortunes," Riker, 1, 436.

[2] Ibid., 1, 436.

[3] Williams, 1, 390.

[4] Correspondence entre Bernstorff et Choiseul, 45, Duke of Choiseul to Bernstorff, July 29th 1759.

[5] Waddington, op. cit., 11, 484, Duke of Choiseul to Kaunitz, January 11th 1759.

dishonourable peace. He was only ready to accept any reasonable proposals of peace.[1] "As time went on," he considered the peace "more necessary for the safety of the State." [2] In addition to the internal troubles of France, which prompted Choiseul to appreciate the urgent need for peace, there were two other factors which exercised a great deal of influence upon his decision. On the one hand he feared that the prolongation of the war might ultimately result in such a crushing defeat to France that it would be difficult for her to recover from it in the future:[3] to negotiate peace now on unpalatable terms, he thought, would be better than to have to accept a dictated peace at the end of a ruinous war. On the other hand, even if the fortunes of a prolonged war were ultimately to favour France, the Duke of Choiseul was anxious to prevent his ally, Austria, from completely destroying Prussia, which after all was her ultimate aim in the continuation of the war. It was part of Choiseul's policy that Austria should not be left without a rival in Europe, lest, once Prussia was destroyed, Austria should seek to renew her old alliance with England, and thus become a menace to France. Consequently, the sooner peace was concluded, the better would be the state of the King of Prussia, whom the Duke of Choiseul found at the end of 1759 "sufficiently weakened".[4]

Fresh disasters only helped to confirm the Duke of Choiseul's views. The fall of Quebec in October of the same year caused him to write to his ambassador in Spain "nos malheurs nous forcent de la [the peace] désirer même désavantageuse." [5] At the same time, his correspondence with the Court of Vienna assumed a different tone from that of his dispatches at the

[1] *Correspondance entre Bernstorff et Choiseul*, 46, Duke of Choiseul to Bernstorff, July 29th 1759.

[2] A.E., M.D., Espagne, 574, f.8r, Duke of Choiseul to Ossun, October 29th 1759.

[3] A.E., C.P., Vienne, 274, f.233r, Duke of Choiseul wrote to Count of Choiseul, November 13th 1759, "Si, au contraire, les deux Cours [France and Austria] ne font la Paix que quand Elles seront abattues, Elles auront de la peine à se relever".

[4] Waddington, *op. cit.*, III, 441, Duke of Choiseul to Ossun, December 24th 1759 (the letter is a valuable source on the advantages of a Spanish mediation, as thought by the Duke, *ibid.*, III, 440-442); see also Flassan, VI, 132-133.

[5] A.E., M.D., Espagne, 574, f.8v., Duke of Choiseul to Ossun, October 29th 1759.

beginning of the year.[1] He wrote on October 29th, urging his ambassador in Vienna to warn Austria that France can no longer suffer disaster for the benefit of her ally:

"nous nous détruirons d'année en année en sa faveur [The Court of Vienna's], *mais il faut la prevenir que nous serons forcés par les circonstances à faire notre paix d'Angleterre dès qu'il sera possible*".[2]

The Empress-Queen, who entered the war ostensibly to recover Silesia from Prussia,[3] became determined to crush Prussia for the sake of Austria's future safety.[4] It was because of that, that the Duke of Choiseul pointed out to his ambassador in Vienna that he had no intention to sacrifice the interests of France to those of Austria.[5] Thus, although Austria did not attain even her first object in the war, France did not seem disposed to postpone peace any more. It should be pointed out that, as far as she was concerned, Austria's refusal to make peace was due as much to her not having recovered Silesia as to the fact that she was not suffering from the strain of the war against Prussia, to the extent that France was suffering from her war against England. The true assessment of the situation is that although the Duke of Choiseul was driven by the state of his country to sue for peace, he should not have forgotten that he was asking Austria to cease fighting before even gaining her minimum war aims.[6]

[1] In his letter of the same date to his ambassador in Austria, he pointed to the disasters which his country had sustained during the last campaign as the reason which made him alter his attitude towards the continuation of the war and towards his commitments for Austria. Bourguet, *Etudes sur la Politique Etrangère du Duc de Choiseul*, 31-35. Referring to Kaunitz, he wrote: "s'il jetta les yeux sur ce qui s'est passé depuis que je suis entré en place, il conviendra que mon courage mérite quelque éloge", *ibid.*, 31.

[2] *Ibid.*, 35.　　　　　[3] Thackery, 1, 454.

[4] Waddington, *op. cit.*, 11, 441, Empress-Queen to the King of France, June 23rd 1758: "Il nous faut une paix qui les mette (nos ennemis) hors d'état. Toute autre serait incompatible avec notre gloire, mais même avec notre sûreté à venir".

[5] Bourguet, *Etudes sur la Politique Etrangère du Duc de Choiseul*, 37.

[6] In his book, *Etudes sur la Politique Etrangère du Duc de Choiseul*, 38, Bourguet tried to justify the Duke of Choiseul on this point: "Si Marie-Thérèse n'était moins 'butée' à vouloir réconquérir cette Silésie qu'elle conservait l'illusion de reprendre, combien de maux épargnés et de ruines évitées. L'espoir de la revanche est certe légitime, et ce n'est pas nous qui voudrions le blâmer. Encore ne faut-il pas y sacrifier aveuglement tout le reste, et c'est à ce point de vue que le ministre avait raison de rappeler la cour de Vienne à la réalité des choses . . . Choiseul accomplissait l'œuvre d'un bon Français et d'un véritable ami de l'humanité".

However, in this critical situation, Choiseul saw that Spain alone could extricate France from all these difficulties, by offering her mediation for peace between France and England.[1]

On the other hand, two years after the appointment of Pitt as Secretary of State, England under his guidance began to reap the fruits of his military plans. 1759, England's *annus mirabilis*, was full of victories for England in all the fields of war. The capture of Goree (December 1758), in West Africa, was the prelude to the year of victories. In the West Indies Guadeloupe and Marie-Galante surrendered to her in the summer. The same year in Germany, the battle of Minden was won by Ferdinand of Brunswick. In India the relief of besieged Madras was considered a very great success.[2] In America the capture of Quebec foretold the conquest of all Canada. Notwithstanding these several victories England was still exposed to the danger of a French invasion.[3] The preparations of France in the French ports, confirmed by intelligence reports,[4] alarmed Newcastle.[5] However Pitt did not let any threat of invasion interfere with his plans. He did not allow one of his distant expeditions to suffer. The campaigns in India, the West Indies, and America were allowed to proceed as if England had nothing to fear at home.[6]

Meanwhile, England's expenditure on war was increasing, the subsidies for the war in Germany as well as the cost of Pitt's military plans were draining the country's resources. Pitt was continually urging Newcastle to find money for the war, and every year the latter asserted that funds could not be raised for another campaign.[7] He complained of Pitt's expenditure on the war, which he considered above the

[1] For the advantages of a Spanish mediation to France, see Waddington, *op. cit.*, 111, 440-442, Duke of Choiseul to Ossun, December 24th 1759.

[2] Ruville, 11, 273.   [3] See *ibid.*, 11, 273.

[4] Waddington, *op. cit.*, 111, 477.

[5] See Corbett, 11, 14.

[6] Williams, 1, 408; by the destruction of Conflan's Brest fleet on November 20th 1759, England was freed from all fear of a French invasion, *ibid.*, 11, 13.

[7] *Ibid.*, 11, 55; B.M., Add. MSS., 32902, f.311v, Newcastle to Yorke, February 22nd 1760, "I dread the Events of this Campaign. And I know *Sufficiently* how difficult It will be to make Another".

capacity of the English Government and complained of the
frequent expeditions and campaigns and Pitt's refusal to listen
to any suggestions for peace. He saw in peace the only remedy
for the situation and urged that every effort should be made to
secure it.[2] But to that he only received Pitt's retort:

> "at any rate we could afford the war better than France, then notoriously
> bankrupt".[3]

Here we find two English Ministers holding opposite views
on the most vital question in their country's affairs: the reason
for this was twofold. There was on the one hand a difference
in their personal character, while on the other each was
following a policy which he thought to be more conducive to
the glory of his country as well as to his own power. The
views of Newcastle and Pitt were in radical conflict; Newcastle
considered peace absolutely necessary to England and held
that his country was unable to bear the steadily increasing
cost of war, for he was

> "haunted by fears; every small incident was the portent of terrible things
> to come; every molehill a volcano".[4]

Moreover he hoped that peace might restore him to his old
power and ruin the influence of Pitt, by putting an end to a war
which was increasing the prestige of his rival,[5] for although he
was First Lord of the Treasury, his position was very unlike
that of Walpole.[6] On the other hand Pitt was "a man of great
merit, weight and consequence", as Newcastle described him
to Granby on November 27th 1759.[7] It was truly said that

---

[1] Waddington, *op. cit.*, 111, 476, "Mémoire du Duc de Newcastle sur l'Etat du
gouvernement", April 19th 1759.

[2] B.M., Add. MSS., 32902, f.311v; Newcastle to Yorke, February 22nd 1760
"Nothing ought to be left untried that can tend to make Peace *This Summer*".

[3] Williams, 11, 55-56; see also Riker, 11, 174, Newcastle to Hardwicke, April
9th 1760, Pitt's answer to Newcastle's complaints, "We are a hundred times better
able than the French".

[4] Namier, 77.

[5] *Pol. Corr*, XVIII, 337, Knyphausen and Mitchell *"au Roi seul"*, June 8th 1759; see
also Ruville, 11, 366.

[6] Namier, 76.

[7] *Ibid.*, 75.

"the Pitt-Newcastle Ministry was virtually Pitt's own Administration."[1] Yet Pitt could not dispense with Newcastle's majorities and his party connections.[2] By 1760, through his conduct of the war and his successful plans, he earned "a well-deserved, nation-wide popularity."[3] These successes and popularity encouraged him to follow his aims in spite of the opposition and the heavy expenditure of the war. His spirit thus

> "appeared to operate with equal vigour in every quarter of the globe . . . he engaged with zeal and alacrity in the continental war, directed his attacks where they were most promptly and severely felt by the enemy".[4]

The question whether his country could well stand the great expenditure of the war was to him a matter of indifference. He had always his eye on France, and whenever he was told that England could no longer afford the expenses of the war in her struggle against that country, he conjectured that the ruin of France, if it were a question of ruin, would be greater than that of England.[5]

This brief comparison between the two countries reveals that on the eve of the Anglo-Prussian declaration of November 25th, 1759, England was in a far more advantageous position than France; moreover, her prospects of success were obviously brighter. On the other hand, the French had much to lose and nothing to gain, and feared the loss of the rest of their colonies in America and in the West Indies. Although it was thus more likely that France should have made the first proposals for peace, it was England, jointly with Prussia, who proposed in their declaration the meeting of a general congress for peace negotiations. Their Prussian and Britannic Majesties declared that they were ready to send plenipotentiaries to any convenient place in order to negotiate jointly a general peace

---

[1] Riker, 11, 149; Professor Namier in *England in the Age of the American Revolution*, 76, describes Pitt's situation in the Government by stating: "Pitt did the work of Secretary of State; otherwise there was no real government".

[2] Riker, 11, 149.

[3] Namier, 75; Newcastle acknowledged the growing popularity of Pitt, in his notes of September 4th 1759: "More popular every day than ever", *ibid.*, 75.

[4] Coxe, IV, 246-247.

[5] Riker, 11, 174, footnote 65.

with plenipotentiaries appointed by the belligerent powers.[1]
Why did England and Prussia take this step and how far was
Pitt sincere in his declaration? England, as already indicated,
was then just starting to reap the fruits of her military plans and
of her costly expeditions. Furthermore, from all evidence
available, the most important and influential member of the
Government, Pitt, then a Secretary of State, appeared to be in
favour of the continuation of war. To suppose that he, who
was so desirous to secure for England "an indisputable
supremacy at sea",[2] who was not satisfied with France brought
to her knees, but wished her to be thrown on her back,[3] "was
seriously considering . . . 'peace' would be utterly to mistake
the objects of his real effort, his energy and his ambition";[4]
for he himself declared, in the King's speech of November
1759, that the only way to secure an honourable peace was "to
pursue the war in all its parts." [5] He also told Newcastle, a few
months later "We don't want a peace." [6] Walpole believed that
no "subsequent step of Mr. Pitt speak him cordial to the business of peace." [7] Even the desperate situation of the King of
Prussia would not have then convinced Pitt to accept the
renewal of Prussia's proposals for peace, if another important
factor did not enter into the scene.

During 1759, Frederick, the King of Prussia showed on
several occasions his desire of putting an end to the war.[8] In
June of the same year, on the advice of his ambassadors in
London,[9] he had proposed to the King of England the issue of a

---

[1] See the Declaration of their Prussian and Britannic Majesties, Thackeray, 11, 470.

[2] Ruville, 11, 277.   [3] Memoirs of George II, 111, 236.

[4] Ruville, 11, 278.

[5] Williams, 11, 17, King's speech, November 13th 1759 (just a few days before
the Anglo-Prussian Declaration).

[6] Riker, 11, 174-175, Newcastle to Hardwicke, April 9th 1760.

[7] Memoirs of George II, 111, 236.   [8] Riker, 11, 173.

[9] The idea of a Congress originated from His Prussian Majesty's representatives in
London, who, in their letter of June 8th, pointed out to their master the advantages of
such a declaration to Prussia: Knyphausen and Michell to the King alone, June 8th
1759, Pol. Corr., XVIII, 337-339; for details of the conferences of the Prussian
representatives and the English Cabinet, see Waddington, op. cit., 111, 478-482,
486-488.

joint declaration to the belligerent powers proposing a general peace Congress.[1] The campaign of 1759 was disastrous to Frederick of Prussia, and the defeat of Kunersdorf was a great blow to his fortunes.[2] Frederick began then to regard the congress as "his sole means of salvation."[3] He therefore ordered his ambassador immediately after the battle of Kunersdorf to resume the proposals for a congress.[4] Pitt stood almost alone in his intention to continue the war until France was utterly defeated and the conquest of America completed.[5] He was aware of the despondency of the King of Prussia and considered his ally's situation as embarrassing everything.[6]

It was only when Charles of Naples [7] made his move towards mediation [8] between the two belligerents that Pitt in spite of his disagreement with the idea of peace,[9] found in his ally's proposals for a congress a refuge from a new situation which he realised to be more embarrassing. He found in it a means of avoiding the Spanish mediation without categorically refusing it[10] and offending Spain. Pitt found in the Congress a con-

---

[1] *Pol. Corr.*, XVIII, 341, Frederick to George, June 20th 1759.

[2] Walpole describes this defeat in his *Memoirs of George II*, 111, 203: "All his Generals were killed or wounded, all his cannon taken, the flower of his troops slaughtered or dispersed".

[3] Ruville,11, 281.

[4] *Pol. Corr.*, XVIII, 511-512, Frederick to Knyphausen, September 1st 1759.

[5] Ruville, 11, 282.

[6] Yorke, 111, 58, Newcastle to Hardwicke, September 19th 1759. He related to him his conversation with Lady Yarmouth to whom Pitt said, with regard the desperate situation of Prussia "that he [Pitt] had flattered himself that he should have been able to have 'given, or laid before, the King, America, the West Indies, Africa', and such a situation of affairs in Germany, as might enable His Majesty to make 'what peace he pleased', but that the distress of the King of Prussia had embarrassed everything".

[7] It should be noted that Ferdinand VI of Spain dying on August 10th 1759, without leaving a son, his step brother Charles King of Naples was to succeed him on the Spanish throne. He only left Naples on October 7th and reached Barcelona ten days later, Rousseau, I, 2, 8.

[8] In spite of His Catholic Majesty's declaration, Pitt could not see that it was a disinterested move on the part of Spain as he declared later, Pitt to Bristol, his ambassador to Spain, December 14th 1759, in Thackeray, 1, 462; See also Muret, 546.

[9] "Pitt, indeed, had resolved upon the continuance of the war for at least another campaign", Yorke, 111, 148; see also Waddington, *op. cit.*, III, 481.

[10] Muret, 546-547.

venient means to crush such schemes as the Spanish mediation, which he wished to fail since he did not sincerely desire peace.[1] Furthermore, by accepting the Prussian plan for a joint peace declaration, Pitt sought to serve other purposes: in addition to appeasing his ally, he was able to disarm his opponents by appearing to be in favour of satisfying the desire to end the war as well as to pose before public opinion as the champion of peace. Nevertheless for several considerations,[2] he was convinced that peace upon a permanent basis was not at that time to be expected.[3]

In order to understand the Spanish mediation, we have to consider the relations between Spain and the two belligerent countries,[4] at the same time, so that we may understand why Charles III of Spain initiated a new foreign policy which played an important role in the struggle between England and France, and how the Duke of Choiseul faced the situation with its advantages and difficulties, in which he sought an alliance with Spain. Between 1756 and 1759, both England and France made efforts to gain the support of Spain. Their fears were not in connection with the military power of Spain, but because each appreciated the importance of trading with Spain and the West Indies for its own commercial prosperity, and consequently for its ability to fight the other.[5] Neither succeeded in its efforts, for the King of Spain, during this period, maintained a strict neutrality. Already a year before war was officially declared between England and France, Rouillé the French foreign minister then predicted this neutrality when he wrote to Duras, the French Ambassador in Madrid that Ferdinand VI:

"demeurera spéctateur tranquille des événemens qu'une rupture entre nous et les Anglais pourra occasioner".[6]

[1] Yorke, III, 149.

[2] For these considerations see Thackeray, 1, 454.

[3] Thackeray, 1, 454.

[4] For earlier relations, and three points of grievances between England and Spain, see Chapter 1, p. 22.

[5] Christelow, "Economic Background of the Anglo-Spanish War 1762", J.M.H., XVIII, 23.

[6] Guillon, 366, Rouillé to Duras, April 2nd 1755.

In spite of his friendship to England,[1] and Pitt's willingness to offer Gibraltar, in 1757, in order to secure a close commercial and political alliance with Spain, Ferdinand VI, resolved to develop the economic resources of his country in peace, refused to side with England against France.[2] His death on August 10th 1759, and the accession of his step brother, the King of Naples, to the Spanish throne, was a very important event in the orientation of Spanish foreign policy, for the new sovereign adopted a totally different policy from that of his predecessor.[3] Much has been written on this change in Spanish foreign policy, a change from a most strict neutrality so carefully expounded by Eusenada,[4] and so faithfully maintained by Ferdinand VI, to a rapprochement between France and Spain crowned later on by the Family Compact.

Some Spanish Historians hold that Charles III's policy towards the struggle between England and France, was neutrality. Danvila y Collado for example, in his book, *Reinado de Carlos III*, says that

"the predominant part of the policy of Charles III was an armed neutrality".[5]

Ferrer del Rio points out that Charles understood that the best policy for Spain in this struggle between France and England was to remain neutral.[6] Both based their views on Charles III's words in his letter to Tanucci:

"*You know my policy which is to be friendly with all and to make myself respected by them*".[7]

[1] See Chapter 1, pp. 21-22.

[2] Hotblack, *Chatham's Colonial Policy*, 127-128.

[3] Renault, 22.

[4] A.E., M.D., Espagne, 97, ff. 63r-63v; M. le Baron de Boislecomte, "Etudes sur les relations politiqes et commerciales suivies entre les deux pays depuis l'établissement de la maison de Bourbon en Espagne (1700-1827)." (In 1751, Eusenada presented to the Cabinet of Madrid the best political system, in his opinion, for Spain to adopt. Pointing out that France and England will always be enemies, and consequently no peace will last between them, Spain would be courted by both, for she could turn the scale, so the right policy for her was to remain neutral).

[5] Collado, 11, 68.

[6] Ferrer del Rio, I, 281.

[7] The letter is dated February 5th 1760, Ferrer del Rio, 1, 281, also in Collado, 11, 68.

They almost agree[1] that the Duke of Choiseul was responsible to a great extent for persuading Charles III to abandon his neutrality; that by using his skill, Choiseul was able to serve his purpose by taking advantage of

"the good nature of the new King of Spain, his amour propre, the nobility of his soul, his natural generosity, and above all, his extreme love to his family and his zeal in maintaining its honour".
and thus Choiseul "concentrated his batteries against" Charles "*the man*, and succeeded as was expected and reaped the benefits which he desired from" Charles, "*the King*". [2]

Ferrer del Rio adds that Choiseul did not only appeal to the sentiment of the Spanish King as an individual, but also to his duties as a sovereign.[3] Thus these Spanish Historians considered that the response of Charles III to the French approach was partly caused by his affection and love of his family due to the generosity of his character. Fernan Nuñez goes so far as to indicate that the Family Compact was not only a "noble and generous act" but an action based on a "disinterested generosity" merely for the sake of giving succour to a defeated neighbour and ally.[4] Moreover Ferrer del Rio [5] indicates that the French Foreign minister exploited the fact that Charles III was very resentful of the aggressive attitude of England in 1742, during the war of the Austrian Succession, when, still King of Naples, he started to help his brother in the conquest of Parma, and an English fleet, under Commodore Martin appeared in the Bay of Naples, and threatened to bombard the capital if Charles would not withdraw his troops. Choiseul, therefore, spared no effort to urge his ambassador in Spain to exploit the unfriendly attitude of the King of Spain towards England in order that he should join France immediately against England.[6] Moreover the Spanish Historians seem to agree also that Charles III's response to France was but a necessary measure of defence

---

[1] Except Collado.

[2] Nuñez, 1, 160; Ferrer del Rio quotes Nuñez' words, I, 286-287, footnote 1. See also Appendix 3, for a further discussion of this matter and for the influence of Fernan Nuñez on the views of later historians.

[3] Ferrer del Rio, 1, 286.

[4] Nuñez, 1, 161.

[5] Ferrer del Rio, 1, 281.

[6] *Ibid.*, 1, 286.

against the encroachments of England and her illegal settlements in the Bay of Honduras in America;[1] Ferrer del Rio [2]
and Collado [3] attribute also Charles III's policy of rapprochement to France to the fact that his possessions in America
were exposed to the danger of being invaded by the English:

> "the only matter which troubled the King of Spain was the *English
> victories in America (invasiones Americanos)*".

as Charles III pointed out in his correspondence.[4] Furthermore, Ferrer del Rio regards the death of Queen Amelia of
Spain as hastening the end of the neutrality of Spain.[5]

It appears that the Spanish Historians generally, in assessing
Charles III's policy and the motives which led him to it, were
to a great extent influenced by the results of that policy, which
were disastrous to Spain and caused her to incur some sacrifices. Had the results of this policy of rapprochement between
the two branches of the House of Bourbon been favourable, the
Spanish Historians' judgments would have probably been very
different. Considering Charles III's policy disadvantageous to
Spain, they tried to free him from all responsibility by pointing
out that his policy was originally to be neutral and friendly with
all, and by attributing the change to some or all of the following
factors: to the generosity of the Spanish King and his love and
his affection to his family; to the influence of the Duke of
Choiseul; to the illegal settlements of England in the Bay of
Honduras in America; to English victories in America; to her
aggressive policy towards him in Naples in 1742; and to the
absence of the vigorous influence of Queen Amelia on the
Spanish King.

Let us now examine the accounts given by the Spanish
Historians: first and foremost let us consider what they claim
to be an important factor in the formation of the King's policy,
namely that the Duke of Choiseul was responsible, to a great

---

[1] Collado, 11, 166; see also Ferrer del Rio, 1, 283; and Beccatini, 11, 15.

[2] Ferrer del Rio, 1, 286.

[3] Collado, 11, 110.

[4] *Ibid.*, 11, 110.

[5] Ferrer del Rio, 1, 284.

extent in making Charles III abandon his neutrality. By attributing the change in Charles III's policy to Choiseul's efforts and influence, the Spanish historians left very little to the personality of Charles III and condemned him as a states-man. In their estimation, he must have been a very weak character. It is true that the Duke of Choiseul aimed at including him in a system which he had designed especially for the glorification of the senior branch of the Bourbon Family and that he exploited all the grievances which Charles III had against the English in order to attain his immediate object of obtaining an honourable peace for France in spite of her disastrous war. Yet Charles III was not at all the simple victim of the French foreign minister's scheme. On the contrary his response to Choiseul was based on several motives and, in particular, on the preservation of his county's interests in Europe as well as in America;[1] for he "means solely to pursue the Interest of the Throne on which He is placed."[2] Besides he was "very far" from being a weak person[3] and consequently was not likely to be easily influenced by the Duke of Choiseul. However, in order to give his action for a union with France a gesture of generosity, Charles III took great care to conceal his own interests in such a union and to make it appear disinterested.[4] The King of Spain was therefore a willing and equal partner, to reap at least as great advantages as the other side,[5] and a minute examination of the French and Spanish correspondence during the six months which preceded the signing of the Family Compact and the Secret Convention, as will be indicated in the following chapter, shows that Charles III appeared at times more anxious for these alliances than the Duke of Choiseul. An acquaintance with the Instructions given to Grimaldi on the eve of his departure to his post as

[1] See infra, pp. 41-43.

[2] P.R.O., G.D., 12, Bristol to Pitt, February 11th 1760.

[3] P.R.O., S.P., F., Spain, 166, Rochford to Halifax, January 13th 1764.

[4] See Simancas, Estado-Leg. 3457, n.38, Instructions of January 14th 1761 to Grimaldi for his embassy in Paris, in Chapter III, pp. 110-111.

[5] The Duke of Choiseul, three years after the conclusion of the Family Compact, was very clearly of the opinion that Spain had secured the best of the bargain, Brown, 14-15, Choiseul to Ossun, December 16th 1764.

D

ambassador to the Court of Versailles also proves a matter of
great significance. At that time when France was likely to
open her peace negotiations with England, Grimaldi was to
try to conclude an offensive as well as a defensive alliance with
France.[1] Charles III was not, therefore, a simpleton,[2] a puppet
in the hands of the Duke of Choiseul and his ambassador in
Spain. Far from being a puppet in the hands of Choiseul, he
realised that:

" All the French were seeking was to secure their interests ",
and he declared to Tanucci, the Sicilian minister that,

"such people do not agree with either my inclination or my way of thinking".[3]

All that could be said on this point is that the Duke of Choiseul
played his part, but Charles III did not succumb, and that if
Choiseul succeeded, Charles succeeded also.

Secondly, Charles III was not thrown into this policy by his
love and affection to his family; neither did Ferrer del Rio and
Nuñez base their statements on this point on any documents or
proofs. Yet they were not alone in making this mistake, for
two other historians[4] referred to Charles's affection for his
family though they did not make it the main spring of his
action. It was "fear for Spain, not love for France", in spite of
the influence of the Queen and his chief minister, Wall, which
made him declare in December 1759, to the French ambassador

"Il faudra bien qu'ils [les Anglais] fassent la paix, sinon ils me contrain-
dront, quoique contre mon envie, à faire la guerre; mais, de façon ou
d'autre, je ne souffrirai pas qu'ils restent les maitres en Europe et en
Amérique".[5]

It is worth quoting here Collado's statement, that the Family
Compact was never being a matter of love *"affaire de coeur"*,[6] on

---

[1] See Instructions of January 14th 1761 to Grimaldi for his embassy in Paris,
Chapter III, p. 111.   For the original draft see Appendix 4, pp. 235-243.

[2] "Il a des lumières, de la pénétration, beaucoup de justesse dans le rasionnement et
dans les combinaisons", Ossun to Duke of Choiseul, September 10th 1759, in
Waddington, *op. cit.*, 111, 431.

[3] Collado, 11, 108, July 12th 1760.

[4] Ruville, 11, 279; Soulange-Bodin, 136.

[5] *Recueil des Instructions, Espagne III.*, XII bis, 338, Ossun to Duke of Choiseul,
December 7th, 1759.

[6] Collado, 11, 103; see also *ibid.*, 166.

the contrary as Blart points out it was "l'alliance de raison." [1]
It was not even "la conciliation de ses affections et de ses
intérêts, qui occasionnait la réserve des ses décisions", [2] as
Flassan said, for the Spanish and Italian interests provided the
overwhelming considerations in the decisions which he took
in the struggle between England and France.

Thirdly, the disputes between England and Spain about the
illegal British settlements in Honduras, the depredations on
Spanish shipping, and the Newfoundland fisheries—of which
the first was the most important and of long standing [3]—
contributed indirectly to the motives which persuaded Charles
to adopt this policy, as both Ferrer del Rio and Collado admit.
It was with regard to these points of dispute that Charles III's
pride was offended by Pitt either by the latter's delay in
answering memoirs relative to them or by his arrogant style. [4]
In June 1760, Fuentes, the Spanish ambassador in London
presented a memoir concerning the prizes which Pitt did not
answer until the beginning of September, [5] and thus

> "being offended by this long silence, all that mortified him from the
> Court of London became magnified in his mind". [6]

Until the end of 1760, England still remained undecided and
had not given Charles III the answer for which he asked. [7]
Charles III had as a consequence of this silence,

> "in his heart the thorn that England would not answer his claims, and by
> its silent offence, he was stimulated to continue the conferences about an
> alliance with France". [8]

[1] Blart, 16.

[2] Flassan, VI, 284. "His Predilections are only Spanish without any Prepossession
in favour of that Nation where the Head of His Family reigns", P.R.O., G.D., 12,
Bristol to Pitt, February 12th 1760.

[3] McLachlan, "The Seven Years' Peace and the West Indian Policy of Carvajal and
Wall", E.H.R., LIII, 472.

[4] In his letter of September 26th 1760 to Bristol, Pitt described the right claimed
by Spain for fishing in Newfoundland as "a sacrifice which can never be made" and
refused in energetic words even to discuss it, see Thackeray, 1, 487-492; from the
Instructions given to Grimaldi on January 14th 1761 before his departure to his
embassy in Paris, it is obvious that Spain, at that time seemed to be offended by the
English government's reaction to the several memoirs regarding her grievances with
England, Simancas, Estado-Leg. 3457, no. 38, See Chapter III, p. 76.

[5] Thackeray, 1, 484, Pitt to Bristol, September 5th 1760.

[6] Ferrer del Rio, 1, 285.

[7] Collado, 11, 108-109, Charles III to Tanucci, December 9th 1760.

[8] Ferrer del Rio, 1, 289-290.

Yet Pitt knew that by "amicable Negotiations alone", the
disputes between his country and Spain could be settled.[1] He
was, therefore, to a certain degree responsible for the hostile
attitude which Spain adopted towards England at the end of
1761. It was not at all impossible that a more prudent and
careful diplomacy and a greater regard to the interests and
susceptibilities of Charles III, immediately on his succession,
might have mitigated his fears and jealousy of Great Britain,
and might have retained the support of Wall,[2] who pointed
out even before the accession of Charles III to the throne of
Spain the best way of keeping the "entente cordiale" between
the two countries:

> "donner quelques satisfactions aux réclamations constantes du governe-
> ment de Madrid au sujet des agissements des vaisseaux de guerre et de
> corsaires britanniques et avoir recours, en cas de négotiations pour la
> paix, à la médiation du roi de Naples qui succéderait bientôt au trône
> d'Espagne".[3]

At the same time, predicting the danger of neglecting the
Spanish grievances, Wall asked the English to help him in his
policy of supporting their interests in Spain, but "No attention,
however, was paid to this advice and no serious effort was made
by Pitt to gain the new sovereign." [4] Nevertheless it is worth
adding that Charles would not have been so susceptible to
England's attitude towards these three points of grievances and
especially that of Honduras, if a much more important factor
did not enter the scene: England's successes in the war seemed
to foretell the destruction of the French colonial empire and
to indicate that the Spanish empire might soon be threatened
by English aggression. The policy adopted by Charles at this
critical moment and the motives that inspired it are largely
revealed in the instructions given to the Marquis of Grimaldi
on his appointment as ambassador to the Court of Versailles.
They show that Charles was desirous of bringing about an

---

[1] B.M., Add. MSS., 36807, f.84r., Pitt to Bristol, April 24th 1761.

[2] Yorke, III, 143-144.

[3] Waddington, *op. cit.*, III, 428-429.

[4] Yorke, III, 143; see also Waddington, *op. cit.*, III, 429.

offensive and defensive alliance between France and Spain, because he held that Spain needed such an alliance.[1]

As to the offence of Commodore Martin to Charles when he was still King of Naples, although it was humiliating at the time to have his foreign policy dictated at the cannon's mouth, it is clear that sentiments such as resentment, however, seldom play a great part in the formation of foreign policy.

The motives of the policy of Charles III become clearer when we realise that at that time Spanish interests agreed to a great extent with those of France. The two main objects which pre-occupied Madrid were the security of the Spanish Princes ruling in some of the Italian states, and that of the American colonies. Although Spain had attained her ambitions in Italy, yet the House of Austria was closely watching the suitable moment to recover its lost Italian territories. When Charles III became King of Spain in 1759 he ceded his throne in Naples to his son Ferdinand, and not, as stipulated by the treaty of Aix-la-Chapelle to his brother Philip.[2] He therefore considered it necessary, in order to prevent a possible Austrian intervention in his family's affairs, to secure his son's position in the kingdom of the Two Sicilies.[3] It was also quite evident that Charles III, alarmed at the victories of Austria over Prussia, greatly feared a total annihilation of Frederick the Great, which would mean that, once Austria had finished with Prussia, and was left without a rival German State to counter-balance her power, she would become too powerful, and dangerous to the Spanish interests in Italy.[4] Thus both France and Spain, for different reasons, then agreed on the necessity of not allowing Prussia to be completely destroyed by Austria.[5]

[1] See Simancas, Estado-Leg. 3457, no. 38, Instructions of January 14th 1761 to Grimaldi for his embassy in Paris (in chapter III, pp. 76-77).

[2] "Phillip was compensated at the expense of Austria and Sardinia, an arrangement carried out without difficulty", Ruville, 11, 279; see Waddington, op. cit., 111, 451-453.

[3] Blart, 5-6.

[4] (As Wall declared to Ossun), Flassan, VI, 131; see also Rousseau, 1, 38.

[5] When Ossun acquainted him with Wall's views on this matter, the Duke of Choiseul answered Ossun on December 24th: "*Je vous confierai que nous sommes dans les mêmes principes*", Flassan, VI, 132. The Duke of Choiseul also tried to gain Charles to his side by indicating that Spain and France had the same views on this matter, Rousseau, 1, 44.

In America, Spain was faced by the enemy of France, England; her vast colonial Empire was threatened by the British successes in America.[1] The sudden disturbance of balance altered the prospects of Spain: as long as France was powerful the danger of hostilities with England was minimised, but with a ruined and defeated France, Charles III was perfectly aware of the dangers to which his colonies would be exposed.[2] Charles III's blood ran cold when he heard the news of the capture of Quebec by the English.[3] Moreover the maritime power of England caused permanent injuries to Spanish commerce, for, in spite of the prohibitions imposed by the laws, forbidding foreigners to trade with the Indies, the English carried a contraband trade to get bullion, not only in the West Indies but also on the coasts of Spain itself.[4] Their illicit export of silver and gold was facilitated by the privileges they acquired by their commercial treaties with Spain.[5] It was reckoned that the English made far more profits from the Spanish Empire than did the Spaniards themselves,[6] and Charles III was convinced of the danger of the British contraband to the Spanish interests, for in the course of his early investigations in Spain, he was presented with a report in which the British were described as

"by far the worst offenders in that contraband trade which is the root of so many disorders in your Majesty's dominions".[7]

The British smugglers were represented to him as

"the principal defrauders" of the revenues of his country, and as "responsible for most of the disturbances in the Indies".

[1] Blart, 6.

[2] Bourguet, *Le Duc de Choiseul et l'Alliance Espagnole*, 46.

[3] Rousseau, 1, 56.

[4] Blart, 7.

[5] Christelow, "Economic Background of the Anglo-Spanish War of 1762", *J.M.H.*, XVIII, 23-24.

[6] Christelow, "French Interest in the Spanish Empire during the Ministry of the Duc de Choiseul 1759-1771", *H.A.H.R.*, XXI, 532, in a memoir by the French Consul (Béliardi) in Spain.

[7] *Ibid.*, 532.

The British treaties with Spain were said to have inhibited the growth of Spanish industry.[1] This contraband trade so detrimental to Spanish prosperity, was a hinderance to the reforms which the Spanish Sovereign intended to introduce into the economy of Spain. Charles III thought, therefore, that by a policy of union with France against England, he would be able to get rid of these British treaties and as a consequence to restore Spanish industry, recapture the Indies trade for the Spaniards and extinguish the British interloping trade.[2]

It is also worth pointing out that Charles III had "two important places" to reconquer "Gibraltar and Port Mahon",[3] and in particular Gibraltar which was still in England's hands, and which "created an irritation that was never healed throughout the century" [4] and which became

"a vital factor in the formation and maintenance of the Family Compact between France and Spain". [5]

Thus partly because of his pride being offended by the English Government and partly because of his Spanish and Italian interests, Charles III considered joining France in what he thought an inevitable struggle the wisest policy to pursue. He saw, in a family alliance between the members of the House of Bourbon, the means of facing the growing power of England, which had already threatened him in Naples in 1742. Fear lest Spain be isolated in an English-ruled world provided the greater part of the driving power which impelled him towards union with France. He understood the danger to which his country would be exposed, once England had dealt with France and become able to concentrate all its power against his isolated country.[6] He also understood the necessity

[1] Christelow, "Economic Background of the Anglo-Spanish War of 1762", *J.M.H.*, XVIII, 25.

[2] Christelow, "Great Britain and The Trades from Cadiz and London to Spanish America and Brazil 1759-1782", *H.A.H.R.*, XXVII, 9.

[3] Flassan, VI, 258.

[4] Conn, 27.

[5] *Ibid.*, 2.

[6] See Bourguet, *Le Duc de Choiseul et l'Alliance Espagnole*, 46.

of helping France to conclude a reasonable peace with
England and decided that he must have a share in making
that peace,[1] because he feared that England might impose too
ignominious terms on France and extend her American
interests, possessions and trade in a way that would threaten
gravely the Spanish Indies.[2] Moreover he thought that it was
an opportune moment to settle his own country's disputes
with England. This explains his dissatisfaction with the Anglo-
Prussian Declaration of November 25th 1759,[3] which meant
the exclusion of his good offices between France and England,
and his decision to dispatch Grimaldi to the Hague, to watch
the progress of the negotiations there.

Let us now turn to the Spanish mediation and circumstances
which led up to it. The Duke of Choiseul, whose critical
position has already been explained, regarded a Spanish
mediation as of the greatest importance. He considered this
mediation for a separate peace between France and England
an essential step towards the realisation of his aims.[4] If the
negotiation for peace succeeded, France would be able to
withdraw from the war before losing all her colonies and
before Prussia was entirely crushed,[5] and without openly
breaking her engagements with the Court of Vienna.[6]
Furthermore, according to an account given by the English
ambassador in Spain, the Duke of Choiseul thought he could
thus secure "a better Peace"[7] for he was "under the illusion
that the English would be seriously alarmed at a new alliance
between Spain and France."[8]

[1] Collado, 11, 108, Charles III to Tanucci, May 6th 1760; Tanucci the Sicilian
Ambassador was of the same opinion, Ferrer del Rio, 1, 287; Grimaldi also believed in
the same thing, P.R.O., G.D., 12, Grimaldi to Fuentes, September 13th 1761.

[2] Conn, 172.

[3] Waddington, op. cit., 111, 347, Ossun to Duke of Choiseul, December 7th, 1759.

[4] On the advantages of a Spanish mediation to France, see Duke of Choiseul's
letter to Ossun, December 24th 1759, Waddington, op. cit., 111, 440-442.

[5] Ibid., 111, 441 see supra, p. 41.

[6] Corbett, 11, 73.

[7] P.R.O., S.P., F., Spain, 159, Bristol to Pitt, February 12th 1759.

[8] A.E., M.D., Espagne, 189, f.28r, (a translation).

On the other hand, if the Spanish mediation was refused, it was very likely to provoke Spain to a war against England.[1]

The mediation of Charles, the future King of Spain, was suggested even before his departure from Naples, for

"he was reckoned to be in favour of a rapprochement with his cousin the King of France, and to have not forgotten being humiliated by the English during the war of the Succession".[2]

but, as he was credited with a fair amount of perspicacity,[3] and, consequently, political considerations might outweigh family ties, the Duke of Choiseul did not neglect to urge his ambassador to appeal to both in his endeavours to gain Charles.[4] It was not Charles III who took the initiative in approaching France about the mediation. The fact that the Duke of Choiseul was the first to press Charles for his mediation is pointed out in "Analyses Historiques des Negotiations entre la France et l'Espagne depuis 1746-1776."[5] It was stated that

"il [Duke of Choiseul] l'[Charles] avoit pressé d'offrir sa médiation à l'Angleterre; et en même tems, par une de ces petites lutes diplomatiques dont il se glorifioit, il mettoit de l'importance à ce que la France ne parât pas faire les premières propositions".[6]

Finding in this move an excellent means of veiling his real intentions, Charles "seized the opportunity with eagerness",[7] and ordered the Sicilian Ambassador (Sanseverino) in London, a few days before the death of Ferdinand VI,[8] to inform Pitt

---

[1] Soulange-Bodin, 122, Duke of Choiseul to Ossun, October 25th 1759: "Il n'est qu'un parti honorable pour Charles III : c'est de proposer sa mediation ; si elle est acceptée, on travaillera avec célérité, au rétablissement de la paix; si elle est refusée, l'Espagne déclarera la guerre et combinera ses forces avec celles qui restent encore à la France".

[2] Waddington, *op. cit.*, 111, 430-431 (a translation).

[3] *Ibid.*, 111, 431, Ossun to Duke of Choiseul, September 10th 1759, see also Collado, 11, 166.

[4] Soulange-Bodin, 118-119, Duke of Choiseul to Ossun, October 25th 1759; see also *Recueil des Instructions, Espagne* 111, XII bis, 349-350, Duke of Choiseul to Ossun, September 7th 1759.

[5] A.E., M.D., Espagne, 189, ff.12-65.

[6] *Ibid.*, Espagne, 189, f.27r.

[7] *Ibid.*, Espagne, 189, f.27r (a translation).

[8] Thackeray, 1, 421.

that his master was ready to mediate peace between His Britannic Majesty, jointly with his allies, and the King of France. Considering the matter "of the greatest delicacy", Pitt pointed out to Sanseverino that the issue of important operations of the campaign, especially in America, was not yet known and that it was necessary that it should be known in order to guide the judgment for a future peace. He also added that whenever peace should be under consideration, His Britannic Majesty would, in the first place, consult his ally the King of Prussia. Pitt realised the importance of avoiding this mediation which

> "from the recent event of the demise of the late King of Spain, (which soon followed the overture . . . ,) is become an object more interesting and important" for ". . . the King of Naples might find himself at the head of the Spanish monarchy, and consequently possessed of all that due weight inseparable from that crown, which cannot but greatly effect the system of Europe". [1]

A few days after the death of Ferdinand VI, Sanseverino repeated more strongly than before, to Pitt, insinuations of the same nature as those in his first conversation, in reply to which, Pitt replied in substance, in the same language. [2]

Meanwhile, after his defeat at Kunserdorf, Frederick hoped that a congress would enable him to emerge from this desperate war without any loss of territory, and perhaps with some gain, through the influence of his triumphant ally. He, therefore, ordered his representatives in London to resume the proposals for a congress. [3] His representatives, in their conference of September 1759, with the English ministers, succeeded in securing permission to draft the declaration. Pitt, however, demanded that it should not be issued to the other countries till the decisive news had arrived from America. [4]

At this moment, Charles III made a second attempt to intervene in the question of peace and asked His Britannic

---

[1] *Ibid.*, 1, 421-422, Pitt to Bristol, September 14th 1759.
[2] *Ibid.*, 1, 422-423.
[3] Ruville, 11, 281-282.
[4] *Ibid.*, 11, 284.

Majesty, through Sanserverino for "the conditions which might, in the opinion of Great Britain, serve as a basis for peace." Pitt after assuring him of "the just sense, which the King had of his Catholic Majesty's friendship and pure intentions", pointed to the fact that

" how very premature and rash it would be, before the final conclusion of the campaign, to form, even to ourselves, an idea of the conditions of a future peace".

He thus declined the offer of his Catholic Majesty. However, in order to assure him of his pacific intentions, he asked Bristol, his ambassador in Madrid, to acquaint His Catholic Majesty with the important measure which England, jointly with Prussia were taking for the meeting of a congress for a general peace.[1]

When Charles III entered Spain towards the end of October, and was informed of the fall of Quebec, he ordered his ambassador in London, Abreu, to send a memorial to Pitt in order to explain

"that his Catholic Majesty could not regard with indifference the disturbances by the English conquests of the balance of power in America, as established by the peace of Utrecht; he was therefore anxious to see the naval war concluded by a peace in which England would show generosity and moderation, and was himself ready to act as intermediary".

Abreu executed the orders without delay.[2] Pitt replied to the Spanish ambassador's letter on December 13th, in a "calm and dignified language",[3] pointing out the fact that His Catholic Majesty had already been acquainted with their Britannic and Prussian Majesties' declaration (which was made public on November 25th 1759) for a congress, which proves His Britannic Majesty's inclination to enter on negotiations for peace.[4] Yet in his letter [5] on the same subject to his ambas-

---

[1] Thackeray, 1, 459-460, Pitt to Bristol, November 20th 1759.

[2] Ruville, 11, 284-285.

[3] Ibid., 11, 285.

[4] P.R.O., S.P., F., Spain, 160, Draft of an answer to Abreu, December 13th 1759.

[5] Thackeray, 1, 461-463, Pitt to Bristol, December 14th 1759.

sador in Spain, Pitt considered His Catholic Majesty's declaration that he could not be indifferent to the British successes in
America

> "very little consistent with the expressions in other parts of that piece,
> where Spain desires to be considered as in a pure neutrality, and as a
> disinterested equal friend",

and expressed his surprise at the attitude taken by His Catholic
Majesty, and asked his ambassador in Madrid to find out

> "what may have given rise to a measure of such high moment, taken as it
> were at a start and upon the road"; [1]

Pitt's appreciation of the fact that Charles III was neither
neutral nor disinterested in this move of mediation can be
shown to be correct by His Catholic Majesty's instructions to
Abreu.

> "Bien que le roi d'Espagne . . . ait pour les Anglais les sentiments d'une
> sincère amitié et qu'il désire conserver avec eux une parfaite union, s'ils
> devenaient trop menaçant pour l'Europe entière et s'ils refusaient de se
> prêter à un accommodement avec la France, il craindrait de se trouver
> obligé de prendre un parti de vigueur". [2]

He spoke in similar terms to the French ambassador in Spain,
as reported by the latter in his letter of December 7th 1759 to
the Duke of Choiseul. [3]

As to the Anglo-Prussian Declaration, [4] it was delivered, on
November 1759, by Prince Louis of Brunswick, in the name
of their Britannic and Prussian Majesties to the representatives
of the powers concerned at The Hague. This declaration was a
proposal to convene a congress, where the courts of London,
Berlin, Vienna, Versailles and Petersburg would be represented, for the establishment of a general peace. [5] When
d'Affry, the French envoy at the Hague, sent it to the Court of
Versailles, the Duke of Choiseul was flattered that the
English were the first to propose peace negotiations; [6] but he

---

[1] *Ibid.*, 1, 462.

[2] Bourguet, *Le Duc de Choiseul et l'Alliance Espagnole*, 47.

[3] *Recueil des Instructions*, *Espagne* 111, XII bis, 338 (see *supra*, p. 38).

[4] As decided in a Cabinet meeting on October 29th, Waddington, *op. cit.*, 111, 486.

[5] A copy of the Declaration in Thackeray, 11, 470-471.

[6] *Correspondence entre Bernstorff et Choiseul*, 106-107, Duke of Choiseul to Bernstorff, December 1st 1759.

suspected the sincerity of this declaration [1] and foresaw the difficulties which usually confront such projects of congress meetings. He doubted also the efficacy of this means for making peace, for he anticipated the disadvantages of such a measure in causing misunderstandings among the allies, and in alienating the mediators. [2] He also regarded the congress to be against the interests of France, for, during the negotiations, England would be able to deprive her of the rest of her colonies, and Austria would continue her successes and victories over Prussia, regardless of the fate of her ally. [3] On the other hand, he considered the best and only way for the interests of France "to engage England in making her separate peace with France through the Spanish mediation". [4]

Notwithstanding his fears and doubts, the Duke of Choiseul hastened to write to d'Affry, acknowledging the receipt of the Anglo-Prussian declaration and asking him to inform Prince Louis of Brunswick that France would jointly with her allies send their reply to the declaration. [5] Losing no time, he wrote, on the same day to the French ambassadors in Vienna and Petersburg, asking for the views of the two Empresses on the declaration and requesting them to decide in favour of the separation of the two wars. [6] The Duke of Choiseul had important reasons for his request to institute two separate negotiations: one between France and England and the other for the rest of the belligerent countries. He was aware of the difference in the nature and aims of the two wars: the maritime war between England and France, and the continental war which was being fought by the rest of the belligerents. He, therefore, wished to avoid the difficulties, and loss of time, which would arise in a conference dealing with them both. By

---

[1] *Ibid.*, 109; see also *Memoires du Duc de Choiseul*, 386, (Mémoire justificatif presenté par Choiseul in 1765).

[2] Waddington, *op. cit.*, 111, 492, "Mémoire rédigé de la main du Duc [of Choiseul] pour l'Impératrice", December 2nd 1759.

[3] *Ibid.*, 111, 442, Duke of Choiseul to Ossun, December 24th 1759.

[4] *Ibid.*, 111, 441.

[5] Bourguet, "Les Pourparlers de La Haye", *R.H.D.*, XVII, 458, Duke of Choiseul to d'Affry, December 1st 1759.

[6] *Ibid.*, 458.

separating the two wars and insisting upon two separate negotiations, he would also be able to make room for a Spanish mediation which he was anxious not to abandon in favour of the Anglo-Prussian declaration.[1]

By then, Austria had neither attained her aim of completely destroying the power of the King of Prussia nor even fulfilled her ostensible aim of the war, namely recovering Silesia. She was also in an advantageous position to continue war and was not likely to abandon an enterprise upon which her future safety depended.[2] Nevertheless, she did not reject the declaration and accepted the Duke of Choiseul's point of view in the separation of the two wars, but she was reluctant to agree to a continental peace, because of her victories and her hopes and confidence in a forthcoming complete defeat of her enemy.[3] Yet the Empress-Queen and her Chancellor were reassured by the idea that England would neither abandon the King of Prussia nor accept the Spanish mediation.[4] Russia, on her part, did not object to the proposal of their Britannic and Prussian Majesties,[5] for her policy was influenced by the Court of Vienna.[6]

Several weeks after the delivery of the Anglo-Prussian declaration, the Duke of Choiseul was convinced, as he assured Ossun, that the English did not yet want peace and that Pitt was preparing to expel the French from America. The more he realised the disinclination of England to peace, the greater importance he attached to the Spanish mediation.[7] He further added that, if the Spanish mediation was once more rejected:

"c'est alors que vous devés forcer tous les moyens pour engager le Roi d'Espagne de prendre des mesures de guerre avec la France".[8]

[1] For more details on all these reasons, see *Correspondence entre Bernstorff et Choiseul*, 108-109, Duke of Choiseul to Bernstorff, December 1st 1759.

[2] *Ibid.*, 112-113, Bernstorff to Duke of Choiseul, December 18th 1759.

[3] Waddington, *op. cit.*, 111, 493.

[4] *Ibid.*, 111, 493, Count of Choiseul to Duke of Choiseul, December 14th 1759.

[5] For more details on this point see Waddington, *op. cit.*, 111, 494-496.

[6] *Recueil des Instructions*, Russie, 11, IX, 32.

[7] A.E., M.D., Espagne, 574, ff.15r-16r, Duke of Choiseul to Ossun, February 8th 1760.

[8] *Ibid.*, Espagne, 574, f.16r.

Fortunately for the Duke of Choiseul the more the English were victorious and disinclined to come to terms with France by means of a Spanish mediation, the more Charles III became inclined to come closer to France, and even to join in war with her against England.[1] When the news of the congress was communicated to him, he was not pleased, and assured the French ambassador of his desire to insist on being a mediator between France and England.[2] By expressing himself in that way, Charles III was adopting a policy totally different from that of Wall, his Prime Minister,[3] who as already pointed out, moved by economic and military considerations, regarded friendly relations between his adopted country and England as being of the greatest importance to the former.[4] It was thus quite natural that in his first conversation with Ossun, he indicated to him that Spain was not sufficiently interested in trying to impose her mediation on England, which mediation he assured him England would reject.[5] As he anticipated the danger that an offer of mediation would lead His Catholic Majesty into war against England, he objected to any mention of Spanish mediation in the counter-declaration, though the Duke of Choiseul insisted on inserting it. Wall's objection was based on a twofold reason: he feared that this mediation might compromise his King's relations with England and be a hindrance to the reconciliation of France and England.[6] Choiseul naturally saw in the first objection an advantage to France, as he confessed in a confidential letter to Ossun. As to the second objection, he pointed out that he was quite determined not to believe an opinion so contrary to the reality of His Catholic Majesty's sentiments and to his own country's

[1] *Recueil des Instructions, Espagne* 111, XII bis, 338, Ossun to Duke of Choiseul, December 7th 1759, see *supra*, p. 38.

[2] Pitt had already foreseen the dissatisfaction which his joint declaration with Prussia would cause to Charles, Pitt to Bristol, November 20th 1759, Thackeray, 1, 461.

[3] Waddington, *op. cit.*, 111, 437.

[4] See *supra*, p. 22.

[5] Waddington, *op. cit.*, 439, Ossun to Duke of Choiseul, December 15th 1759.

[6] A.E., C.P., Vienne, 275, ff.326v-327r; Wall to Massones, March 3rd 1760, sent to Count of Choiseul March 20th 1760.

interests.[1] In spite of Wall's objection the Duke of Choiseul and Ossun succeeded in persuading Charles III to consent to let Louis XV word the counter-declaration as he pleased.[2] However it was not until four months had elapsed that the counter-declaration was delivered to Prince Louis of Brunswick; it contained the proposal of separating the negotiations connected with the two wars as well as Spanish mediation with regard to the settlement of peace between England and France;[3] but the Duke of Choiseul, who feared that the reference to Spanish mediation might be a hindrance to the conclusion of peace between his country and England,[4] told d'Affry to inform General Yorke, the English Envoy at the Hague, that in spite of the insertion of the Spanish mediation in the counter-declaration for the particular peace between England and France, His Christian Majesty would not reject any other way of treating this peace between France and England.

At the Hague soon after the Anglo-Prussian declaration was delivered, conversations between the French envoy, d'Affry, and the English envoy, Yorke, took place.[5] These conversations which lasted about five months, apart from not being official,[6] were not successful. The two envoys were full of good intentions and were disposed to serve the cause of peace and consequently to serve their own ambitions by bringing themselves into prominence. They were not responsible for the failure of their conversations, which right from the beginning were bound to come to that end because the views of the two countries were so opposed on the question of the

[1] *Ibid.*, Vienne, 275, f.329v; Duke of Choiseul to Ossun, March 19th 1760: "cet Inconvénient . . . ne peut que nous être fort avantageux, en indisposant le Roy Catholique contre la Cour de Londres." Sent to Count of Choiseul on March 20th 1760.

[2] Soulange-Bodin, 131-132; for what passed between Ossun and Charles III on this question, see Rousseau, 1, 47-49.

[3] Bourguet, "Les Pourparlers de La Haye", *R.H.D.*, XVII, 546-547.

[4] A.E., C.P., Hollande, 503, f.282r; Duke of Choiseul to d'Affry, March 31st 1760.

[5] For the history of these conversations, see Bourguet, "Les Pourparlers de la Haye", *R.H.D.*, XVII, 456-468, 541-556; and Waddington, *op. cit.*, 111, 499-545.

[6] They could be called "Semi official".

separation between the two wars.[1] To the objection of the
English ministers to this principle, d'Affry replied that they
either feared a mediation which would force them to conclude
a fair peace, or that they desired to relieve the King of
Prussia from his difficulties.[2] Pitt objected to this principle
not only because he did not then want peace[3] but also because
he anticipated that once a separate peace had been concluded
between England and France, the King of Prussia would not
be able to get great assistance if any at all from England, for
Parliament would in the altered circumstances refuse to grant
subsidies which would only be for the benefit of Prussia.[4]
While Hardwicke gave Pitt "*great weight*" in his reasoning on
the subject,[5] Newcastle, though admitting that there was
"great Weight" in it, was persuaded that, if a separate peace
was not concluded between France and England, no peace
could be obtained,[6] and considered a separate peace as the
means of bringing about a general one.[7] Though Newcastle
was justified in his views, since as will be indicated, the
separate peace between France and England was followed by
the general one, yet it should be pointed out that this only
happened when all the powers seemed to be disposed to
peace. During these first conversations only France and
Prussia were really desirous of peace though not on any
humiliating conditions in spite of their desperate situation,
while England, Austria and Russia were not yet prepared to
make peace. It was quite natural for Pitt to desire the realisation of the enterprises and plans which he started, and, in his
country's advantageous situation to want to acquire for her an

---

[1] Since their first conversation in the House of the Russian ambassador, Golowkin,
when d'Affry indicated, that "il croyait nécessaire de 'tenir les deux guerres séparées
en les términant comme elles l'avaient été dès le commencement'. L'Agent Anglais
riposta, avec beaucoup de vivacité, qu'il valait bien mieux 'tout términer ensemble' ",
Bourguet, "Les Pourparlers de La Haye", *R.H.D.*, XVII, 459.

[2] See *ibid.*, 463.

[3] See *supra*, pp. 30-32.

[4] B.M., Add. MSS., 32901, f.42v; Newcastle to Hardwicke, January 2nd 1760.

[5] *Ibid.*, 32901, f.49v; Hardwicke to Newcastle, January 3rd 1760.

[6] *Ibid.*, 32901, f.42v.

[7] *Ibid.*, 32901, f.407v; Newcastle to Yorke, January 22nd 1760.

E

indisputable maritime supremacy. Yet the plan of separating the negotiations concerning the two wars was reasonable since it was more practicable and it corresponded to the situation. In spite of the fact that some of the interests of France and England were connected with the negotiations of the rest of the belligerent countries, the two wars were of distinct nature, arising from different causes. This idea which did not seem to be timely then, was the basis of the negotiations of 1761, and ultimately of the treaties of Paris and Hubertsburg.

So the Anglo-Prussian declaration failed to be accepted by France and her allies as a basis for peace negotiations; the only step taken on the strength of it being the 'semi official' conversations between d'Affry and Yorke. While these conversations were in progress, the Duke of Choiseul, doubting the sincerity of Pitt's desire for peace, and consequently being uncertain of their outcome, was exerting himself to secure Spanish mediation. After the rejection of the Spanish offer through Abreu, no answer was made from the Court of Madrid, and there was no more question of His Catholic Majesty's intervention during the first months of 1760.[1] No results came from this mediation save that the Court of Vienna adopted the plan of a separate peace.[2] But this did not satisfy the French Foreign Minister. He kept Charles III acquainted with all the conversations at the Hague, submitted to him the draft of the answer of France and her allies to the Anglo-Prussian declaration; and according to the policy which he indicated to Ossun to follow, the latter was to seize every opportunity to cultivate the good dispositions of His Catholic Majesty towards France, and to embitter his feelings against the English and their disguised refusal of His Catholic Majesty's good offices.[3]

Having thus lost all hope of an immediate peace, the Duke of

---

[1] *Correspondence entre Bernstorff et Choiseul*, 132, Duke of Choiseul to Bernstorff, March 27th 1760.

[2] *Ibid.*, 132, stating the importance of this result he continued: "de sorte que si la négociation avec l'Angleterre a jamais lieu, je serai moins embarrassé de nos alliés".

[3] Waddington, *op. cit.*, 111, 442.

Choiseul was resigned to continue the war alone,[1] until such time as he could obtain an honourable peace. He realised more than ever before the necessity of an alliance with Spain and declared to Ossun that it would be his policy as long as he remained in the King's service "d'avoir pour principe invariable de politique d'être uni avec la Couronne d'Espagne",[2] for he considered this alliance as the only path to glory to both branches of the House of Bourbon.[3] Feeling already, at the prospect of a future alliance with Spain, in a stronger position, he denied that peace was so much wanted in France as was believed in the other countries of Europe, he even assured his ambassador that His Christian Majesty

"ne mettra pour cet object ni empressement, ni faiblesse dans sa conduite".[4]

While, thus, the Duke of Choiseul was exerting his efforts with the King of Spain, efforts which were to be crowned by the Family Compact, the war continued to rage.

[1] A.E. M.D., Espagne, 574, f.27r., Duke of Choiseul to Ossun, June 2nd 1760.

[2] *Ibid.*, Espagne, 574, f.26r.

[3] *Ibid.*, Espagne, 574, f.26v., "il n'y aura de grandeur dans la maison de France, de gloire, de vraie sûrete et de vraie tranquilité, que lorsque les deux Couronnes ne cesseront d'avoir pour guides de leur conduite de Systême nécessaire à leur grandeur".

[4] *Ibid.*, Espagne, 574, ff.26v-27r.

THE STANLEY-BUSSY NEGOTIATIONS

NEARLY a year had elapsed since the rupture of the Hague Conversations before other endeavours for peace were made. Meanwhile the continued disasters to the French arms, the collapse of their trade and navy and the impoverishment of their country compelled them to turn again to hopes of peace. The Duke of Choiseul took over Marshal Belleisle's duties as war minister on February 25th 1761 after the latter's death. In doing so he became Minister for war as well as Foreign Minister in France, and was now only too eager to bring the hostilities with England to a close. The situation of French affairs demanded a speedy peace.[1] France had suffered much in her conflict with England, and was not in a condition to endure indefinitely a prolongation of hostilities. The French nation was eager for peace. The prospects of a continuation of war were not at all bright; on the contrary further losses were more likely to make an avoidance of the coming campaign necessary. Charles III, though not making any mystery that all his sympathies were on the side of France, and that the continued successes of the English arms were alarming him, was still undecided about the part which he would take in this struggle. It must not be forgotten that France and Spain, after and in consequence of the rupture of the conversations of the Hague, in May 1760, had resumed communications and had been drawing nearer together. By the end of 1760, the French Foreign Minister, however, was becoming impatient with regard to Spain. He did not think then that it was sufficient that the king of Spain should realise the danger to which the Spanish Colonies were exposed in America by the victories of British arms there, but considered it of the

---

[1] A.E., C.P., Autriche, 281, f.47r, "Mémoire sur la manière de procéder à la paix", joined to the letter of Count of Choiseul, January 6th 1761.

greatest importance that His Catholic Majesty should act with "la plus grande célérité et la plus grande vigueur." [1] The Duke of Choiseul, consequently declared to Ossun in the same letter:

"Quoiqu'il en soit, Mr., le Roi Ne doit Ni ne veut rester plus longtemps dans l'incertitude des véritables dispositions de la Cour de Madrid". [2]

He went so far as to declare to Ossun [3] that if His Catholic Majesty made up his mind and joined France in her struggle against England, His Christian Majesty would not think of peace then. [4] He explained in the same letter that:

"Les maux étant extrêmes il n'y a que les remèdes violens qui puissent les guérir".

He forwarded then two plans of attack against some of England's commerical interests: either an attack on Portugal and Brazil, or an appeal to Holland to join France and Spain against England in order that they maintain the liberty of commerce at sea. [5] He further stated that if Spain had no intention to declare herself openly and positively against England, the King would adopt the plan of peace which he had already formed, and would engage his allies

"de gré ou de force d'y concourir". [6] "Si le Roi d'Espagne ne peut pas se déclarer éfficacement le roi sera forcé de suivre coûte que coûte la négociation de la paix". [7]

At the end of the letter, Ossun was urged to find out what were His Catholic Majesty's final decisions on which the French Foreign Minister, as he declared, depended much in planning with his allies, for either peace or war. [8] Thus at the end of

---

[1] *Ibid.*, Espagne, 530, f.237v; Duke of Choiseul to Ossun, November 25th 1760.

[2] *Ibid.*, Espagne, 530, f.238r.

[3] *Ibid.*, Espagne, 530, f.196r; Duke of Choiseul to Ossun, November 14th 1760.

[4] Sautreau in his "Analyses Historique des Négotiations entre la France et L'Espagne depuis 1746 jusqu'en 1776" thinks that if the Duke of Choiseul "étoit sûr du Roi d'Espagne et de ses ministres, il ne seroit pas même tenté d'ouvrir des Négotiations pour la paix", A.E., M.D., Espagne, 189, f.35r.

[5] Bourguet, *Le Duc de Choiseul et l'Alliance Espagnole*, 161-162. This letter of November 14th 1761, which is almost all published by Bourguet, is an outline of Choiseul's views on his policy towards England and Spain, (*Ibid.*, 159-164).

[6] A.E., C.P., Espagne, 530, f.198r.

[7] Bourguet, *op. cit.*, 160, the same letter.

[8] *Ibid.*, 163-164.

1760, the matter of war or peace in France rested chiefly on the decisions of Charles III. When Ossun waited on the latter in order to acquaint his court with his decisions, the King of Spain, after assuring him of his willingness to join France in her struggle against England, pointed to his unpreparedness which made it impossible at this time to fulfil his desire.[1] He did not even indicate the time which he required for preparing his country for the struggle,[2] because, as he declared, he did not want to make France, through doubtful hopes, decline a peace or continue alone a war which might cost her more losses.[3] When Charles III's answer reached the Duke of Choiseul, the latter, appreciating very much the frankness and justice of the Spanish monarch, decided to take the necessary measures for making peace with as easy conditions as possible.[4] Although regretting much that Charles III was not able to join France against their common and natural enemy,[5] he was relieved that His Catholic Majesty did not fix a certain date for making common cause with France, for as he was not then willing to involve France in any sort of commitments,[6] he realised that such engagements would have embarrassed France very much.[7]

Charles III, though appreciating much the advantages of his

[1] *Recueil des Instructions*, *Espagne*, III, XII bis, 339. "Bien résolu à ne plus souffrir les insolences britanniques, avant de s'engager dans une lutte qu'il savait devoir être périlleuse, il voulait remédier au désordre dans lequel il avait trouvé le royaume, en réconstituer les forces maritimes et militaires, et en rétablir les finances."

[2] Simances Estado, Leg. 3457, no. 38, Instructions of January 14th 1761 to Grimaldi for his embassy to Paris. The persistent request of France for His Catholic Majesty's answer was indicated when explaining the position of Spain's relation with France.

[3] Bourguet, *op. cit.*, 165-167, Ossun to Duke of Choiseul, November 28th 1760, see also *Recueil des Instructions*, *Espagne III*, XII bis, 339-340.

[4] A.E., C.P., Espagne, 530, f.306v, Duke of Choiseul to Ossun, December 9th 1760.

[5] *Ibid.*, Espagne, 530, ff.340r-340v, Duke of Choiseul to Ossun, December 16th 1760.

[6] *Ibid.*, Espagne, 530, f.130r, Duke of Choiseul to Ossun, October 28th 1760. "Mais vous devez éviter avec une extrême attention de rien articuler de précis sur les engagemens que Nous pourrions prendre avec l'Espagne. Vous sentez que leur Nature et leur étendue dépendroient nécessairement de Notre situation actuelle".

[7] *Ibid.*, Espagne, 530, f.306v, Duke of Choiseul to Ossun, December 9th 1760.

union with France against England, had his reasons for not joining France immediately in her struggle against that country. First and foremost, as he often repeated to Ossun, he needed some time in order to prepare his country and his colonies for the strife. He also, very likely, did not want to appear as the aggressor towards England, and preferred to lean in his "measures" against England on "a Solid Support." [1] He therefore, while preparing to take up arms against England, was waiting for a written answer to his claims from Pitt,[2] though he could hardly expect this answer to please him, for he had already known Pitt's opinion on these questions through Fuentes, his ambassador in London, who replaced Abreu at the beginning of 1760, and who was charged in particular to settle his country's grievances with England.[3] He tried during that year to reach an agreement with Pitt on these points of dispute. In June, he made a formal complaint of the arbitrary acts of the English at sea, forwarding at the same time a complete list of the Spanish ships seized by the English men of war, or privateers since 1756.[4] In September of the same year, he presented two more memorials: one on the usurpations of the English settlers in Honduras, and the other on the fisheries.[5] It was only at the beginning of September 1760 that Pitt answered the first mentioned memoir.[6] His answer to the other more important questions of the fishing right and the cutting of logwood in Honduras was a concise but a sharp answer.[7] As to the fishery question, he asked Bristol to "let M. Wall understand the utter impossibility of a concession on the part of his Majesty, so destructive to the

---

[1] B.M., Add. MSS., 32918, f.27r, Translation of a letter in cypher from Fuentes to Wall, January 23rd 1761.

[2] A.E., C.P., Espagne, 530, ff.211v-212t, Ossun to Duke of Choiseul, November 17th 1760.

[3] See *Recueil des Instructions*, *Espagne* 111, XII bis, 339.

[4] P.R.O., S.P., F., Spain, 161, Memoir dated June 20th 1760.

[5] *Ibid.*, Spain, 162, Memoirs of September 9th 1760.

[6] *Ibid.*, Spain, 162, Pitt to Fuentes, September 1st 1760, see also Thackeray, 1, 484, Pitt to Bristol, September 5th 1760 (see chapter II, pp. 58-59).

[7] Thackeray, 1, 487-492, Pitt to Bristol, September 26th 1760.

true interests of Great Britain."[1] With regard to the Honduras question,

> "his Majesty is desirous and ready to give all just satisfaction to the Catholic King with regard to fortifications and establishments erected there, and at the same time to adjust and terminate amicably and equitably disputes about cutting logwood, if the court of Spain will enter into negotiation on this last-mentioned point".[2]

A few months later, Ossun asserted to his country that the English were holding the same views. They still considered an assurance of their cutting of logwood a necessary preliminary to any discussion of the Spanish claims.[3] This conditional manner of treating, which the English were using, was but irritating His Catholic Majesty and increasing his hostile feelings towards England. In a contemporary French memoir, His Catholic Majesty's feelings were clearly described in the following words:

> "Ce Prince trouvoit étrange que les Anglois convinssent de leurs usurpations, et en même tems osassent s'en prévaloir comme d'une Compensation avec d'autres Avantages. Il disoit à ce sujet à un de ses ministres 'que la prudence et la nécessité le retenoient encore; mais qu'il faisoit un grand effort sur lui même pour ne pas rompre dans l'instant avec l'Angleterre' ".[3]

At the same time, while waiting for an answer to his claims from England, Charles III hoped that

> "the French would not succumb to one of their overwhelming fits for peace and consequently rush its conclusion".[5]

Thus Charles III, who had an immediate interest in the negotiation pending with France, desired to delay the conclusion of peace between England and France. It was clear that he had no idea of allowing France to make peace with England without the settlement of the Spanish claims.[6] He had

[1] *Ibid.*, I, 488.

[2] *Ibid.*, I, 488-489.

[3] Bourguet, *op. cit.*, 196-197, Ossun to Duke of Choiseul, March 5th 1761.

[4] A.E., M.D., France et Divers Etats, 570, ff.18r-18v.

[5] Collado, II, 108, Charles III to Tanucci, November 4th 1760.

[6] Hotblack, *Chatham's Colonial Policy*, 131.

cause to fear the pacific tendencies of the Duke of Choiseul. The latter would avoid an alliance with Spain as long as he retained hope of peace with England. If peace was, therefore, concluded between France and England, Charles III's hopes of an alliance with France would be dashed to the ground. Charles III's fears also increased when he heard the rumours about the negotiations for peace between England and France. The Duke of Choiseul tried in vain to assure him that although France earnestly desired that peace, no negotiations for it had yet taken place; that if there was any, His Catholic Majesty would have been acquainted with their progress, as he was with those of the year before at the Hague. The King of Spain persisted in his fears: he was aware that he had already proved to England that he was not impartial, and feared therefore to be compelled to sustain alone a war against her.[1] He consequently recalled Massones, the Spanish ambassador in Paris, from his post and replaced him by Grimaldi, the ambassador at the Hague, and known to be a partisan of the French alliance,[2] in order that the latter would watch the development of the negotiations between France and England,[3] and sue for an alliance between France and Spain.[4] Grimaldi, in his letter to Fuentes of March 5th 1761, only expressed his King's fears when he said that it was

"of the Utmost Importance for Us, to assure Ourselves of France; and engage Her, before She makes Her Peace; For afterwards, I don't know, What Inclination She may have to go to War again for our Sake".[5]

Fuentes was no less desirous of the conclusion of an alliance between France and his country when he declared that Spain had lost much time, but assumed that it was then their

---

[1] A.E., M.D., France et Divers Etats, 570, ff.22r-22v.

[2] P.R.O., S.P., F., Spain, 159, Bristol to Pitt, March 5th 1759.

[3] Bourguet, *Le Duc de Choiseul et l'Alliance Espagnole*, 188.

[4] Simancas, Estado Leg. 3457 no. 38, Instructions of January 14th 1761, given to Grimaldi for his embassy in Paris (which instructions are superficially consulted by the Spanish History relevant books), for more details on these instructions see *infra*, pp. 76-77, and the original Spanish draft, appendix 4, pp. 235-243.

[5] B.M., Add. MSS., 32919, f.446r.

"Opportunity."[1] The same spirit of distrust prevailed in the Court of Versailles, for the Duke of Choiseul attached great importance to the hostility, which Charles III then showed against England, but suspected the intentions of that Sovereign, whose intention might not be, after all, to declare himself against England. He might be satisfied with just pretending it, in order to obtain some advantages from the two belligerent countries in the future treaty of peace:

"de l'Angleterre par la crainte qu'il lui inspiroit, de la France par la reconnoissance qu'elle lui devroit du zèle qu'il affectoit pour sa cause".[2]

The Duke of Choiseul was not mistaken when he analysed the intentions of His Catholic Majesty in the following words:

"Tout ce que Nous croyons voir jusqu'à présent c'est que la Cour de Madrid voudroit ou que nous Ne fissions pas la paix, ou du moins que les intérêts Espagnols fussent ménagés dans le Traité"

Choiseul did not seem pleased when he came to the conclusion that:

"Ce désir est à peu près le même chés toutes les Nations Neutres, qui sans avoir pris acucune part, avec hazard et aux dépens de la guerre voudroient partager les avantages de la participation".

However, in the same letter, the Duke of Choiseul formulated the policy which France should follow in her relations with Spain. France should manage Spain very carefully so that, if the negotiations of peace with England failed, Spain would come to the rescue of France.[3] Ossun in a letter of February 14th explained clearly this policy and its difficulties,

"La grande difficulté est de trouver des Moyens pour détourner ce Prince ou d'une conciliation ou d'une rupture prematurée, et de l'engager en même tems à Négocier Vis-à-vis de l'Angleterre avec Modération et avec fermeté, et à se préparer à des démarches de Vigueur, sans les mettre en usage".[4]

[1] Ibid., 32920, f.40r, Fuentes to Grimaldi, March 10th 1761, "So good an Opportunity", he asserted, "is not to be lost", Ibid., f.40v.

[2] A.E., M.D., France et Divers Etats, 570, ff.22v-23r.

[3] A.E., C.P., Espagne, 531, f.127v, Duke of Choiseul to Ossun, February 3rd 1761; the Duke of Choiseul hoped that, with the help of Spain in the war, he might be able to repair his country's losses; if the war was unsuccessful he had in view that the losses of Spain would lighten those which France might suffer, Corbett, 11, 185.

[4] A.E., C.P., Espagne, 531, ff.237v-238r.

Clearer still were Ossun's views on this policy when he wrote to Choiseul in another letter of the same date.

"nous devons . . . désirer que Sa Majesté Catholique ne rompe pas actuellement; ou ne s'accorde pas à l'amiable avec les Anglais jusqu'à ce que notre paix soit faite ou manquée".[1]

Spain was not the only country interested in delaying the conclusion of peace. Austria, for different reasons,[2] had the same desire as Spain. Although Maria Theresa seemed then to be more inclined to peace than she had been the year before [3] —or at least the French ambassador in Vienna had thought so for four months [4]—she was actually as averse to it as she had been before. The French ambassador must have felt very annoyed when he realised that he had been deceived and that consequently he had misled his government:

"depuis quatre mois j'abusois le Roy en luy donnant de fausses notions sur une Cour que je devrois connoitre. Je me consolerios volontiers d'estre duppe s'il n'en refuttoit que l'humiliation de mon amour propre, mais Je ne prends pas si aisément mon party quand il s'agit des intérêts du Roy".[5]

However, in order to obtain peace, the Duke of Choiseul was prepared if necessary, to abandon the interests of his ally Austria.[6] When the French ambassador in Vienna discussed with the Chancellor the best means of obtaining a peace, they differed in their views, whereas Austria was for a congress,[7] France was for a separate negotiation with England. At the beginning of 1761, the Duke of Choiseul explained to Kaunitz [8]

[1] *Ibid.*, Espagne, 531, ff.224v-225r.

[2] See Chapter II, p. 27.

[3] A.E., C.P., Autriche, 281, ff 8r-8v, Count of Choiseul to Duke of Choiseul, January 3rd 1761.

[4] *Ibid.*, Autriche, 281, f.256v, Count of Choiseul to Duke of Choiseul, February 15th 1761.

[5] *Ibid.*, Autriche 281, ff.256v-257r.

[6] A.E., M.D., France and Divers Etats, 570, ff.7v-8r, "Dépêche de la Cour", February 21st 1761. See also chap. II, p. 27.

[7] A.E., C.P., Autriche, 281, f,26r, Count of Choiseul to Breteuil (French ambassador in Russia), January 3rd 1761.

[8] *Ibid.*, Autriche, 281, ff.47-52, Memoir of January 6th 1761 to Vienna.

his views on the advantages of a separate negotiation and the
disadvantages of a congress. It was then clear that the French
Foreign Minister preferred a separate negotiation to a congress
not only because, as he indicated, it was the quickest, the
safest and the surest way, but also because he wanted to control
the negotiations of his allies as well as those of his country.[1]
Desiring to save all he could from the wreck of his country's
fortunes, he hoped to make something of the French conquests
in Germany, though they were nominally won for the
Empress.[2] However in his declaration of January 31st 1761,[3]
the Duke of Choiseul reached a compromise between the
wishes of Versailles and Vienna, by proposing the meeting of a
general Congress at Augsburg, and two separate negotiations
between France and England which were to be held in
London and in Paris. Kaunitz not approving of this declaration,[4] the Duke of Choiseul turned his efforts towards his other
important ally, Russia, on whose clear and decisive answer, as
he pointed out, he was then to rely,[5] in order to be able to act,
if Russia approved of his views, without holding any more
discussions on the same question with the Austrian Chancellor.
Breteuil [6] succeeded in making Woronzow, the Russian
Chancellor, accept the French proposals of the separate
negotiations between France and England and of a general
Congress. It was also agreed with the Court of Russia, that
Prince Galitzin,[7] the Russian ambassador in London, should
act as intermediary, in presenting the French overtures for

---

[1] *Ibid.*, Autriche, 281, f.27r, Count of Choiseul to Breteuil January 3rd 1761.
"C'est un point capital de nous rendre maitres de la Négociation, et d'être autorisés
par nos Alliés à traiter directement la Paix".

[2] Williams, 11, 81.

[3] A.E., C.P., Autriche, 281, ff.175-176, this declaration was joined to
Stahremberg's letter of February 9th.

[4] Waddington, *La Guerre de Sept Ans*, IV, 471.

[5] As Count of Choiseul pointed out to Breteuil in his letter of February 10th 1761,
Waddington, *op. cit.*, IV, 472.

[6] For a more detailed account of Breteuil's endeavours with the Russian Chancellor
Woronzow, see *ibid.*, IV, 472-476.

[7] By this choice the Duke of Choiseul "flattoit agréablement la vanité de l'Impératrice
de Russie, qu'il rendoit pour ainsi dire l'arbitre des destinées de la France", A.E.,
M.D., France et Divers Etats, 570, f.35v.

peace to the Court of London. This agreement between the two Courts of Versailles and Petersburg was but to accelerate the peace-move. The Count of Choiseul did not therefore lose much time in showing Kaunitz the authorisation of Woronzow to Prince Galitzin to act as an intermediary. He explained his reasons in a letter of March 12th to the Duke of Choiseul:

"La première [reason] pour mettre ce Ministre (Kaunitz) au pied du mur, et ne luy laisser aucun prétéxte de se refuser à une démarche proposée par la Russie elle-même. La seconde c'est que j'ai cru qu'il n'étoit pas inutile de lui prover par là que la Russie entroit sincèrement dans nos vues, qu'elle étoit plus facile que la Cour de Vienne". [1]

In striving to attain his aim, the Duke of Choiseul was not only confronted with the difficulties of the delicate role which he was to play in his "two games" [2] with regard to England and Spain; but also with the oppositions of his ally Austria, as well as with a powerful faction in France itself pledged to the support of Austrian interests, and anxious to continue the war. The existence of this party could not but exercise an influence on Choiseul's policy. However anxious he might be to free his country from the strain of a long and an unsuccessful war, he was obliged to face the fact that there were those who were ready to accuse him of a too ready a compliance with the demands of England. [3] It seemed, therefore, that there was a very definite limit to concessions beyond which Choiseul could not afford to go. [4] Peace would only be attained if this limit coincided with what the English ministers were willing to accept.

In England, by that time, some fundamental changes had taken place: George II, who died on October 25th 1760, was

---

[1] A.E., C.P., Autriche, 281, ff.443v-444r.

[2] Corbett, II, 185.

[3] Temperley in his article on "The Peace of Paris", asserted that the Duke of Choiseul, "Though dependent on the favour of Louis XV and La Pompadour, he had also appealed for support to the French public, and could not consent to humiliating terms", The Cambridge History of the British Empire, 1, 489-490.

[4] When the fisheries question was at issue in the negotiations between England and France, the Duke of Choiseul assured Stanley that: "that total exclusion of France from any share whatever in that branch of commerce was a condition no minister ought nor durst comply with", Thackeray, 11, 574, Stanley to Pitt, August 6th 1761.

succeeded by his grandson, George III. At his accession to the
throne, he found an administration

"powerful from the possession of great talents and the combination of
parties, and popular from uninterrupted success". [1]

Nevertheless the new Sovereign was anxious to restore peace
to his country. [2] His Groom of the Stole, Bute, was not less
anxious to bring the war to an end. They were also as desirous
of getting rid of Newcastle as of Pitt, but were wise enough to
see that both united were irresistible and thus took every
advantage of their differences to play one against the other. [3]
They believed that as long as England was involved in war,
Pitt, to whom the successes which had attended the English
arms were almost exclusively attributed, seemed indispensable;
hence they thought that only peace with France could enable
them to get rid of Pitt. [4] However the first six months of the
new reign were largely occupied by the general election and
the ministerial changes. [5] The accession of Bute to the post of
Secretary of State for the Northern Department was a notable
triumph for the King and his favourite, since they succeeded in
making Newcastle give his consent to this change and consequently in widening the breach between Newcastle and Pitt.
Bute stood, by his views on peace, midway between Newcastle
and Pitt. Bute was as anxious as Newcastle to see peace restored
and would perhaps have been ready to make some sacrifice to
secure it, [6] in order that his master might reap all the benefits
of the popularity of having inaugurated his reign by conferring
the blessings of peace upon a nation wearied by a long struggle
and also that he might be able to dispense with Pitt's services

[1] Adolphus, I, 5.

[2] *Ibid.*, I, 19.

[3] Williams, 11, 68-69.

[4] Winstanley, 29-30, Winstanley points out here the fact that George III and Bute
wanted peace in particular in order to enable them to act with greater freedom in
recovering the powers of the Crown; Professor Namier and Sedgwick, on the other
side, are of the opinion that George III in reality "carried on, to the best of his more
than limited ability, the system of government which he had inherited from his
predecessors", *Letters from George III to Lord Bute 1756-1766*, XLII.

[5] For the different changes in the Government, see Winstanley, 30-33.

[6] Ruville, 11, 366.

whenever he felt necessary.[1] Yet he had reasons for divergence upon this point. In the first place he was to consider national opinion, as he did not want to endanger the popularity of his master,[2] for although the greater part of the nation was anxious for peace,[3] yet the long series of victories made them regard the maintenance of their conquests as an indispensable condition. Bute was thus obliged "to steer a middle course",[4] and to aim at bringing about a peace which would satisfy national ambition and yet be acceptable to France. The attitude which Bute was to take between the two ministers, Pitt and Newcastle, was of great importance to the decisions of the English Cabinet during the negotiation of peace with France. It will be noticed that as long as Bute took the side of Pitt, the latter kept his predominant position in the cabinet and his views prevailed on the Cabinet decisions, but when Bute changed front, important alterations took place in the character of the decisions of the Cabinet meetings with regard to these negotiations.

Pitt, who was then in a better position for bargaining on England's behalf than in the spring of 1760,[5] had no wish needlessly to prolong the war; but though ready to make peace, he intended it to be of such a character as would cause it to rank amongst the most glorious in English history. He was determined to turn an unusually advantageous position to the utmost advantage.[6] He made no secret of the terms which he would expect France to accept: the cession of

"all Canada, Cape Breton, the islands, the harbours, the fisheries, and particularly the exclusive fishery of Newfoundland".

He asserted that, if he was capable of signing a treaty without it, he should be sorry he had ever regained the use of his right

[1] Winstanley, 46.

[2] See Williams, 11, 85.

[3] B.M., Add. MSS., 32918, ff.120-121, Anonymous letter of January 29th 1761 to Newcastle; see also Ibid., 32920, f.40v. Fuentes to Grimaldi, March 10th 1761.

[4] Winstanley, 46.

[5] See Williams, 11, 81.

[6] Ruville, 11, 365.

hand.[1] The following narration of the peace negotiations will indicate how the question of the fisheries proved to be the most important point of difference between Pitt and the Duke of Choiseul. None in the cabinet, except Temple, shared Pitt's uncompromising views. Of the others, Bute was the nearest to him in the first stage of the negotiation. Bedford was his "most formidable opponent." He held fundamentally different views on foreign policy. He had no belief in increasing the colonial possessions of England. He also opposed Pitt's policy of destroying the French navy. He thought that it was not a natural step to take and that it was dangerous for it must excite all the naval powers of Europe to enter a confederacy against the English.[2]

In spite of the fact that the energy of Pitt and the increasing glories of the British arms and the depression of the French power contributed to render the war popular, by the end of 1760 the greater part of the English nation was anxious for peace. Public opinion started to blame the project of carrying on a German war, and treated it as "a dangerous delusion."[3] In the autumn of that year, Israel Maudit published an important pamphlet: *Considerations on the Present German War*.[4] It set forth the impolicy of the English measures in Germany. The subsidy to the King of Prussia was represented in a most injurious light; he received six hundred and fifty thousand pounds a year to fight his own battles, whilst England was bound to defend him without the slightest commitment on his part.[5] Mauduit considered that policy as "ruinous and impracticable."[6] This shrewdly and ably written pamphlet had at that time

"more operation in working a change on the minds of men, than perhaps fell to the lot of a pamphlet".[7]

[1] Albemarle, I, 23-24, Newcastle to Hardwicke, April 15th 1761.

[2] Williams, 11, 85.   [3] Adolphus, 1, 19.

[4] Williams, 11, 67; it is believed that it was published with the countenance of Hardwicke, *Memoirs of George III*, 1, 25.

[5] Adolphus, 1, 21; Mauduit thought that Frederick was doubtless a man of great abilities, one of its clearest proofs was making England to pay him that large subsidy "for nothing", Mauduit, 68.

[6] Mauduit, 95.

[7] *Memoirs of George III*, 1, 25.

However anxious the English people were for peace, they desired it to be of such a character that it would secure the unchallenged supremacy of England;[1]

> "a long series of victories had so raised their self-esteem that they regarded the permanent maintenance of their conquests as an indispensable condition".[2]

They wanted the peace to be not only advantageous to England, but disastrous to France. As to the terms of peace, there were two views: one supporting the idea of keeping Canada and another for keeping Guadeloupe. In Beer's *British Colonial Policy*, the different pamphlets on each side are enumerated as well as the arguments which each party put forward in support of its views.[3] However, generally speaking, British opinion, as recorded both in private letters and in the press, inclined to favour the keeping of Canada; considerations of security and distrust of the French being in people's minds.[4] As to the English ministers, there was nothing to show that in 1760 any of them had any settled views on the choice to be made between conquests, still less that they tried to force any such views on their adherents. Peace or no peace was at various times an issue, but not whether preference in the peace treaty should be given to Canada or to Guadeloupe. It was but slowly that opinion matured on this point and even then it did not become an issue as between parliamentary groups.[5] It was in 1761 that Pitt declared his desire of acquiring all Canada, with the islands and the exclusive fisheries.[6] The French Minister possessed a very clear understanding of the opinion prevailing in the British Ministry and had made up his mind that peace could be attained only by the sacrifice of Canada,

---

[1] In *The Public Ledger*, London, December 24th 1760, 1189, an impartial Spectator, as he called himself, could not see why England should be so complaisant to France as to return any conquests she had made.

[2] Ruville, 11, 367.

[3] Beer, 134-152; see also Alvord, 1, 56-63.

[4] Namier, 321. It is worth pointing out here that it was long before the pamphlet warfare ceased, that the ministers had taken their decision, Alvord, 1, 63.

[5] Namier, 317-318.

[6] See Albemarle, 1, 23-24, Newcastle to Hardwicke, April 15th 1761, see *supra*, pp. 67-68.

F

and this he acknowledged by his first proposal for peace on
March 26th 1761, that the basis of the peace negotiations
should be the *uti possidetis* on certain dates.[1]

Frederick, the King of Prussia, was growing more and more
inclined for peace. In spite of occasional victories, he was
becoming weaker with every campaign. Recognising that the
condition of including Prussia in the treaty between France
and England, was impossible, he agreed that Pitt should make
a separate peace with France on condition that France consented to evacuate Wezel and all other possessions on the
Rhine and confine her assistance to the Empress-Queen to
24,000 men, and that he himself received an increased
subsidy from England.[2]

It was on the last day of March 1761, that the Russian
ambassador, Prince Galitzin, communicated to Pitt the
overtures of peace proposed by France and her allies. The two
Empresses, the Kings of France, Sweden and Poland jointly
invited the Kings of Great Britain and Prussia to take part in a
congress which was to meet at Augsburg.[3] But the more
material paper was a "Mémoire", by order of the King of
France, enclosed in a letter from the Duke of Choiseul to
Pitt.[4] This memoir [5] set forth that, as the delays of a European
congress are proverbial, the attainment of peace might be
facilitated if the particular interests of England and France
were considered separately. As a basis of discussion the French
Foreign Minister suggested the principle of the *uti possidetis*,
that the two countries should remain in possession of the
territory they occupied in various parts of the world at certain
fixed dates. In Europe, May 1st 1761 was the date named as
determining possession, in the West Indies and Africa,
July 1st 1761, and in the East Indies, September 1st 1761.
These epochs, however, were not to be taken as final or

[1] Alvord, 1, 63. The Duke of Choiseul acknowledged it also in his instructions to
Bussy of May 23rd 1761, see Waddington, *op. cit.*, IV, 517.

[2] Williams, 11, 81-82; Waddington, IV, 405-406.

[3] See *Parliamentary History of England*, XV, 1021-1022.

[4] *Ibid.*, 1023.

[5] *Ibid.*, 1023-1025.

beyond discussion. They, as well as the question of compensation to be given for the surrender of the conquests of each country, were to be subjects of negotiation. These terms were not disadvantageous to England; and Newcastle, overjoyed and even surprised that France would at the outset offer such terms, wrote to Devonshire:

"I will then Rejoice with you upon the Contents of the enclosed Papers; which (If We make a proper Use of Them, which I much doubt,) would secure us a good Peace, even this Summer". [1]

Devonshire was not less surprised. Nevertheless he could not believe that Minorca alone would content France in lieu of the places, which had been taken from her, nor could he imagine that France was so distressed as to submit to such terms. [2] Pitt was not so enthusiastic, for he suspected that Choiseul might intend to consider England's allies' territories on the continent, which had been occupied by the French, as conquests wrested from Britain. [3] However this declaration received a prompt answer on April 8th; [4] accepting the proposal for a congress in Augsburg, and promising the appointment of ambassadors. A memoir of the same date to the French government was transmitted to Choiseul, together with a letter from Pitt, in which the English minister explained his views concerning the separate proposals of the Court of Versailles. Pitt declared his agreement with the principle of the *uti possidetis*, and requested the dispatch of a special ambassador, he disagreed, however, with the French proposals with reference to the definition of dates. [5] Pitt desired, during the negotiations, not only to conclude the operations which had begun, but also to begin further enterprises, the success of which would justify an increase of his demands. At the moment when he dispatched his answer to the French proposals, he

[1] B.M., Add. MSS., 32921, f.272r, Newcastle to Devonshire, April 2nd 1761.

[2] *Ibid.*, 32921, ff.311v-312r, Devonshire to Newcastle, April 4th 1761.

[3] Waddington, *op. cit.*, IV, 498-499.

[4] See *Parliamentary History of England*, XV, 1025-1026.

[5] Waddington, *op. cit.*, IV, 500-501.

sent therefore an expedition against Belleisle, in order to
obtain a compensation for Minorca.[1]

The second interchange of memoirs of April 19th and 28th [2]
produced no agreement about the epochs. However it was
agreed that both countries should exchange plenipotentiaries
for conference with the respective ministers of foreign affairs.
Whereas Hans Stanley [3] was chosen by the English Government to confer with the Duke of Choiseul, Bussy [4] was
appointed by the French government to confer with Pitt. In
his letter of May 4th,[5] the Duke of Choiseul, recommending
Bussy to Pitt, expressed regret that he could not negotiate
directly with the English Secretary of State. At the same date,
already in this early stage of the negotiations, because of the
English expedition against Belleisle, he expressed his fears
about Pitt's sincerity for peace, and also feared that this
conquest might become an invincible obstacle to peace:

"car Je doute que le Roi soit dans l'intention de traiter avant que
Beleisle lui soit remis".[6]

The instructions given to Stanley for his mission to Paris were
discussed in a meeting of the English Cabinet on May 13th
1761.[7] Although it was agreed, at this meeting, that Stanley
"was to hear; and That the Business . . ." was to "be done" in
London, it was necessary to provide him with the necessary
instructions which would enable him to converse with the
French Foreign Minister. In spite of the fact that his powers as

---

[1] A.E., C.P., Angleterre, 443, f.103v, Galitzin to Duke of Choiseul, London,
May 11th 1761; Flassan VI, 385, "Cette manière adroite d'opérer, tendait à laisser les
Anglais en possession de tout ce qu'ils avient pris à la france"; Bedford's comments on
this conquest, Bedford Correspondence, III, 16-17.

[2] See Parliamentary History of England, XV, 1028-1033.

[3] About Stanley, see Albemarle, 1, 21-22; Yorke, 111, 268 (footnote 5); Bedford
Correspondence, 111, 151 (footnote); Waddington, IV, 521-525; Grant, 10; Bourguet
"La Mission de Bussy à Londres", R.H., LXXI, 4-5.

[4] About Bussy see Yorke, 111, 268 (footnote 4); Williams, 11, 88; Waddington,
op. cit., IV, 520-521; Grant, 11-12; Bourguet, op. cit., 5; Albemarle, 1, 22.

[5] Waddington, op. cit., IV, 510.

[6] A.E., C.P., Angleterre, 443, ff.100r-100v, Duke of Choiseul to Prince Galitzin,
May 4th 1761.

[7] Account of which is given by Newcastle in his letter of May 14th 1761 to Hardwicke, B.M., Add. MSS., 32923, ff.63-72.

plenipotentiary were formally confirmed, his actual power was very limited, for he was not to agree to anything without special orders from one of the Secretaries of State. Stanley was not, even if asked by the French Foreign Minister, to make any proposals for peace. He was to tell the Duke of Choiseul, if asked, that His Britannic Majesty having accepted the proposals of the French government, it was not at all likely that he (Stanley), should be charged to make any other on his country's behalf.[2] The English ministers did not thus desire to be the first to suggest the preliminary terms of peace. However, the English plenipotentiary was asked to take "*ad referendum*" any views or notions which the Duke of Choiseul may entertain for the separate peace between the two crowns or for that of the conciliation of the other belligerent powers. He was also recommended to:

"give a watchful attention to the conduct and motions of the Spanish Ambassador there".[3]

As to Bussy's instructions, they were drawn up by the Duke of Choiseul in a memoir of May 23rd 1761,[4] in which it was indicated that Bussy's first and most important aim should be the conclusion of a reasonable peace regardless of the ambitions of the two Empresses. However Russia, represented by her ambassador, should be considered because she helped in bringing about the negotiations between France and England. It was also of great importance that Bussy should keep on good terms with the Spanish ambassador, with whose country France wanted to maintain her friendship and to propose an alliance. Bussy, however, was not to listen to proposals for any aggressive policy against England, if the negotiations for peace with her were taking a favourable course. This part of the instructions concerning the attitude which Bussy was to take towards the

---

[1] Thackeray, 1, 508, Stanley's instructions of May 18th 1761. All his instructions are *ibid.*, 1, 506-509.

[2] *Ibid.*, 1, 507.

[3] See *ibid.*, 1, 507-509.

[4] See Bourguet, "La mission de Bussy à Londres", *R.H.*, LXXI, 6-7, and Waddington, *op. cit.*, IV, 512-517.

different foreign countries' representatives during his mission in London, was ended by the following directions:—

"Apporter pour le succès de la paix tous les moyens de conciliation qui seraient conformes à la justice et à la dignité du Roi, sans se laisser amuser par une négociation vague".[1]

The second part of the instructions was relative to the conditions of the separate peace between France and England: the question of the dates, at which the principle of the *uti possidetis* was to be applied, was an important question to settle. Approximate compensations with regard to the acquisitions of England in America and Africa were indicated. However, they were not to be definite and Bussy was to obtain from England the "propositions catégoriques et par ecrit."[2] It is clear that both the English and the French Foreign ministers did not then wish to be the first to make offers for the conditions of peace.

The two main points of difference existing then between the two countries were the epochs and the compensation principle. Though apparently minor, they were very important. Protracting the decision on the dates of the *uti possidetis*, in France's exhausted state meant more losses to her and more gains for her enemy. It was clear that Pitt did not decide on this point immediately, because he intended to include Belleisle in the *uti possidetis*, consequently when this island surrendered on June 7th, Pitt was able to propose new dates for the *statu quo*.[3] As to the second point, it was important for France,[4] who had beside her acquisitions in Germany, nominally conquered for her ally Austria, nothing else but Minorca to bargain with in the negotiations, to know whether the principle of the *uti possidetis* was to include merely the losses of the English Crown or also those of her German allies. After several meetings of the English cabinet,[5] this question was decided in favour of

[1] Bourguet, "La Mission de Bussy à Londres", *R.H.*, LXXI, 7.

[2] Waddington, *op. cit.*, IV, 516-517.

[3] See Rousseau, 1, 59.

[4] The Duke of Choiseul acknowledged its importance in his letter to Bussy, of June 19th 1761, A.E., C.P., Angleterre, 443, ff.225v-226r.

[5] On these discussions see Ruville, 11, 370-371.

France. The losses of the allies were to be considered in the separate peace, but France was specially informed that England made the concession out of desire for peace, and in order to remove obstacles to an agreement, and not because she regarded the occupation of German territory as any real loss to England. However, though this decision was reached on May 20th 1761,[1] before the dispatch of Bussy to London, the Duke of Choiseul did not seem to be acquainted with it a month later.[2]

At the same time that these peace negotiations were going on between France and England, negotiations of another nature were proceeding between France and Spain. The Duke of Choiseul, considering Pitt's character and views on peace a threat to the negotiations, and desiring[3] to insure the safety of his country in case of a rupture of the peace negotiations with England, entered into an exchange of views with Spain. He hoped by this means to secure the diplomatic support of Spain during the course of the negotiations; and if France were to make peace, to obtain the King of Spain's guarantee for the stability of the treaty; or if on the contrary they failed to attain peace, the Duke of Choiseul's plan was that Spain should be drawn into the war, and that France would be able to profit by the events which this situation might produce and repair her losses. Finally if the event proved unfortunate, he had in view that the losses of Spain would lighten those which France might suffer.[4] It has been truly observed that this policy was so "Machiavellian" and so selfish that it compels a certain admiration.[5] The Duke of Choiseul was thus starting to play a double game, a difficult and dangerous game, for the French Foreign minister was negotiating for peace and war at the same time, yet he was first and foremost anxious to attain peace. He

[1] *Ibid.*, 11, 371, Newcastle to Devonshire, May 20th 1761.

[2] See A.E., C.P., Angleterre, 443, ff.221-230, Duke of Choiseul to Bussy, June 19th 1761, see *infra*, p. 83.

[3] A.E., C.P., Espagne, 532, ff.273r-273v, Duke of Choiseul to Ossun, May 26th 1761.

[4] Corbett, 11, 185; see *Memoires du Duc de Choiseul*, 387, Mémoire Justificatif presenté au Roi par Choiseul en 1765.

[5] Corbett, 11, 185.

therefore tried not to let his negotiations with Spain go too far, and become an obstacle to his peace negotiations with England; but, as events were to show, it was not an easy plan to carry out; and when England offered more moderate conditions of peace to France, the latter was too far committed in her engagements with Spain to be able to accept them.

From the outset of the negotiations between France and Spain, things were not easy. Grimaldi, who was appointed Spanish ambassador in Paris in the place of Massones, seized the first opportunity to propose an offensive alliance against England, which proposal surprised and frightened the Duke of Choiseul,[1] who believed that the ambassador was ahead of his court. The instructions given to Grimaldi, before his departure to Paris, threw light on this question. The general impression conveyed by the original draft of these instructions [2] is that Spain was at this time offended by the English government's reaction to the several memoirs regarding his points of grievances with that country, and presented by Fuentes, the Spanish ambassador in London; it also shows that Spain thought then that the only way left to her in order to get any satisfaction for her grievances against England was to join France in her struggle against England before it became too late. However it is obvious that Spain still hesitated about taking such a hazardous step. After indicating to Grimaldi, in this memoir, the state of his country's relations with both England and France, he was, in the first place, requested to find out whether there was any negotiation for peace between France and England, and if there was, how far it had gone. He was also asked to take advantage of an opportune moment, when the French Foreign minister would complain to him of Spain not joining France in the struggle against England in order to renew that minister's hopes of a close union between the two Countries. Great stress was laid upon the fact that he should make His Catholic

---

[1] Bourguet, *Le Duc de Choiseul et l'Alliance Espagnole*, 188, Duke of Choiseul to Ossun, February 17th 1761.

[2] Simancas, Estado-Leg. 3457, no. 38, Instructions of January 14th 1761, to Grimaldi for his embassy in Paris; for the original Spanish draft of these instructions see Appendix 4, 235-243.

Majesty's action of joining France appear only as a generous gesture of that King for succouring his cousin, the King of France, and on no account to mention any of His Catholic Majesty's real motives for that union. Grimaldi was also to suggest, as his own opinion, that France should offer Minorca to Spain in order to facilitate agreement on terms for a union between the two Courts. Moreover, Grimaldi was to put forward on his own initiation, without committing his country, proposals for a union between the two Courts. However, Grimaldi was authorised to take whatever action he judged best for the interests of his country. In conclusion, he was instructed to use forthwith in Paris his zeal and industry and so perhaps to open a way to great political enterprises. This phrase was explained by an interline clause "qual fuera en caso de la necesidad que tenemos immediata, un Pacto de union con la Francia ofensivo y defensivo."[1] This categoric statement in the concluding words of the instructions make it very clear that any offensive and defensive alliance proposed by Grimaldi was certainly not the result of his unaided initiative: he could only be criticised as being too hasty in reaching a point that he was fully instructed to press. He had his reasons for hastening this proposal.[2] Charles III was so pleased with the results of Grimaldi's first conversations with Choiseul that he wrote to Tanucci, asserting that Grimaldi has done

"In three days since he arrived in Paris, much more than what the previous ambassador did during the whole time of his embassy". [3]

Choiseul, on the other side, anxious not to lose such an opportunity, for which he had been working almost two years, prepared a project of a treaty of alliance between the two Courts. Although it was difficult for him to decide the nature of the engagements between them, he drew up a memoir,[4] advocating an offensive and defensive alliance between the two

[1] This very important explanation was added between the lines in order to unfold the ambiguity of "the greatest justifiable achievements".

[2] See Rousseau, I, 55.

[3] Ferrer del Rio, I, 289, Charles III to Tanucci, February 24th 1761.

[4] Bourguet, *Le Duc de Choiseul et l'Alliance Espagnole*, 192-193, Memoir of March 3rd 1761 set to Ossun.

countries together with a treaty of commerce. Further, Ossun
expressed his satisfaction that the Duke of Choiseul did not miss

"cette précieuse occasion de fixer invariablement le système politique
et l'union intime d'intérêts, de vues et de moyens des deux monarchies".[1]

In May, Charles III authorised Grimaldi definitely to propose a
general treaty of alliance between France and Spain.[2] When
Grimaldi presented to him a project of the defensive alliance
between France and Spain, the Duke of Choiseul noticed an
item which was most likely to affect the negotiations of peace
between his country and England. Grimaldi, fearing that
France might conclude her peace with England and leave Spain
in the lurch, suggested that Spain should join France in her
negotiations with England in order that she might settle her
own grievances. Aware of the difficulties which such an
interference might produce, Choiseul declared to Ossun:

"Il est cependant très vraisemblable que si le Roi Catholique étoit admis
à y discuter ses droits et ses prétentions, cet épisode pourroit occasioner
plus de difficultés et de longueurs que le parti qu'elle prendroit de venir
enfin au secours de la France . . . si la Cour de Londres ne se prete pas
aux vues et aux intentions pacifiques de Sa Majesté".[3]

In the same month, in his instructions to Bussy, the Duke of
Choiseul emphasised the subordination of a Family Compact
to the attainment of an immediate peace:

"s'il trouvait le ministère britannique aussi conciliant qu'il devrait l'être
il ne perdrait pas de vue, que le premier object de sa mission est de
parvenir à une paix raisonnable et que ce ne peut être que lorsque nous
en perdrons l'éspérance, que nous serons obligés de nous livrer aux idées
de l'Espagne, dans tous les cas très embarassantes.[4]

On May 12th, Choiseul forwarded to the Spanish Court a
counter-proposal. He suggested that two treaties should be
made between the two countries. One, which he proposed to
call the "*Pacte de Famille*", was to be a general and intimate
alliance between the two courts and to have no relation to any

---

[1] *Ibid.*, 198, Ossun to Duke of Choiseul, March 16th 1761.

[2] Corbett, 11, 186, who, however, does not quote his authority.

[3] A.E., C.P., Espagne, 532, f.301v, the Duke of Choiseul's "Observations sur le
projet d'un Traité d'alliance défensive à conclure entre le Roi et le Roi d'Espagne",
May 1761 (*ibid.*, ff.299-302).

[4] Waddington, IV, 515-516.

other Power. The other would regulate their relations with the rest of Europe.[1] It was only in the following month (June 2nd) that the latter treaty of alliance was defined by the Duke of Choiseul. This special Convention was to meet the actual situation. He suggested that Spain should undertake to declare war on England on May 1st 1762, if by that time peace had not been concluded, and on this condition France was ready to include the settlement of the Spanish grievances in the separate negotiation that she was carrying on with England.[2] Grimaldi, very pleased with the idea, was for signing at once. But Choiseul held back.[3] He did not want to commit himself and his country until the result of the existing negotiation with London was known. However cautious was the Duke of Choiseul in not signing on the spot, these new proposals could not but complicate the situation which was already difficult because of Pitt's views on peace, and the differences which were still existing between the two courts about the epochs and the compensation question. Evidence will prove later on the serious inconveniences of these new proposals on the negotiations of peace between France and England. Mixing the grievances of a friendly power with those of a belligerent one was not likely to be acceptable to England. It was very natural that Grimaldi sprang at these proposals and was for signing at once, and that Charles III welcomed them. These proposals provided for Spain, at the time that Fuentes' negotiation with Pitt in London was not likely to come to any satisfactory conclusion, the only two possible ways left to Spain, through which she might obtain satisfaction for her grievances. An intervention by France in her favour might give Spain this satisfaction. If this means failed, only forceful means were left to Spain to obtain satisfaction for her claims.

Such was the state of affairs between France and Spain, when Bussy started his conferences with Pitt on the 3rd of June. He

---

[1] See Bourguet, *Le Duc de Choiseul et l'Alliance Espagnole*, 206.

[2] A.E., C.P., Espagne, 532, ff.334-338, "Mémoire particulier sur la Circonstance Présente", sent to Ossun, June 2nd 1761.

[3] A.E., M.D., France et Divers Etats, 570, f.84r.

related to the Duke of Choiseul in his "grande lettre",[1] his first
interviews with Pitt on the two important questions of the
epochs and of the setting off of the French conquests in Germany, against the English conquests elsewhere.[2] As to the first
question, Pitt pointed out that it was not possible to fix the
epochs before signing the Treaty as had been previously indicated in His Britannic Majesty's Memorial of April 28th.[3]
Pitt's answer on the second question was not more favourable,[4]
although, as pointed out, this question was already agreed upon
by the English ministers.[5] Bussy in his private letter complained
of Pitt's attitude, of his uncompromising answers, and described
him as only ready to take all possible advantages from the
French proposals of March.[6] Nevertheless Bussy seemed very
impressed by the personality of Pitt:

> "Ce ministre, Monseigneur, me parait avoir de grands talents, une
> fermeté singulière, beaucoup de méthode et de suite dans l'esprit.
> Quoiqu'on le dise haut et dur, j'ai éprouvé qu' il est maitre de lui-même
> quand il veut".[7]

Meanwhile Stanley, on the other side of the Channel, was
conversing with the Duke of Choiseul. From the outset of their
conferences, which started on June 7th,[8] Stanley formed a very
favourable opinion of the French Foreign minister:

> "I must confess that in the whole course of this conversation the Duc de
> Choiseul spoke with very fair appearances of candour, as well as that I
> think him a person of very good natural abilities".[9]

Choiseul agreed to allow the epochs to be made a subject of
negotiation, but told Stanley that as His most Christian Majesty
had already named the first days of September, July, and May,

[1] As Bussy referred to it in his private letter to Choiseul, A.E., C.P., Angleterre,
443, f.195r, Bussy to Choiseul, June 11th 1761.

[2] Waddington, op. cit., IV, 526-527, Bussy to Choiseul, June 11th 1761.

[3] Ibid., IV, 526.

[4] See ibid., IV, 526-527.

[5] See Ruville, 11, 371.

[6] A.E., C.P., Angleterre, 443, ff.195r-196r.

[7] Waddington, IV, 527.

[8] Thackeray, 1, 514-519, Stanley to Pitt, June 8th 1761.

[9] Ibid., 1, 519.

His Britannic Majesty should either accept the appointed days or name others more agreeable to his intentions. Nevertheless the French Foreign Minister complained "with civility but with anxiety", that Stanley was too inflexible in laying constantly and unremittingly upon France the burden of speaking first, which appeared to him very unequal and unmerited after the frank and ample proposal which he had made.[1] In his discourse with Stanley upon the preference given by some of his countrymen to Guadeloupe and by others to Canada, the Duke of Choiseul fixed his utmost attention upon Stanley's countenance, aiming at penetrating Stanley's thoughts upon the alternative, but the latter did not afford him any foundation for "the most remote suspicion".[2]

Limited in his power and not authorised to make any proposals about the epochs or to give a definite answer about the compensation question, Stanley's first conferences with Choiseul did not come to anything of importance as Choiseul indicated in his letter to Bussy:

"Tel a été le précis d'une conversation de plusiers heures qui a abouti, comme vous voyez, à très peu de choses et qui me fait craindre que nous ne restions longtemps à nous voir venir".[3]

Neither did Bussy's interviews with Pitt produce any agreement about these two questions. However, by that time the fall of Belleisle (capitulated June 7th) enabled the English ministers to offer terms for peace. In a cabinet meeting of June 16th,[4] the epochs were decided. They were two months later than those proposed by France, so arranged as to include Belleisle amongst the English possessions.[5] It was also stipulated that the peace, as regards England, should be separate and distinct from whatever is concluded at Augsburg and that the treaty must be

[1] *Ibid.*, 1, 528, Stanley to Pitt, June 12th 1761.

[2] *Ibid.*, 1, 531.

[3] Waddington, *op. cit.*, IV, 524, Duke of Choiseul to Bussy, June 7th 1761.

[4] See *Grenville Papers*, 1, 367, Jenkinson to Grenville, June 16th 1761; the same to the same, June 18th 1761, 368-369. The news of the surrender of Belleisle arrived in England on June 13th, *Jenkinson Papers*, 1.

[5] Instead of Choiseul's dates, the following were proposed, July 1st, September 1st and November 1st.

signed by August 1st. These terms were never discussed, for the Duke of Choiseul, before receiving them, realised from his first conferences with Stanley that the English were not at all likely to make the first offers with regard to the future compensations of conquests,[1] and desired to promote his peace negotiations with England, and to know their dispositions to his terms of peace in order to fix his attitude towards Spain.[2] He therefore summoned Stanley, and assuming an air of agitation, enumerated to him the terms which France was prepared to accept in her treaty of peace with England. When Stanley asked the Duke to give him these terms in writing, in order not to make any mistakes or slips, the Duke took him to his office and dictated to him [3] what is referred to as the "little leaf" by Professor Williams. Choiseul stressed very much the necessity of secrecy. He recommended that his offers should only be communicated to those ministers whom it was absolutely necessary to trust.[4] In these new proposals, the Duke of Choiseul abandoned the principle of *uti possidetis* and sketched out a settlement. Guadeloupe, Marie Galante and Goree were to be exchanged for Minorca. England was to retain the whole of Canada, with the exception of the island of Cape Breton, which was to be returned to France on the condition that it should not be fortified. The French were still to enjoy the fishing privileges off the coast of Newfoundland, in accordance with the peace of Utrecht. The boundary of Canada on the side of Louisiana was to be fixed. France would return all the territory which she had occupied in Germany.[5]

These elaborate airs of secrecy were put on to persuade Stanley and Pitt that Choiseul was ready to make greater

[1] Stanley made it clear to Choiseul in his conference of June 12th, Thackeray, 1, 529-530: Choiseul was right, Pitt stressed that point in his letter to Stanley of 19th, Thackery, 1, 535-536.

[2] By then negotiations on the secret convention were going on as well as on the Family Compact.

[3] Waddington, IV, 532; see also Thackeray, 1, 540, Stanley to Pitt, June 18th 1761.

[4] Waddington, *op. cit.*, 531. The Duke of Choiseul went as far as to pretend that he did not intend to acquaint Bussy with the "little leaf".

[5] See Paper of June 17th 1761, communicated by Duke of Choiseul to Stanley, Thackeray, 1, 543.

concessions than anyone else in France and that they had better accept his terms without prolonged discussion.[1] However, in spite of the fact that Choiseul exaggerated their secrecy, there is reason to believe that he was sincere in his desire to keep these offers secret for fear of the faction who schemed to continue the war,[2] and for fear of his Austrian ally, for he was disposing without her consent of the conquests of France in Germany, conquered originally for his ally's sake. He had indeed promised only three weeks previously that Wesel and the Prussian territories on the Rhine, which were then being administered in the Empress's name, would never be the subject of negotiation by France.[3]

Two days after dictating the "little leaf" to Stanley, the Duke of Choiseul acquainted Bussy, in a private letter, with all he had said to Stanley with regard the terms of peace, but asked him to pretend that he was not acquainted with them[4] and sent him, officially, the following instructions. Bussy was to propose to Pitt to sign his agreement to the following points : that the *uti possidetis* was the base of the negotiation; that the allies of England in Germany were included in the *uti possidetis*; that England was to indicate the epochs of the *uti possidetis*, provided that those epochs would not be decided for later than six months. Expecting difficulties on the second point from Pitt, the Duke of Choiseul informed Bussy to tell Pitt, if he raised any objection to it, that he did not expect that France, in proposing the *uti possidetis*, meant only to accord to England all the advantages and to neglect her own: namely her successes in Germany.[5] Choiseul's proposals of June 17 had defined his policy more precisely than he had done before. For the sake of peace he was ready to give up important colonial possessions but he wished to maintain the fishing rights on the Newfoundland banks to make his offers less distasteful to his fellow countrymen.[6] Stanley thought that these terms were the best that could be made with France; that they were considerable

[1] Williams, 11, 91-92.   [2] Winstanley, 54.
[3] Williams, 11, 92.   [4] Waddington, IV, 534.
[5] *Ibid.*, IV, 535-536, Duke of Choiseul to Bussy, June 19th 1761.
[6] Winstanley, 55.

concessions as preliminary terms. Stanley asserted that
Choiseul was sincere in his offers, but foresaw that the French
Foreign Minister would struggle hard for the fisheries and
would rather part with almost anything else.[1] Pitt was not
taken in by Choiseul's airs of secrecy, and told Stanley that

> "this little leaf is so loose and void of precision as to the objects it does
> mention, and so defective from its total silence as to matters of the
> highest importance".[2]

However, these offers indicate a critical stage in the negotiations between the two countries. The events of the following
weeks were to decide whether peace was to be concluded. In
London their importance demanded two lengthy cabinet
meetings which were held on June 24th and 26th.[3] In these
meetings, the French proposals were to be discussed and a
counter-project to be drawn up. All the ministers agreed in
refusing to allow the boundaries of Canada to be defined as
Choiseul proposed and in repudiating the demand that Cape
Breton should be restored to France, but they were willing
that England should sacrifice some of her conquests in order to
redeem the French conquests in Germany. They disagreed over
Choiseul's demand that France should retain the Newfoundland fisheries. Pitt was for refusing; he declared that he would
spend sixteen millions, and fight many campaigns to wrest the
right from France. In his opinion:

> "a demand of this most valuable benefit, founded on a treaty which
> subsists no longer, cannot but meet with the utmost difficulty, nor will
> ever be consented to without some great and important compensation".[4]

In accordance with the decision of these cabinet meetings,
Pitt forwarded a dispatch to Stanley,[5] in which the French
proposals on many points were rejected: The demolition of
Dunkirk according to the Treaty of Utrecht was demanded.
France was to surrender Canada in its entirety; to cede

---

[1] Thackeray, 1, 542, Stanley to Pitt, June 18th 1761.

[2] *Ibid.*, 1, 544, June 26th 1761.

[3] On these meetings, see Waddington, *op. cit.*, IV, 538-541, and *Grenville Papers*,
1, 371-373, Jenkinson to Grenville, June 25th and 27th.

[4] Thackeray, 1, 546, Pitt to Stanley, 26th June 1761.

[5] *Ibid.*, 1, 543-549, see also Waddington, *op. cit.*, IV, 540-541.

Senegal and Goree; and to restore Minorca and all that she had conquered in Germany. The neutral islands were to be left wholly neutral, or an equitable partition of them to be fixed in the future treaty. These articles were *sine qua non* [1] and all the rest was left to Stanley for further negotiation. This dispatch, sent to Stanley demanding "le monopole le plus absolu", [2] proved to be the turning point of the negotiations. [3] It worked an immediate change in Duke of Choiseul's policy, [4] as will be indicated later. As soon as Stanley received Pitt's new instructions he had two conferences with the French Foreign Minister, the results of which conferences he reported to Pitt in his letter of July 1st. [5] Stanley reckoned that, although Choiseul seemed ready to make some concessions in certain articles, yet he declared his intention to insist very definitely upon the Newfoundland fisheries. This question weighed heavily upon him, he also expressed himself very distinctly on this matter to Bussy, in his account to him of his latest conferences with Stanley: [6]

"L'abandon de la pesche étant regardé comme une perte immense et irréparable pour le Royaume, le Roi ne peut faire cet abandon que lorsque la France ne sera plus absolument en état de faire la guerre". [7]

He pleaded also for a defenceless port in Cape Breton, and only

---

[1] Criticising the style of Pitt's letter of June 26th Newcastle wrote to Devonshire: "I wish, We have not put too Many *Sine Qua non*; and that the Letter had been wrote with more seeming confidence, Friendship, and Desire of coming soon to a Conclusion and Complimenting M. Choiseul upon the Advance He had made towards it; which I own, I think a very great One". B.M., Add. MSS., 32924, f.320r, Newcastle to Devonshire, June 28th 1761.

[2] Grant, 17.

[3] Yorke, 111, 269; two days after its despatch, Newcastle reckoning its importance wrote to Devonshire: "Whenever The Answer to This Letter comes from France, then will be decided the great Point, *Peace, or War*", Newcastle to Devonshire, June 28th 1761, f.321r.

[4] Grant asserted in his article on *La Mission de Bussy à Londres*, 20, that the Duke of Choiseul: "était tout d'abord absolument sincère dans son désir de conlure la paix, . . . on peut fixer au 30 juin 1761 la date où il a changé d'idée, c'est-à-dire le jour même où il recevait la résponse de Pitt (26 juin)".

[5] Thackeray, 11, 532-542, Stanley to Pitt, July 1st 1761.

[6] A.E., C.P., Angleterre, 443, ff.324-327, Duke of Choiseul to Bussy, July 4th 1761.

[7] *Ibid.*, Angleterre, 443, f.325r.

G

after a long struggle, which nearly ended in a breach,[1] did he propose the name of another harbour where French fishermen could find shelter. On this other important point he wrote also to Bussy in the above mentioned letter:

"Cet article seroit seul l'occasion d'une rupture, si les Anglois ne trouvent pas moyen en cas qu'ils ayent la manie de garder l'isle Royale, de nous donner une autre isle et Port qui serviroit d'abri à nos Pêcheurs".[2]

Although these two points were not the only points on which the two countries disagreed, yet they were the most important ones and the only ones which were most likely to affect the negotiations. The Duke of Choiseul expressed his willingness to negotiate on the other two points of difference with regard to the Western African Coast and Dunkirk. Nothing could better explain Choiseul's views on the terms of negotiation for peace with England than his letter of July 4th to Ossun.[3] He expressed his readiness to make concessions in other points in his negotiations with England, if France was granted the fishing privileges and the "abri." There was now a danger of a deadlock. Both countries refused to make any concessions on this point. Choiseul considered the fisheries a *sine qua non* [4] condition. He had set his heart on them and was determined not to yield on this point. He told Stanley "que la pêche est sa folie." [5] On the other hand, Pitt, aware of the importance of these fisheries, was not less persistent in desiring to deprive France of any share in them. Choiseul had, thus, discovered that peace with England could only be bought by the surrender of the fisheries, and the price was more than he could afford. France had not been reduced to such extremities as to be forced to submit to this demand; and Grimaldi, by his side, was very anxious to conclude with him the two different treaties of alliance. As the hope of peace faded, the value of the Spanish alliance increased. With a new ally, France might be able to continue the war for another

[1] See Thackeray, 11, 534, Stanley to Pit, July 1stt 1761.
[2] A.E., C.P., Angleterre, 443, f.324v.
[3] See Waddington, *op. cit.*, IV, 541-543.
[4] *Ibid.*, IV, 543.
[5] Thackeray, 11, 542, Stanley to Pitt, P.S., July 5th 1761, to his letter of July 1st.

campaign, which might render the British cabinet more reasonable. Thus, although the Duke of Choiseul continued the negotiation for peace with England, he showed greater compliance towards Spain. Having failed to conciliate his opponents, he possibly endeavoured to intimidate them. In his conference with Stanley of July 4th,[1] he warned him that if war was prolonged, France would have new allies.[2] On the same day in his letter to Bussy, Choiseul drew the latter's attention to the necessity of not treating with England on the question of the Neutral Islands without the consent of Spain who had interests in these islands.[3] Pitt must have been furious, when Bussy communicated to him his Foreign Minister's instructions:

"Oh, Mon Dieu . . . J'éspère bien que cela n'arrivera pas; L'Espagne n'a rien à voir dans la négociation entre les deux Couronnes, et l'Angleterre ne permettra jamais qu'il y soit admise".[4]

It was precisely this delicate point of interference in favour of Spain which the Duke of Choiseul raised in his letter of the fifteenth of July to Bussy.[5] He foresaw England's refusal to accord him any satisfaction on the fisheries question and pre-occupied himself with the future rupture between the two countries. However, he recommended Bussy not to rush his return to France, for he aimed at prolonging the negotiation with England for two more months.[6] It was therefore on purpose that he delayed his dispatches of the middle of July, and that he made the French Memoir bear the character of a proposal for discussion and not of an ultimatum. He explained his reasons to Bussy: it was in order that these negotiations would bring him to September when the season of hostile attacks from England on the French coasts should be over; and as it would be then nearly time for the opening of the English parliament, the French could break the negotiations

[1] P.S., July 5th 1761, Stanley to Pitt, ibid., 11, 540-542.

[2] Ibid., II, 541.

[3] A.E., C.P., Angleterre, 443, f.327r, Choiseul to Bussy, July 4th 1761.

[4] Waddington, op. cit., IV, 544, Bussy to Duke of Choiseul, July 9th 1761.

[5] See ibid., IV., 544-545.

[6] "l'idée maitresse de Choiseul à cette époque était de gagner du temps", Grant, 17.

with England "avec éclat."[1] Choiseul was already thinking
of the publication of the different memorials and letters
exchanged between the two countries in the course of these
negotiations in case of a rupture, when he recommended
Bussy not to be contented with a verbal answer from Pitt, but
to ask him for a written one.

In his Memoir of July 13th,[2] the Duke of Choiseul demanded
again a share in the Newfoundland fisheries and the cession of
Cape Breton; the Convention of 1754 was proposed as a basis
for the settlement of the East India conflict. Stipulations were
made for the return of the African settlements, either Senegal
or Goree, whereas the Duke of Choiseul had formerly been
willing to accept a third harbour. Although France agreed to
surrender its conquests from the German allies of England, an
exception was made of the territories of the King of Prussia.
It was argued that as those had been conquered and governed
in the name of Austria, they could not be restored without the
consent of that power. Choiseul had not formerly been so
conscientious towards his allies when he was seriously anxious
for peace. Minorca was to be restored to England in exchange
for Guadeloupe and Marie Galante. Choiseul ended his memoir
by asking for the restoration of Belleisle without any equivalent. Dunkirk[3] was purposely not mentioned in the memoir.
Bussy was to leave it to the end of his conversations with Pitt.
This dispatch, which conveyed the French proposals, was
followed by two other separate memorials: a request for the
settlement of the Spanish grievances,[4] where the three
grounds of complaint by Spain were enumerated in strictly
moderate and inoffensive language. The other memorial[5]
pointed out that the consent of the Empress-Queen to the
separate peace had just been under two conditions: that all

---

[1] Waddington, op. cit., IV, 544, Duke of Choiseul to Bussy, July 15th 1761.

[2] See Thackeray, 11, 546-552.

[3] Bourguet, "La Mission de Bussy à Londres", R.H., LXXI, 14; referring to the
demolition of Dunkirk, Duke of Choiseul wrote to Bussy: "C'est un moyen dernier et
qu'il faut réserver pour la fin de la négociation soit en bien soit en mal".

[4] See Thackeray, 11, 552-553.

[5] Ibid., 11, 553.

conquests from the King of Prussia should be retained and that neither France nor England should give succour of any kind to their respective allies in Germany.

In spite of his pessimistic predictions indicated in his letter to Ossun in Spain and to Bussy in London, the Duke of Choiseul still clung to peace, for in his country's wholly exhausted condition, even with the aid of an additional ally, he would not have wished for a continuance of war. A few days before sending those memorials to England he wrote to Ossun:

> "Vous ne cacherez pas au roi d'Espagne et à son ministre que nous avons besoin de la paix dans ce moment-ci; et que nous comptons que les engagements que nous prenons n'éloigneront pas cette paix nécessaire, si nos ennemis deviennent traitables sur les conditions". [1]

Was not he also of the opinion that Bussy should not present the memorial concerning the Spanish grievances at the same time as the French memorial? He therefore advised Bussy to leave the Spanish memorial till Pitt answered the French proposals. If Pitt accepted the French terms of peace, which was not very likely, there will be always means to adjust them. If Pitt, on the other hand, was not prepared to make any concessions and the negotiations were broken off, it would not be a wise policy to give England such a long warning about Spain's intimacy with France. [2] In spite of his wise views on deferring the date of the presentation of the memorial relative to the Spanish grievances, the Duke of Choiseul, apparently, had to give way to Louis XV's desire of giving Fuentes the last word in deciding the date of its presentation. [3] When Bussy consulted Fuentes on the matter, the latter insisted on presenting the Spanish claims without delay. [4] Bussy's en-

---

[1] Waddington, *op. cit.*, IV, 553, Duke of Choiseul to Ossun, July 7th 1761.

[2] Bourguet, "La Mission de Bussy à Londres," *R.H.*, LXXI, 16.

[3] Rousseau, 1, 64; Bourguet, *op. cit.*, 16-17. No evidence is available to indicate what exactly happened as regards that important decision and how Louis XV's views prevailed on that question. The lack of minutes on the French "Conseil d'Etat" is responsible for this ambiguity. See Appendix 2, on "Conseil d'Etat".

[4] It is believed that Charles III insisted that the Spanish claims should be presented without delay, A.E., M.D., France et Divers Etats, 570, f.131r. On the arguments put forward by Fuentes for not delaying that presentation and his conversation with Bussy on this question on July 22nd, see Waddington, IV, 561.

deavours to persuade him to follow the wise policy of the
Duke of Choiseul were useless. However, taking into consideration the importance of "managing" Spain, Bussy yielded to
Fuentes;[1] and presented the memoir concerning the Spanish
claims, as well as that relative to Germany. Such an extra-
ordinary act convinced the British Ministry that the Bourbon
Courts were contemplating hostilities. Pitt with his usual
sagacity, at once perceived, as well as if he had read the letter
of Choiseul to Bussy of July 15th, that hostilities were inevitable
and that a rupture was delayed merely to bring on winter,
render the English fleet less dangerous and get the Spanish
treasure ships safely into port.[2] Pitt, therefore, considered the
memorial about the Spanish claims "as a thing incompatible
with the sincerity of the negotiation", and indicated that His
Britannic Majesty

> "will not suffer the disputes with Spain to be blended, in any manner
> whatever, in the negotiation of peace between the two crowns".[3]

The other memorial about Germany was regarded

> "as totally inadmissible . . . as implying an attempt upon the honor of
> Great Britain, and the fidelity with which his Majesty will always fulfil
> his engagements with his allies".[4]

As to the English answer to the French Memoir, it was far
from conciliatory and was

> "more consistant, perhaps, with the situation in which this country
> [England] stood from the advantages of conquest, than with the pacific
> sentiments which were supposed to give rise to the treaty".[5]

Many of the French demands were rejected. The right of
fishing within the Gulf of St. Lawrence and the possession of
Cape Breton were again refused. The French were not to
continue enjoying their privileges in the Newfoundland

---

[1] A.E., C.P., Angleterre, 444, ff.33v-35v, Bussy to Duke of Choiseul, July 21st
1761.

[2] Lecky, III, 195-196.

[3] Thackeray, II, 554, Pitt to Bussy, July 24th 1761.

[4] Ibid., II, 554.

[5] Adolphus, I, 39.

fisheries unless they were prepared to demolish the fortifications of Dunkirk. Belleisle was offered as an equivalent to
Minorca.[1] If in substance Pitt's demands were unaltered, the
language in which they were worded, abandoned all effort at
conciliation; Pitt wrote this answer "as a conqueror to a
humiliated rival".[2]

It is difficult to believe that the Duke of Choiseul expected
his new proposals to be accepted unmodified and that the two
other memorials would not have any effect on the course of the
negotiation. It is far more probable that the French Foreign
minister aimed at serving some other purposes! Realising in
his conferences with Stanley and in the memorials and letters
from Pitt, the impossibility of attaining the terms which he
desired for peace and specially those of the fisheries, the Duke
of Choiseul was playing a desperate game with his last cards.
He was trying by new means either to obtain peace or to
strengthen his country's situation with regard to her allies,
Austria and Spain, in order to prepare her for the continuation
of war, if the negotiations with England were broken.
Whereas he was trying to frighten England by vaunting the
intimacy between France and Spain in order to obtain better
conditions,[3] he was proving to Spain that France was risking
the hope of peace with England because of her interest.
Whereas he was endeavouring to prove to England that France
was not standing detached from Austria, he was proving his
loyalty to his ally Austria. However, if Choiseul hoped to
frighten the English government, he must be counted to have
failed. His proposals were met with a serious rebuff. The Duke

---

[1] For the rest of the proposals see Thackeray, 11, 557-560. The answer of the British
Court to the Memorial of the French propositions of July 25th 1761 (according to
B.M., Add. MSS., 32925, f.339v where it is stated that it was sent on July 25th) in
Thackeray, 11, 557, it is dated July 29th.

[2] Williams, 11, 96.

[3] Ossun's opinion on presenting the Spanish claims with the French Memorial:
"On pense icy, et je confesse que Je pense aussy, que cette Méthode bien loin
d'Eloigner la conclusion de la paix, l'auroit accélérée et peut être rendue meilleure
pour la France, parcequ'il est très vraisemblable que les Anglois éviteront, à quelque
prix que ce soit de rompre avec l'Espagne". A.E., C.P., Espagne, 533, ff.206r-206v,
Ossun to Duke of Choiseul July 31st 1761.

of Choiseul also considered the English answers to his proposals offensive both in form and matter and he described them:

> "plutost des lois dictées par un vainqueur que des conditions de paix proposées entre Puissances égales". [1]

Meanwhile the relations between France and Spain were growing strained. The delay of the signature of the Secret Convention was but increasing the fears of Charles III[2] and rendering him suspicious of the intentions of the Duke of Choiseul. It was clear that the more or less favourable aspect of Choiseul's negotiations with England, caused the variation of his language towards Spain. Wall was penetrating Choiseul's game far enough to suspect that if, under a threat of a Spanish intervention, France could obtain a favourable enough peace with England, she would certainly leave Spain and her grievances in the lurch. He consequently declared to Grimaldi that he had not the least doubt that France :

> "n'eut cherché uniquement qu'à s'étayer de l'appui de L'Espagne pour rendre les conditions de la paix plus supportables". [3]

Wall also called attention to the free hand with which France was dividing the West Indies with England without consulting Spain. Charles III himself expressed the same sentiments to Ossun on this question. This strained position was intensified by what was regarded as "the half-hearted" [4] way in which Bussy had presented the Spanish claims to Pitt. The King of Spain complained that His Most Christian Majesty did not mention the Spanish grievances in his ultimatum presented to Pitt, and that although they were presented in an obliging way to Spain in a separate memoir, yet they were not

> "menagées de façon à faire connoitre au Ministère Britannique que la France ne suspendra pas la conclusion de la paix quand bien même l'Angleterre refuseroit de satisfaire Sa Majesté Catholique". [5]

---

[1] *Ibid.*, Espagne, 533, f.176r, Duke of Choiseul to Ossun, July 30th 1761 (holograph).

[2] *Ibid.*, Espagne, 533, ff.145v-146r, Ossun to Duke of Choiseul, July 27th 1761.

[3] A.E., M.D., France et Divers Etats, 570, f.122v; see also Wall to Grimaldi, July 31st 1761, Ferrer del Río, 1, 300.

[4] Corbett, 11, 187; All these points of complaint of Spain are explained by Ossun in his letter of July 31st 1761 to Duke of Choiseul, A.E., C.P., Espagne, 533, ff.179-194.

[5] *Ibid.*, Espagne, 533, f.184r.

The effect of the haughty answers of Pitt was immediate. The Duke of Choiseul, with scarcely a hope of peace, was menaced by a near prospect of losing Spain. There was no room for hesitation and he made his decision forthwith and sent word to Ossun

> "Le tems de l'union des deux Couronnes est arrivé, si Sa Majesté Catholique est aussi touchée de l'orgueil et du déspotisme à craindre de l'Angleterre que l'est le Roi, Sa Majesté vous ordonne de dire à ce Prince qu'elle regarde le Traité et la Convention comme conclus entre elle et le Roi son cousin".

He recommended his ambassador in the same letter:

> "d'échauffer le Roi d'Espagne et son Ministère le plus qu'il vous sera possible, pour qu'il prenne avec autant de promptitude que de hauteur son parti".[1]

In Spain the message was received in the same spirit that it was sent.[2]

The negotiations for peace continued but the Duke of Choiseul was no longer sincerely concerned to make peace. He was only anxious to protract negotiation until his treaties of alliance with Spain were concluded. This was no easy task. To prevent the English ministers breaking off negotiations before he had concluded his alliance with Spain, he had to avoid demanding terms which would be rejected out of hand and to offer those which would at least be an excuse for further and perhaps protracted negotiations.

The French Ultimatum which reached London early in August 1761 was inspired by these principles. France was willing to accept another island in exchange for Cape Breton, and thus made some show of peaceful intentions, but as regards German affairs, she maintained her former attitude.[3] In his letter to Bussy of the same date, Choiseul declared the decision of the French Government to continue war "avec la plus grande vivacité", if the French Ultimatum was not accepted.[4] The

---

[1] *Ibid.*, Espagne, 533, ff.176v, 177r, Duke of Choiseul to Ossun, July 30th 1761, (holograph).

[2] Corbett, 11, 188.

[3] Ruville, 11, 396; see Thackeray, 11, 566-569, Ultimatum of France in Reply to that of England 5th August 1761.

[4] Bourguet, "La Mission de Bussy à Londres", *R.H.*., LXXI, 22.

Duke of Choiseul found himself then in a very critical position. Had the English Cabinet accepted his ultimatum, the Spanish grievances would be an evident hindrance to peace, and Choiseul, by his precipitate Spanish policy would be considered the cause of breaking off the negotiations of peace when his country needed it very urgently. Also would not his policy be attacked by those ministers who were still for peace with England? [1] If he was to satisfy this party, and accept peace regardless of Spain, he would dishonour his country by breaking her engagements with Spain; and lose her friendship and help which he regarded very important for France. [2] As a matter of fact, the Council of the King complained more than once of Choiseul's impatience and precipitation in treating with Spain. The Duke of Choiseul, however, had been very careful in preparing the instructions to be sent to Bussy to govern his conduct towards England in connection with the Secret Convention about which he was informed at the same time. By this Convention, it was stipulated that His Christian Majesty was not to conclude peace till Spain had obtained satisfaction for her grievances from England. Bussy was instructed not to mention the Convention, if the French Ultimatum was rejected, for there would be no point in giving another pretext for breaking off the negotiations. If the French Ultimatum would become a subject of discussion, Bussy was to try to predict the issue of the negotiations. If they were not likely to come to a favourable conclusion, he must keep the same silence with regard to the Convention; on the other hand, if he thought that the discussion would come to a favourable conclusion, he should point out the importance of settling the Spanish grievances at the same time. If Pitt accepted the French Ultimatum, he should be shown the Secret Convention and

[1] Grimaldi related to Fuentes in his letter of August 4th 1761 that a violent discussion took place in the French Cabinet meeting between the partisans of peace and those of war, when the Duke of Choiseul's Ultimation of August 5th was prepared, Collado, 11, 129.

[2] "Je n'ai qu'un système politique qui est d'être uni et d'aimer l'Espagne, de tout sacrifier à cette union". Duke of Choiseul to Ossun, February 23rd 1762, A.E., M.D., Espagne, 574, f.647v.

THE STANLEY-BUSSY NEGOTIATIONS

consulted as to the best means of evading it.[1] In the same letter
Bussy was recommended not to show this dispatch to Fuentes,
because Wall had already enough ground to suspect the
sincerity of France.[2]

A few days after sending the French Ultimatum, the Duke of
Choiseul composed a letter for Bussy to present to Pitt, as an
answer to his haughty letter of July 24th. In his letter it was
asserted that

> "tant que l'Espagne l'approuvera, le roi se mêlera des intérêts de cette couronne,
> sans s'arrèter au refus impérieux de la puissance qui s'y opposerait".[3]

The answer to these last French proposals demanded several
meetings of the English Cabinet.[4] The English ministers were
divided in their views on the terms of the answer to the French
Ultimatum. The main point of their division was the fisheries,
and thus the opinion of Stanley.

> "did not fail to make deep impressions at the meeting, and appeared to
> contribute not a little to shake the resolutions of many of their lordships
> with regard to the liberty of fishing in the Gulf of St. Lawrence, and to an
> abri there demanded by France".[5]

It is not our concern here to deal with the deliberation of these
different meetings. It is, however, of most importance to
notice that after the meetings of August 13th and 14th a change
of front on the part of Bute and his master took place. Bute,
who was till then supporting Pitt's views, united with Newcastle, the minister whom he had formerly neglected. This
"cabinet revolution"[6] was not long in making itself felt in the

---

[1] Professor B. Williams was right when he condemned the Duke of Choiseul's
sincerity to his ally Spain, see *ibid.*, 11, 100.

[2] A.E., M.D., France et Divers Etats, 570, f.122r, the letter to Ossun was dated
August 10th 1761.

[3] Bourguet, "La Misson de Bussy à Londres", *R.H.*., LXXI, 18, for the English
translation, see Thackeray, 1, 574-575, Bussy to Pitt, August 5th 1761.

[4] Albemarle, 1, 26-28, Hardwicke gave a brief account of the two meetings of
August 13th and 14th, in his letter of August 15th 1761 to Royston; in his letter of
August 22nd to the same, he indicated the moderate terms which were to be offered
to France, *ibid.*, 1,33-34; a summary of the outcome of these meetings is in Thackeray,
11, 604-608, Pitt to Stanley, August 27th 1761; for notes on the meetings of August
14th and 24th see Yorke, 111, 271-274.

[5] Thackeray, 11, 604.

[6] Winstanley, 67, for more details on this change of front, see *ibid.*, 65-67.

realm of politics. The party in favour of concession and
conciliation became, thus, the stronger and in spite of Pitt
and Temple's objection, the right of fishing in the Gulf of
St. Lawrence, except on the coasts belonging to England, was
granted to France, and the island of St. Pierre was offered as a
shelter for French fishing boats. The privileges of the French
in the Newfoundland fisheries were to continue if the stipulations of the treaty of Aix-la-Chapelle with regard to the
fortifications of Dunkirk were executed. The English minister,
however, still demanded that the French should restore that
part of the territory of the King of Prussia which they had
conquered.[1] Thus the material point of the fisheries had been
decided in favour of France, and in place of the stipulations of
the treaty of Utrecht with regard to the fortifications of
Dunkirk, the more moderate conditions of Aix-la-Chapelle
had been substituted. Had such terms been offered a few weeks
earlier, peace might have been concluded.[2] It was too late;
Choiseul having prematurely despaired of peace, had already
committed himself with Spain. If he was free, he would have
gladly accepted them, but he was too deeply committed to
Spain to be able to accept them. By that time the Family
Compact and the Secret Convention were concluded (on
August 15th 1761).[3] They provided for the closest union
between the two countries (France and Spain) for purposes of
defence and commerce, and engaged Spain to declare war upon
England on May 1st 1762, in case the hostilities between
France and England had not then been concluded. The fact, but
not the exact terms, of the treaty became known to the
English ministers through information from Stanley, and
through the intercepted letters which passed between Fuentes
and Grimaldi, the Spanish ministers in London and Paris.

[1] See Thackeray, 11, 591-597, The Answer of the British Minister to the Ultimatum
of France delivered to Bussy on August 16th 1761.

[2] Albermarle, 1, 34, Hardwicke was not at the time sure whether the moderate
conditions would make peace possible: "Whether this will do now, I don't pretend to
prophesy, but I believe it would have done some time ago. Much will now turn upon
the boasted union with Spain, which I fear has gone a great way", Hardwicke to
Royston, August 22nd 1761.

[3] For the text of the "Family Compact", and the "Secret Convention", see Blart,
appendices 1 and 2, 205-217.

Grimaldi's letters of August 31st and September 13th could leave no doubt in Pitt's mind that the offensive alliance had already been signed and that Spain was only waiting for the arrival of her treasure fleet at Cadiz to declare herself.[1]

Tied by these treaties with Spain, it was not strange, therefore that the Duke of Choiseul did not receive the milder declarations of England with enthusiasm, as he would have done if they had been presented to him a few weeks earlier. On the contrary his attitude and the way with which he treated them gave Stanley reason to believe that Choiseul was indifferent to peace;[2] and to consider a reconciliation between the two Crowns impracticable.[3] The French Foreign Minister treated the concessions of the English ministers as mere points for discussion. With regard to the Island of St. Pierre, he asked for time in order to consult seamen and other persons better informed than himself. He urged also the necessity under which he was of waiting for a dispatch from Bussy before he could give his final answer.[4] It was very clear that he was merely trying to protract the negotiations.

However bright might be his prospects of the help of Spain in the war with England, the Duke of Choiseul must have been very embarrassed to be so near to a conciliation with England on terms to which he would have consented some time ago, and which he was now unable to accept. Stanley seemed also aware of the French Foreign minister's embarrassment. He believed him to be very much embarrassed because many of the conditions offered by England at that time, "though strictly exacted, and though properly enforced by new precautions", were his own, and the island was no longer unattainable. If a rupture took place for the security of the House of Austria, although it would appear a noble and grand measure to foreigners, yet it would not be very well received at home.[5]

---

[1] See Williams, 11, 103-104.

[2] Thackeray, 11, 617, Stanley to Pitt, September 6th 1761.

[3] Ibid., II, 613.

[4] Ibid., II, 610-611, Stanley to Pitt, September 1st 1761.

[5] Ibid., II, 617.

Neither was Newcastle wrong when he summed up the situa-
of the French Foreign minister:

> "We lost *l'Heure de Bergier*; And that I thought from the Beginning. We
> had, or pretended to have, Such a Diffidence of M. Choisuel's Sincerity
> at first, as gave Him Such Doubts of *Our Sincerity*, That He found Himself
> obliged, in Interest, to adopt Another System by way of Resource, That
> new System with Spain, and perhaps some further Engagements with the
> Two Empresses, has embarrassed Mr. de Choiseul So much, That, when
> We grew more Reasonable, and made Our *proper* Concession, He was So
> engaged in His New Measures, That He sent over the last Equivocal
> Memorial, to be presented by Bussy, as the *Ultimatissimum* of Their
> *Ultimatum*; And That Answer, Receding even from many of Their
> former Concessions, *could not be Accepted*". [1]

It was unlikely that the Duke of Choiseul, on receiving these
milder conditions from England, failed to perceive the mistake
which he had committed by his precipitation towards Spain,
and the danger to which he was exposed because of his
Spanish policy. It was time to declare to the "Conseil du Roi"
that rupture of the negotiations with England was inevitable:
this foreshadowed new unhappiness and new expenses for the
State. However, the Duke of Choiseul would be very careful
in making his statement to avoid any accusation of being the
cause of the unsuccessful issue of these negotiations. Also did
he not prepare a "Mémoire Justificatif" [2] which he presented
to the Council of the King on September 6th? [3] He tried to
explain all the reasons which persuaded him to hasten the
signature of the treaties with Spain. He wanted to insure the
safety of France, for he realised from the outset of the negotiations that England was not sincere in her negotiations with
France; that her aim was either imposing an ignominious peace
on France, or continuing war. He pointed to the two objects
which France aimed at, in her negotiations with Spain:

> "Le premier afin qu'elle ne fût pas un motif de rupture à la négociation
> de paix de l'Angleterre avec la France; le second afin que si la paix
> n'avait pas lieu, l'Espagne devint une ressource à la continuation de la
> guerre". [4]

---

[1] B.M., Add. MSS, 32928, f.211v. Newcastle to Yorke, September 18th 1761.
He refers to France's last memoir, dated September 9th and presented by Bussy to Pitt
on September 13th; this memoir is in Thackeray, 11, 619-623.

[2] As referred to in A.E., M.D., France et Divers Etats, 570, f.152v.

[3] See Waddington, *op. cit.*, IV, 590-593.   [4] *Ibid.*, IV, 591-592.

Although it was easy for Choiseul to put forward these two objects, yet it was not as easy to achieve them. In hastening to attain the second object, Choiseul missed the first. However, the Council approved the conduct of the Duke of Choiseul, and a rupture of the negotiations with England was decided. Nevertheless for political considerations, France was to answer the English Ultimatum of August 16th,[1] and not to mention the Spanish grievances. His Catholic Majesty was hurt by this silence on his interests and affected indifference and generosity which are sometimes much more effective than reproaches.[2]

Stanley's reports of his conferences with the Duke of Choiseul arrived on September 11th, and Bussy presented the memoir of the French Government to Pitt, on the 15th.[3] Choiseul asked for the island of Miquelon beside St. Pierre, and for two definite points on the African Coast (Amamaboo and Abra). He declined to give back Wesel and Gueldres etc. . . . and asked for new proposals to determine the further support to be granted to the allies. These terms did not matter much to Pitt. It was sufficient for him that France did not accept England's final conditions. On the same day, a cabinet meeting decided the recall of Stanley, who on September 20th asked for his passports from the French Foreign Minister.[4] Meanwhile Bussy had his last audience with Pitt on the 17th and left London a few days afterwards. Thus by the end of September, the peace negotiations between France and England which lasted for six months came to an unsuccessful conclusion. Nothing better than Flassan's remarks on the negotiations of 1761 could conclude their narration:

[1] Flassan, VI, 441-442, see *supra*, p. 96.

[2] A.E., M.D., France et Divers Etats, 570, f.156v; "Ce Prince donne des facilités à la France qu'Elle peut accépter ou refuser: Il la dispense de remplir un Engagement qu'Elle vient de prendre, tandis que l'Espagne reste engagé de son côté". His Catholic Majesty "s'est porté . . . à laisser à la France la liberté de terminer ses differends avec l'Angleterre sans éxiger, comme condition *sine qua non*, que ceux de l'Espagne le soyent en même tems". A.E., C.P., Espagne, 533, ff.460r, 458v, Ossun to Duke of Choiseul, September 23rd 1761.

[3] Waddington, IV, 595; "The last Memorial of France to England, September 9th 1761" is in Thackeray, 11, 619-623.

[4] Thackeray, 11, 625, Stanley to the Duke of Choiseul, September 20th 1761.

"Cette négociations est belle, et fut conduite avec beaucoup d'art, de la part du ministère français principalement. Toutefois au milieu de plusieurs pensées nobles et grandes, et de vues justes et profondes, on trouve un peu trop de manège et d'intrigue diplomatique. Il est vrai que dans la position où était la France, on tachait de suppléer par l'habileté de la tactique, au désavantage produit par les malheurs de la guerre". [1]

Meanwhile, indignant at the interference of France in the disputes between England and Spain, Pitt immediately dispatched some instructions to Lord Bristol on July 28th. [2] Lord Bristol was to ask Wall whether the memorial, relative to the Spanish claims and delivered by Bussy, was authorised by the Court of Spain. On its being acknowledged, he was instructed to remonstrate "with energy and firmness" about the irregularity of such a proceeding. [3] Bristol was also to demand an explanation with regard to the destination of the Spanish fleets. [4] When Lord Bristol [5] waited on Wall for the purpose of asking these questions, Wall answered that France had voluntarily proposed to attempt the accommodation of differences and spontaneously offered to the Catholic King (in case the disputes between Great Britain and Spain should at any time hereafter occasion a rupture between our two courts), to unite her forces with those of Spain to prevent the English encroachments in America, upon His Catholic Majesty's territory, that Spain was not seeking to provoke England, especially

"at a time that the court of London was in the most flourishing and most exalted situation it had ever known". [6]

This letter from Lord Bristol which was received on September 11th, contained nothing which could justify any hostile intention against Spain. [7]

---

[1] Flassan, VI, 446.

[2] Thackeray, 1, 570-574, Pitt to Bristol, July 28th 1761.

[3] Ibid., 1, 571.

[4] Ibid., 1, 573.

[5] Bristol related his conferences with Wall in a lengthy letter of August 31st 1761, 1, 579-588.

[6] Ibid., 584-585.

[7] Adolphus, 1, 43.

To the surprise, then, of all who were not acquainted with his motives, Pitt, a week after the receipt of this letter, proposed in the Cabinet to order Bristol to withdraw from Madrid and presented a bold plan of operations against the trade and colonies of Spain. This proposition was delivered by writing and signed by Pitt and Temple, as advice to the King.[1] But the cabinet, after three several councils remained unconvinced by the arguments forwarded. The King having rejected the written advice of Pitt and Temple, in favour of the plan, Pitt declared his resolution to resign. He explained the reasons which compelled him to do so in the following words:

> "in his station and situation he was responsible, and would not continue without having the direction. That this being his case, nobody would be surprised that he could go on no longer, and, he would repeat it again, that he would be responsible for nothing but what he directed".[2]

On October 2nd, Pitt took leave of the Council thanking the ministers and the late King for the support they had given to the war and on the 5th, he resigned the Seals. Lord Temple quitted his post on the 9th following.[3] Thackeray in approving Pitt's reasons for resignation stated:

> "He considered responsibility as the first principle of a free government, and the confidence of the people as the true basis of his own administration".[4]

Thus the negotiations for peace between England and France failed in spite of the fact that both the Duke of Choiseul and Pitt desired its conclusion.[5] Several factors contributed in the failure of these negotiations. The question of the fisheries,

---

[1] A copy of this advice, which is dated September 18th 1761, is in *Grenville Papers*, I, 386-387.

[2] Hunt, "Pitt's Retirement from Office, October 5th 1761", *E.H.R.*, XXI, 132 (*Endorsed* St. James's, October 2nd 1761 Minute *and in a later hand* Spanish War).

[3] *Memoirs of George III*, I, 62.

[4] Thackeray, I, 593.

[5] Williams, II, 88; "The Duc de Choiseul does me no small injustice in supposing, as he does, that I wish nothing but to continue war, at any rate", *Grenville Papers*, I, 385-386, Pitt to Temple, August 10th 1761; See also Ruville, III, 95, about Pitt's disposition for peace; "no man has it [wish for peace] more at heart than Choiseul", an extract referring to Stanley's interview with George III on September 30th, *Letters from George III to Lord Bute 1756-1766*, 65.

H

"equally insisted upon on both Sides",[1] although not the immediate cause of the rupture, was responsible, to a great extent, for this unsuccessful conclusion.

"The Point of the Fisheries is, and has been almost the Sole Obstacle to our Peace".[2]

It was only when the Duke of Choiseul thought that England was not prepared to make concessions on the fisheries and that consequently peace with her could only be brought by the surrender of them, that he wavered in his inclination towards peace and drew nearer to Spain.[3] The value of the Spanish alliance then increased in his eyes. With Spain at the side of France, it might still be possible to attain satisfaction on this important point either by intimidating the enemy, or by continuing the war for another campaign. Thus, when a few weeks later, England offered milder conditions of peace and particularly with regard to the fisheries, the Duke of Choiseul was too deeply committed to Spain to be able to accept them.

It is not difficult to discover the reasons for which both the English and the French Foreign ministers set their hearts on the fisheries.[4] The exclusion of the French from the fisheries had been made by Pitt a point of the greatest moment because they were the nursery for the French navy. Pitt, who considered that France was "chiefly, if not solely, to be dreaded . . . in the light of a maritime power",[5] realised that in order to secure England's supremacy, it was necessary "to break beyond hope of resuscitation the naval power of France."[6] He believed that

[1] B.M., Add. MSS., 32926, f.324v, Newcastle to Hardwicke, August 9th 1761; "Both Pitt and Choiseul held the fisheries question to be of prime importance", Hunt, *Political History of England*, 26.

[2] B.M., Add. MSS., 32926, ff.324r-324v; *ibid.*, 32926, f.281r, in his letter of August 7th 1761, to Hardwicke, Newcastle assured him that "The great Point is, That of The Fisheries; The Rest, I Think, may be accommodated".

[3] Stanley reminded Pitt, in his letter of August 6th, that the "extreme attachment to Spain" was never mentioned till the receipt of Pitt's letter of June 26th, in which Pitt refused France "this favourite article" (of the fisheries), Thackeray, 11, 585.

[4] *Grenville Papers*, 1, 342, Jenkinson wrote to Grenville, May 24th 1761 that "the Fisheries were the principal object which made those colonies valuable".

[5] *Parliamentary History of England*, XV, Pitt's speech on the Preliminaries of Peace, 1265.

[6] Beer, 152.

this reduction of the French maritime power could best be achieved by completely excluding France from the New-foundland fisheries,[1] not only on account of their economic value,[2] but also for the greater reason of their strategic importance, being a nursery for training sailors.[3] He therefore declared in a cabinet meeting that the right of France to fish and dry on certain banks of Newfoundland should not be renewed, and that England "should insist upon it as a *Sine qua non*". He went as far as to declare that England should break off negotiations, and risk the continuance of war in that campaign and another rather than give it up.[4] These fisheries, provided then with "the best of schools for the French navy",[5] for deep sea fishing, was recognised as a "great nursery for sailors",[6] and consequently an important factor in increasing and training the naval power of the country who took share in these fisheries".[7]

However, Pitt's conjectures may not seem well grounded, for it might be thought that Pitt, thinking in terms of England's power which lay in her maritime strength, lost sight of the fact that France was much more dependent on her armies than on her navy, and thus the destruction of her navy would not necessarily mean her total downfall. It is true that a maritime strength is more essential for England than for France, and that its destruction in the case of France would not mean the total destruction of her military strength, for she could still have an army and rely on it in her relations with the other European

[1] *Parliamentary History of England*, XV, 1263.

[2] Williams, 11, 84, " The annual value of these fisheries to France was calculated at about half a million sterling, roughly equal in value to all the rest of the produce of Canada".

[3] Innis, 119, confirms Pitt's views on the strategic value of the fisheries: "*The whole increase of the naval greatness of France had its foundation from this trade*".

[4] B.M., Add. MSS., 32924, ff.313r-313v, Newcastle to Devonshire, June 28th 1761.

[5] Williams, 11, 84.

[6] *Public Ledger or Daily Register of Commerce and Intelligence*, March 12th 1760, 205. The Writer considered these fisheries also a source of immense riches and referred to it as "our silver mine".

[7] According to Professor B. Williams, France engaged in this industry of the fisheries, "nearly 3,000 ships and boats, and 15,000 men", 11, 84.

countries. But if we considered more closely what Pitt meant
by a total destruction of the power of France and the principles
on which he based his calculations, we can understand him
better and appreciate his views in that respect. All that Pitt
meant, was to reduce France to such a state which should not
enable her to recover her maritime power and become in the
future of any danger to the supremacy of England in the
colonies and at sea. He, therefore, realised that by making
concessions in the fisheries as well as by restoring to her all the
valuable West-India Islands, England was giving her

> "the means of recovering her prodigious losses, and of becoming once
> more formidable . . . at sea". [1]

His calculations were based on strategic as well as economic
considerations. Although Pitt was right in his estimate of the
real value of the fisheries, yet it is worth pointing out that
depriving France of a share in the American fisheries was not,
at any rate, sufficient to destroy her maritime power, for
although very little would have been then left of her colonies,
what she retained would have contributed towards the
recovery of her navy.

Even if Pitt was correct in his appreciation of the value of
the fisheries, he could not be justified in demanding its monopoly. He was at fault in insisting on depriving France of a
share in the American fisheries, not only because it would not
have totally served his aim of destroying his enemy's maritime
power, but also because this deprivation, so far from preventing
latent disputes in the future, was more likely to excite hatred
and resentment and a sense of revenge on the side of the
enemy. [2] France, who enjoyed for many years a share in the
American fisheries, was likely to resent losing, and to
endeavour to recover this privilege. Favourable as the war had
been to England, it cannot be said that this demand erred on
the side of moderation, for it meant for France a destruction
of her fisheries and a great loss to the French navy. If any
conclusion was drawn from the belief that France in her
exhausted condition must be driven to accept any terms for

[1] *Parliamentary History of England*, XV, 1265, Pitt's speech on the Preliminaries of
Peace.

[2] Professor B. Williams is of the opinion that Pitt was right in principle, 11, 100.

peace, it could not but fail to be erroneous. The proud spirit
of independence which distinguishes that nation was sufficient
to prevent her from accepting mean or degrading terms. The
French always maintained the sentiments worthy of a nation
which could be poor without degrading humility.[1]

"France", as Stanley said, "though *humbled* and weakened was still a power
which had an existence in the world".[2]

Neither was the Duke of Choiseul unaware of the value of
maritime power. Firmly believing that the strength of a nation
depended largely on its commerce, he considered that France,
England, Spain and Holland were for this reason first class
powers while Austria, Russia and Prussia lacking an extended
overseas trade were necessarily of secondary importance in
European politics.[3] Indeed, a year earlier, desperate through
the successive losses of French colonies, he had written
immediately after the fall of Quebec to this same corres-
pondent

"*la France dans la position actuelle, ne peut plus être regardée comme puissance
commerçante et, par conséquent, comme puissance de premier ordre*".[4]

And in a Memoir sent to Madrid at the end of the same year,
he had reiterated the same opinion on the importance to the
maritime power:

"*La supériorité des forces de terre est sans doute d'un grand poids, mais,
depuis que le commerce est devenu l'objet de toutes les puissances, il est
démontré, par le fait, que la preponderance est du côté de celle qui a
l'empire de la mer*".[5]

Aware as he was of the economic and strategic value of
colonies, the Duke of Choiseul was determined not to yield
on the point of the fisheries. He told Stanley "*que la pêche
est sa folie*",[6] and that if he gave it up, he would be stoned in

1 Adolphus, I, 27.

2 Albemarle, I, 45, a note by Hardwicke, written upon Newcastle's letter of
October 18th 1761.

3 See Christelow, "French Interest in the Spanish Empire during the Ministry of the
Duc de Choiseul, 1759-1771", *H.A.H.R.*, XXI, 521, Duke of Choiseul to Ossun,
November 14th 1761.

4 Bourguet, *Le Duc de Choiseul et l'Alliance Espagnole*, 42.

5 Rousseau, I, 39. Memoir by the Duke of Choiseul, sent to Madrid, on December
24th 1759.

6 Thackeray, II, 542, P.S., July 5th 1761, Stanley to Pitt.

the streets of Paris.[1] Pitt was well aware of Choiseul's views since Stanley on several occasions had reported that the fishery would never be given up. Early in July for instance he asserted that

"such is their [the French's] desire of preserving some share in this branch of trade, which I believe is so absolutely necessary to the kingdom, that they would hardly relinquish it totally if an army was in the heart of their country".[2]

At the beginning of August, Stanley was of the opinion that the Duke of Choiseul was ready to adjust the rest of the matters of the negotiations to the satisfaction of England if he was granted an *abri*, and that he seemed "entirely determined to continue the war" if he was refused that concession.[3]

Further, the manner and character of Pitt's dispatches had untoward consequences and met with general disapproval. His tone of triumph and mastery was extremely imprudent in the circumstances and only too likely to justify and increase the fears of the defeated enemy.[4] This haughty tone was noticed all through his negotiations with France, and increased by the presentation of the memorial concerning the Spanish grievances on July 23rd. Stanley himself thought that Pitt's "manner of negotiating spoilt the peace." [5]

Moreover, the attack upon Belleisle [6] at the very time that the negotiations for peace were in progress, was in all probability a serious error, since the conquest of that island could not but raise the suspicion of Choiseul on the sincerity of the English Secretary of State for peace. Did he not also

---

[1] Hotblack, *Chatham's Colonial Policy*, 51.

[2] Thackeray, 11, 540, P.S., July 5th 1761.

[3] Thackeray, 11, 565, P.S., August 1st 1761, to the letter of July 30th 1761, Stanley to Pitt.

[4] For more details on this point, see Yorke, 111, 284-285. Professor B. Williams is of the same opinion on this point, 11, 101. He considered "his [Pitt's] blunt and haughty language" his chief fault as a negotiator. Waddington agrees "il est évident que la raideur du ministre anglais et le ton de sa correspondance contribuèrent beaucoup à l'insuccès", Waddington, *op. cit.*, IV, 601.

[5] Albemarle, 1, 45, Note written by Hardwicke upon Newcastle's letter of October 1st 1761.

[6] See Bedford's views on this conquest, Bedford to Bute, June 13th 1761, *Bedford Correspondence*, 111, 16-17.

express his fears to Prince Galitzin: that this conquest might become an invincible obstacle to peace? [1]

If we add to all these reasons the helpless situation in which France was at that time, it became easier to discover the motives which impelled the Duke of Choiseul to adopt a policy of duplicity. If the war was still to continue, France must win Spain as an ally and if he tried to include the Spanish claims in the French terms of peace, it was in order to show Pitt that France would have new allies, and was not thus compelled to accept conditions of absolute surrender. Drawing nearer to Spain had not by any means as its main object continuing war against England, for it is hardly to be supposed that France, wholly exhausted in her resources, would, even with the aid of an additional ally, have wished to continue hostilities. This policy was adopted by the French Foreign minister as a precautionary measure upon which France might rely in case of a failure of the negotiations. Neither did the Duke of Choiseul make any secret about it. In a letter in his own handwriting he asked Ossun not to conceal his desire for peace from Charles III and to tell him that the French hoped that their new engagements with him would not hinder peace which was very necessary to them; he added in the same letter:

> "Ce n'est pas la guerre proprement dite qui fait désirer au Roi la paix; Il seroit peut être même avantageux, vu la liaison et l'intimité de la France et de l'Espagne, de continuer la guerre, mais nous avons des troubles intérieurs qui fatiguent le Roy à l'excès . . . et qu'ils ne peuvent être reprimés que par la paix". [2]

Two weeks later, the French Foreign Minister still held the same opinion, for he told Ossun:

> "M. de Grimaldi parait très opposé aux sacrifices que le Roi veut bien faire pour se procurer cette paix, mais il ne connait pas nos maux intérieurs, ils sont tels qu'ils augmentent la nécessite de la paix sans que nous puissions les dévoiler aux Cours etrangères". [3]

---

[1] A.E., C.P., Angleterre, 443, ff.100r-100v, Duke of Choiseul to Galitzin, May 4th 1761, see *supra*, p. 72.

[2] A.E., C.P., Espagne, 533, f.35v, Duke of Choiseul to Ossun, July 7th 1761.

[3] A.E., M.D., Espagne, 574, f.44r, Duke of Choiseul to Ossun, July 21st 1761.

He added, however, that if England refused to accept his offers:

"il faudra bien nécessairement continuer la guerre, et c'est alors que nous aimerons la bonne volonté que marque l'Espagne pour se déclarer contre nos Ennemis". [1]

Nevertheless, if Pitt was to blame for his persistence in excluding the French from the fisheries, and his expedition to Belleisle and his haughty language, it must be pointed out that the Duke of Choiseul contributed also to the failure of the negotiations by his precipitate engagements with Spain, engagements which were the immediate cause of their unsuccessful conclusion. Both Waddington and Yorke held Pitt alone responsible for the failure of the negotiations, yet the Duke of Choiseul had his share in bringing the negotiations to an unsuccessful end. His simultaneous negotiations for war and for peace were fatal to the latter. His suggestions of June 2nd of including the Spanish grievances in the negotiations for the separate peace between France and England was disastrous to his projects of peace. It is true that Choiseul in his instructions to Bussy and to Ossun had emphasied the subordination of the Family Compact to the attainment of an immediate peace. [2] It is true that the Duke of Choiseul recommended his ambassador in Spain not to commit himself in any sort of engagements with that country. It is also true that the Duke of Choiseul in July 1761 was of the opinion that the claims of Spain should not be presented at the same time as the French memorial and that he deferred the signature of the Convention with Spain till he received the answer to his Ultimatum from England. In a word, it is true the Duke of

---

[1] *Ibid.*, 44v.

[2] Choiseul's instructions to Bussy with regard to Spain, A.E., M.D., France et Divers Etats, 570, ff.51v-52r, "M. de Bussy trouvera à Londres M. le Comte de Fuentès. Cet Ambassadeur irrité des lenteurs de M. Pitt, ne respire que la guerre; son maitre animé du même Esprit de Vengeance a proposé au Roi un traité offensif et défensif. Dans l'incértitude du succès de la Négociation actuelle avec l'Angleterre, le Roi réduit ce traité à une alliance purement défensive. Si M. Pitt témoigne trop de roideur dans les Conditions de la paix, alors M. de Bussy échauffera le ressentiment de M. de Fuentès, parceque la crainte que les Anglois concevroient d'une déclaration de guerre de l'Espagne, les porteroit à modérer leurs prétentions à l'égard de la France. Cet objet est très délicat. Il faut que M. de Bussy ne s'engage ni trop, ni trop peu avec M. de Fuentès."

Choiseul's first object was peace and he tried, by all possible means, not to let his negotiations with Spain affect those of peace with England; but the task was very hard to undertake:

"in playing with the Spanish alliance, Choiseul was playing with fire". [1]

and in spite of his able and shrewd plans and cautiousness, he failed in fulfilling his aim. Thus, whereas at the beginning of July, there existed an even chance for peace and war, this balance was suddenly destroyed by the inclusion of the Spanish grievances in the negotiations.[2] This fact was admitted even by the French themselves:

"Malgré la différence des sentiments des deux Cours, on pouvoit absolument espérer qu'elles se concilièroient sur tous ces points; mais l'intervention de l'Espagne opposoit désormais entr'elles une barrière insurmontable". [3]

If the Duke of Choiseul thought that the inclusion of the Spanish grievances in his separate negotiations with England were likely to intimidate Pitt, and render his terms of peace more moderate, events proved that he was wrong in his calculations.[4] Pitt who had measured better than Choiseul Spain's weakness,[5] far from fearing her, when later on he suspected an offensive alliance between her and France, he demanded an immediate attack on her colonies.[6] After the rejection of the memoir concerning the Spanish grievances, the Duke of Choiseul faced by the danger of losing Spain, who was growing more and more suspicious, could not do otherwise than decide to continue the war and to hasten

[1] Hotblack, "The Peace of Paris 1763", *R.H.S.T.*, Series 3, II, 251.

[2] Grant admits that peace was still possible before the inclusion of the Spanish grievances in the negotiations, Grant, 18.

[3] A.E., M.D., France et Divers Etats, 570, f.146r.

[4] See *supra*, pp. 91-92. The Duke of Choiseul was not then aware of the weakness of Spain, Choiseul to Ossun, December 16th 1764, see *Receuil des Instructions, Espagne III*, XII bis, 354.

[5] Williams, 11, 106.

[6] A.E., M.D., Espagne, 97, 67v; Grant, 17, assured us that Pitt: "savait très bien qu'il risquait de pousser Louis XV dans les bras de l'Espagne; mais non seulement il méprisait ce danger, il le souhaitait même. 'Je tiens pour certain', écrivait à sa cour le 1er Juin le chargé d'affaires Napolitain, 'que Pitt sera plus l'ennemi de l'Espagne que de la France; il mésure sa haine au nombre des vaisseaux qu'il voit en mer, et certes, à l'heure présente, il en voit plus d'espagnols que de français' "; See also Namier, 341, Newcastle to Hardwicke, August 6th 1761.

the conclusion of his treaties of alliance with Spain. Sautreau[1] indicates this difficulty with which Choiseul was then faced in the following words:

> "que devenoient nos engagemens avec l'Espagne? Le traité n'étoit pas encore signé; mais il n'en existoit pas moins. . . . Le Roi d'éspagne avoit marqué tant de confiance qu'il étoit impossible de faire un pas en arrière sans se déshonorer, et sans s'intérdire à jamais toute éspèce de secours de la part de cette Couronne". [2]

Thus even before the signature of the treaties with Spain, the Duke of Choiseul had gone so far in his engagements with that country that it became difficult to retreat from them. By the time the terms of peace with England became milder, the Duke of Choiseul was already committed to his engagements with Spain, and Charles III was ready to take up arms against that country. Sautreau realised the uneasiness of such a situation when he wrote:

> "Ces deux opérations étoient dìrèctement contradictoires; elles le jettèrent dans un embarras inéxtricable en reussissant toutes les deux. . . . Il étoit sur le point d'y [peace] parvenir, en obtenant des Anglois les seules conditions qu'il pût espérer; mais la négociation de l'alliance avec l'Espagne étoit aussi à son point de matûrité". [3]

The Duke of Choiseul had no alternative than to continue the war unless he decided to lose not only the alliance, but also the friendship of Spain, which alliance he considered of the greatest importance to his country. [4] The Duke of Choi-

---

[1] Sautreau de Marsy, Claude Sixte, man of letters, born in Paris in 1740, particularly known by his articles in many newspapers of his time: L'Année Littéraire, Journal des Dames, Journal de Paris. He died in Paris on August 5th 1815. He published many works, i.e. "L'Almanach des Muses", (1765-1793) in 28 volumes; "La Nouvelle Anthologie française" (1769-or 1787) in 2 volumes etc. . . ., Biographie Universelle, Ancienne et Moderne, XXVII, 269-270. He wrote a valuable Memoir "Analyses des négociations entre la France et les Autres Puissances de l'Europe (1748-1788)" which is still in manuscript form and kept in the Archives of "Le Ministère des Affaires Etrangères, Paris", under the following reference: Affaires Etrangères, Mémoires et Documents, Espagne, 189. As this memoir is not published it has not been mentioned in the aforesaid biography. According to information from the "Ministère des Affaires Etrangères, Paris", Sautreau, in that ministry, filled the post of Director of the department of "Traductions de Documents au Service des Archives" during the Revolution and the First Republic.

[2] A.E., M.D., Espagne, 189, ff.40r-40v.

[3] Ibid., Espagne, 189, f.35r.

[4] See A.E., C.P., Espagne, 533, f.394r, Duke of Choiseul to Ossun, September 8th 1761.

seul's policy was thus dictated to him by circumstances as his cousin Count of Choiseul[1] indicated later to his ambassador in Vienna:

"Notre sistême est très simple et n'est ni de choix ni d'adoption ; ce sont les circonstances et la nécessité qui nous l'ont prescrit ; nous avons désiré la paix l'année passée ; nos alliés y ont consenti ; nous avons engagé une négociation dirècte avec l'Angleterre. . . . Cette négociation a manqué, la continuation de la guerre est devenue un parti nécessaire". [2]

It was natural that the Count of Choiseul did not refer to the engagements with Spain as a reason of this rupture, however Ossun realized that France's engagements with Spain were responsible for the failure of the negotiations for peace between France and England.

"La dernière réponse de la France se raproche si fort des prétentions de l'Angleterre, qu'il est naturel de présumer que notre Paix particulière ne manquera pas à l'occasion des intérêts directs des deux Puissances. Ce sont ceux de nos Alliés ou les engagemens que la France vient de contracter avec l'Espagne qui paroissent devoir éloigner notre réconciliation". [3]

The only consideration, however, which might justify the Duke of Choiseul in committing such imprudent measures would be :

"l'idée de saisir l'*unique* occasion de conclure le pacte de famille, qui, s'il ne pouvoit être avantageux dans le moment, pouvoit l'être dans la suite". [4]

Also did he not assert to Ossun the importance of such an alliance when he wrote to him in the following year :

"Nous perdrons il est vrai le Canada, mais nous nous mettrons en Etat de jouir et de profiter de l'avantage inéstimable du Pacte de Famille, que Cette guerre nous a procuré et qui est plus intéressant mille fois pour la France que la Colonie du Canada". [5]

The Duke of Choiseul, aware of his imprudence, hastened, as already indicated, to explain his policy in his memoir to the

---

[1] Count of Choiseul became the Foreign Minister in October 1761, Flassan, VI, 326.

[2] A.E., C.P., Autriche, 286, ff.278r-278v. Count of Choiseul to Count of Chatelet (the French ambassador in Vienna), February 14th 1762.

[3] A.E., C.P., Espagne, 533, f.458r, Ossun to Duke of Choiseul, September 23rd 1761.

[4] A. E., M.D., Espagne, 189, f.45r.

[5] *Ibid.*, Espagne, 574, f.76v, Duke of Choiseul to Ossun, May 17th 1762.

French cabinet on the 6th September,[1] and to set forth in thirty-six hours the "Mémoire Historique" about the negotiations between France and England during the six months from March to September 1761.[2] Choiseul's aim was to justify his policy, to evade any accusation of his precipitate Spanish policy, and to prove to the French and the English people as well as to the rest of the European countries[3] that the English were totally responsible for the failure of these negotiations. Although very honest in putting down, in this memoir, all the official letters and ultimata exchanged between the two countries during these negotiations,[4] the Duke of Choiseul presented them so as to form an apologia.[5] The French Foreign minister made a point of impressing the English people by indicating what a beneficial peace the English might have had if they had treated France with less haughtiness,[6] and of pointing out to the European Countries and particularly to those interested in the liberty of commerce

"Le Contraste que forment le désir extrême du Roi de rétablir la paix, et l'obstination des Anglois à continuer la guerre".[7]

On reading this "Mémoire," Voltaire declared:

"Ce mémoire échauffera tous les honnêtes gens, tous les bons citoyens".

President Henault[8] assures us also that:

"Ce mémoire eut tout l'effet que l'on en devait attendre, et tout Paris y applaudit".

Neither Voltaire's predictions nor Henault's assurances were true for the largest part of the French people remained perfectly indifferent to this appeal. Barbier, who used to write on

---

[1] See supra, pp. 98-99.

[2] Jobez, V, 444; the Pamphlet's title is *"Actes et Mémoires Authentiques des Négociations faites pour La Paix en 1761 entre les Cours de Londres et de Versailles".*

[3] This memoir was known to the different countries of Europe, see A.E., C.P., Portugal, 93, Duke of Choiseul to St. Julien, December 15th 1761.

[4] I have made a careful collation of the original letters and ultimata with those of the memoir and it is clear that nothing was altered.

[5] A.E., M.D., France et Divers Etats, 570, f.160r, reckoned also by Flassan, VI, 446.

[6] See *Walpole's letters,* 111, 459, Walpole to Horace Mann, November 10th 1761.

[7] A.E., C.P., Portugal, 93, Duke of Choiseul to St. Julien, December 15th 1761.

[8] Charles Henault became "president de la première Chambre des enquêtes" in 1710, Perey, 9.

many of the current affairs in his journals, did not seem to have been acquainted with the existence of this "mémoire".[1] In England it "open'd many people's eyes",[2] and many went as far as to call it "La condamnation *of a late minister*";[3] it also put the English government under a certain obligation to give England and the world an answer to it,[4] The task was entrusted to Charles Jenkinson, Bute's Under-Secretary of State[5] who was given:

> "Ordre exprès de représenter les faits avec toute la modération et le ménagement possibles".[6]

The reasons for preparation of this answer could be easily explained by the fact that at that time Bute had re-opened secretly the negotiations of peace with France through the channel of Viry and Solar the two Sardinian Envoys in London and Paris.[7] Jenkinson prepared a lengthy answer to show that France was the aggressor and to prove the fallacy of allowing her to compensate for British conquest in America by the restoration of her own conquests from Hanover and from the German allies; but no use was made of this answer,[8] and it has never been published.[9] An explanation of the non-publication of this essay might be found in Viry's letter of December 15th 1761 to Solar. Viry declared to the latter that whereas the English government was strongly soliciting the publication of that memoir, a well-intentioned person for peace of that ministry was working at delaying its publication for a few weeks, because he thought that:

---

[1] Jobez, V, 444-445.

[2] *Life and Letters of Lady Sarah Lennox*, 52.

[3] A.E., C.P., Angleterre, 444, f.349r, with a letter of M. John Malan of November 14th 1761, November 6th 1761.

[4] L.H. MSS., 9, ff.24-25, Viry to Solar, London, December 15th 1761.

[5] *Jenkinson Papers*, footnote 2, 15 (This answer is in B.M., Add. MSS., 38336, ff.161-268).

[6] L.H. MSS., 9, f.25.

[7] As explained in the following chapter.

[8] *Jenkinson Papers*, 15, footnote 2.

[9] *Jenkinson Papers*, XII (Introduction).

"il conviendroit mieux qu'on ne donne ce Mémoire au Public que dans
le Tems qu'on sera d'accord, ou du moins prêt à l'être, pour que l'effet
qu'il pourroit avoir ici sur les Esprits, ne ralentit pas les Dispositions
Pacifiques qu'on prend soin d'insinuer dans [un] nombre de Membre
du Parlement". [1]

It is obvious that that well-intentioned person could not be
anybody else but Bute, who, at that time, was already
negotiating secretly peace with France. It is most likely therefore that the difficulties with which he was confronted in these
negotiations persuaded him not to publish the answer at all.

In spite of the fact that these negotiations were broken and
that they came to naught, they proved to be useful for the later
negotiations, for they furnished the basis on which the final
treaty of peace was concluded a year later. [2]

---

[1] L.H. MSS., 9, f.25.

[2] *Mémoires du Duc de Choiseul*, 388, Duke of Choiseul in his *Mémoire Justificatif* of
1765, acknowledged that fact: "La paix, qu'a faite Votre Majesté, a eu pour base ma
première négociation"; see also Beer, 153.

CHAPTER IV

THE NEGOTIATIONS OF 1762

First Stage

HAVING failed to achieve peace with England for his country in the March–September negotiations, the Duke of Choiseul, convinced of the necessity of peace for France, was preparing for new negotiations. His position then was different from what it had been during the previous discussions; although apparently strengthened by new alliances with Spain, yet these engagements were inevitably to render him less free in his actions and decisions, as events were to prove; for, naturally, there were always Spanish interests to consider, for which the Duke of Choiseul did not seem always to have much consideration. His sole aim, all through, was to obtain an honourable peace for France and to benefit as much as possible from his new engagements with Spain, by obtaining for his country better conditions of peace than those previously offered. Thus, as soon as the Bussy-Stanley negotiations had been broken off, he urged his ambassador in Spain to exert all his efforts to persuade His Catholic Majesty to advance the date of his declaration of war against England,[1] which declaration, according to the "Secret Convention," was to be on May 1st, 1762. The Duke of Choiseul had many serious reasons for insisting on this advancement of Spain's declaration of war against England. The French Foreign Minister, aware that his country, in her exhausted situation, even with the help of an additional ally, was not capable of continuing the war for a long time, and thinking that fresh negotiations for peace with England might be resumed during the winter of the same year,[2] considered that the sooner Charles III joined his arms to

---

[1] A.E., C.P., Espagne, 533, ff.475-476, Duke of Choiseul to Ossun, September 29th 1761; *ibid.*, Espagne, 534, ff.87-88, Duke of Choiseul to Ossun, October 19th 1761.

[2] *Ibid.*, Espagne, 533, f.475v.

those of France the better. More important still was his desire to reap the benefits of his Spanish policy before it was too late, especially as, at that time, in England, the pacific views of the new Secretary of State and the other ministers caused him to fear that they might succeed in settling the Spanish grievances, so as to prevent Spain from joining France in the struggle against England or at least to delay hostilities.[1] Besides, a defeat of the Austrians in Silesia might dishearten the Empress-Queen and persuade her, as well as Russia, to make peace, at the Congress of Augsburg. He feared that in this event France would be left on her own in the struggle against England; thus isolated, he thought, her position would be as humiliating as it was disadvantageous.[2] Whereas, if the King of Spain had an ambassador at Augsburg, who was united in his interests with those of France, the latter country would be in a very advantageous position, as the Duke of Choiseul declared in the following words:

> "nous y jouerions le rôle pour les affaires d'Espagne et de France, qui nous conviendroit, en nous rendant les maîtres absolus de notre négociation avec l'Angleterre".[3]

Moreover, he believed that, if Spain entered the conflict against England at an earlier date the English Parliament would be hampered in raising funds and that a sudden and well-timed entry could also surprise Portugal[4] and force her either to alliance or to certain defeat.[5]

Meantime, some ministerial changes took place in the French cabinet. On October 13th, 1761, a few days after the resignation of Pitt, the Count of Choiseul, a cousin of the Duke, at that time French ambassador in Vienna, became the French Foreign minister, leaving the Duke in direct control of his country's relations with the Bourbon powers in Spain,

---

[1] *Ibid.*, Espagne, 534, ff.48r-48v, Duke of Choiseul to Ossun, October 13th 1761.

[2] *Ibid.*, Espagne, 534, f.49r.

[3] *Ibid.*, Espagne, 534, f.49v.

[4] Portugal was to be the first object of the combined military operations of France and Spain.

[5] Aiton, "The Diplomacy of the Louisiana Cession", *A.H.R.*, XXXVI, 710-711.

Naples and Parma, as well as with Portugal. The latter combined with his duties as war minister those of Minister of marine.[1] It must be pointed out, however, that the Count of Choiseul was called to the ministry of foreign affairs only in order to relieve the Duke; and that, in spite of these changes, the latter did not lose his influence in the conduct of Foreign Affairs in France.[2]

At the same time, Charles III was not anxious to declare war against England before the appointed date; on the contrary he believed in the advantages of not advancing the date of declaration as indicated in his memoir which was sent to France with Ossun's letter of October 15th 1761.[3] His reluctance to adhere to the views of the French Foreign minister was not due to lack of willingness but to very real deficiencies in the Spanish military establishments.[4] In the same memoir Charles III declared the necessity of being prepared, in order that:

"Nous puissions au Moins tirer tout le parti possible de la surprise".[5] The Duke of Choiseul seemed resigned to the attitude of Charles III when he wrote to Ossun:

"nous ne sommes en droit que de représenter, la lettre de la Convention à fixer l'époque; nous devons nous y soumettre et faire seuls des efforts en Amerique cet hiver".

In the same letter, however, he could not hide his fears of the attitude of Spain:

"Dieu veuille que d'icy là il ne se rencontre pas de nouveaux obstacles à cette déclaration".[6]

Considering the eagerness with which the Duke of Choiseul was working to accelerate a break between Spain and England, one could appreciate the satisfaction with which he received

[1] Bourguet, "Le Duc de Choiseul et l'Alliance Espagnole, après le Pacte de Famille", R.H., XCIV, 6-7.

[2] Waddington, La Guerre de Sept Ans, V, 281; see also L.H. MSS., 9, f.129, Count of Choiseul to Egremont, April 16th 1762, also in P.R.O., G.D., 1.

[3] A.E., C.P., Espagne, 534, ff.71-80; it is a French translation of the original Spanish Memoir.

[4] Aiton, "The Diplomacy of the Louisiana Cession", A.H.R., XXXVI, 711.

[5] A.E., C.P., Espagne, 534, f.77r.

[6] Ibid., Espagne, 534, ff.144v, 144r, Duke of Choiseul to Ossun, October 27th 1761 (holograph); also in ibid., ff.142v, 141r (a copy of this letter).

the news that a rupture was imminent. He feared lest this "démarche maladroite" of the English Court should entangle him in toils from which they could never extricate themselves. The great advantage of a rupture was that it would end an ambiguous position which hampered Franco-Spanish policy and prevented them from gathering the fruits of the Family Compact.[1]

Meanwhile, on the other side of the Channel, Bute, who came to power to make peace and to make it at any price, within a short time of Pitt's fall, started his task by taking secret steps to re-open the negotiations at the point where they had been broken off. The intermediaries whom he employed were Count of Viry,[2] the Sardinian Envoy in London, and his colleague in Paris, the Bailli of Solar.[3] The correspondence exchanged in this transaction was conducted apparently with the utmost secrecy. It began with a letter from Viry to Solar, on November 17th,[4] in which he spoke of Pitt's fall as a great surprise and indicated that a certain person of credit wished that it had taken place before Stanley and Bussy had been recalled. In this letter the delicate work of negotiating peace between France and England was begun, and in about a month's time, just when England and Spain were on the eve of breaking off relations, negotiations were actually on foot. On December 8th, the Duke of Choiseul formally accepted the mediation of the Sardinian Envoys.[5] Thus at the same time

[1] Ibid., Espagne, 534, f.323r, Duke of Choiseul to Ossun, December 25th 1761; see also Bourguet, "Le Duc de Choiseul et l'Alliance Espagnole, après le Pacte de famille", R.H., XCIV, 23.

[2] On Viry, see Albemarle, 1, 94-97; Bedford Correspondence, 111, 82 (footnote); Life and Letters of Lady Sarah Lennox, 1, 68-69 (footnote 3); Fitzmaurice, 1, 137-138.

[3] On Solar, see Albemarle, 1, 97; Bedford Correspondence, 111, 81 (footnote).

[4] L.H. MSS., 9, ff.5-6. This letter is written November 17th and not October 17th as stated by Corbett, 11, 285. It is true that the "9bre" looks like "Obre", but a letter from Viry to Solar, of December 13th 1761 confirms the fact that the above mentioned letter was written in November and not in October (L.H. MSS., 9, f.13).

[5] Ibid., 9, ff.10-12, Duke of Choiseul's letter of December 8th was joined to Solar's of December 13th to Viry (Ibid., 9, ff.7-10). Ibid., 9, f.12, some "Observations" were added to the Duke of Choiseul's letter by Solar. He told Viry that the name of the King of Sardinia was menioned only as a simple term of politeness and that "il ne faut y faire nulle attention", for he repeated his desire that the two Sardinian Envoys should act simply as individuals.

that the Duke of Choiseul was anxious to persuade Spain to break off relations with England and declare war against her, he was willingly accepting the overtures of peace offered by the latter country. The explanation of this rather contradictory conduct of the Duke of Choiseul becomes easier when we realise that, although he was anxious to obtain peace, yet in the new circumstances he was not at all prepared to accept the same terms that he would have accepted before, when he was not very sure of Spanish assistance and when he had to negotiate with Pitt:

"le Roy n'est plus disposé à accorder à l'Angleterre les avantages offerts pendant la négociation dernière. Il faudroit avoir à traiter avec un second Pitt, pour oser négocier sur de pareilles propositions". [1]

He therefore urged Spain to break with England so that France might benefit from the joint operations of the two countries against England by obtaining in her peace negotiations with England more advantageous terms than those which were offered the previous year. He seemed then certain that most of the English ministers desired peace, yet he realised the difficulty with which they would be faced if they accepted any less advantageous terms than those of the previous negotiations.

"Il est certain que la plupart des ministres Anglois désirent la paix, mais Il n'est pas moins certain que si l'on veut réfléchir à leur position et à celle de la France, Cette paix si désirée n'est pas faisable, car le Roy n'acquiescera pas aux propositions qui ont esté faites dans la dernière négociation, et Il n'y a pas un Ministre Anglois assez hardy pour consentir à des conditions moindres, que celles qui ont esté proposées par la France". [2]

It was, therefore, natural that the Duke of Choiseul was very pleased as soon as he was acquainted with the decision of Spain to break off with England and declared that their principal object was to operate offensively as well as defensively against their common enemy in all parts but that their main offensive plan should be that against Portugal. [3] The reasons which made an attack against Portugal a main aim in the

---

[1] A.E., C.P., Espagne, 534, ff.182v-183r, Duke of Choiseul to Ossun, November 17th 1761 (holograph); also in *ibid.*, Espagne, 534, f.180v (a copy of this letter).

[2] *Ibid.*, Espagne, 534, f.306v, Duke of Choiseul to Ossun, December 15th 1761.

[3] *Ibid.*, Espagne, 534, f.323v, Duke of Choiseul to Ossun, December 25th 1761.

Franco-Spanish military operations against England were mainly based on economic factors. England was to be attacked at the different sources of her strength. Charles III, who complained of the British contraband which reached his empire through Brazil, attached great importance to the conquest of the Portuguese Empire, which would rob the British of

> "a valued market, a source of bullion and an important route for contra-
> band trade with the Spanish Empire".

The Duke of Choiseul regarded Portugal as an English colony and on that ground alone she was, in his opinion, the enemy of France.[1]

Meanwhile the secret negotiations between France and England continued. The correspondence exchanged in these transactions was according to its importance carried to its destination by a special messenger, or by a trustworthy traveller on his way through Paris and London, or sent by ordinary post.[2] Before receiving Choiseul's answer of December 5th, in which the Duke of Choiseul agreed to use the two Sardinian Envoys, or even before receiving an answer to his first letter of 17th of the previous month,[3] Viry took advantage of the presence of his son, as he indicated in the letter, and used him in writing a letter to Solar, communicating to the latter some confidential information.[4] He assured him, first of all, that the important ministers of the English Government were well disposed to peace in these words:

> "tout le Ministère actuel, et surtout les Personnes qui ont le plus grand
> crédit sont très bien disposées pour conclure une Paix particulière
> entre la France et l'Angleterre".[5]

[1] Christelow, "Economic Background of the Anglo-Spanish War of 1762", *J.M.H.*, XVIII, 26-27 (Portugal was attacked by Spain only during the last week of April, A.E., C.P., Espagne, 536, f.34r, Ossun to Duke of Choiseul, April 19th 1762).

[2] Viry and Solar used some trustworthy persons to carry their letters during their passage through Paris and London. Fox, son of Fox ex-Secretary of State carried Viry's two letters of December 13th and of the 15th to Solar on January 4th 1762. George Pitt, on his way to his embassy in Turin was asked to carry Viry's letters of January 5th, 8th and 12th. These persons were not acquainted with the contents of the letters nor the negotiations. Less important letters, namely Viry's letter of January 22nd etc. were sent by ordinary post.

[3] Viry received this answer dated December 4th on December 15th, Viry to Solar, L.H. MSS., 9, f.18.

[4] *Ibid.*, 9, ff.13-16.   [5] *Ibid.*, 9, f.14.

He was also persuaded that the two nations would reach agreement in a short time if they took the last *Ultimatums* as a basis
for the new negotiations, provided that no more English
victories took place in America. Nevertheless, in a very
important letter, two days later,[1] Viry recommending Solar
to act circumspectly in this affair, told him not to conclude
from what he had previously written that things were so easy
in England in connection with peace for there was in England
a quite considerable party who did not want peace or at least
desired it on impracticable conditions.[2] However, in order to
accelerate these negotiations, Viry suggested that France
should send secretly to London:

> "quelqu'un qui passeroit pour un Marchand bien instruis et munis des
> pouvoirs nécessaires, et il se pourroit de cette façon que la Paix se trouvat
> signée ou du moins des Préliminaires, avant que le Public en eût le
> moindre vent".[3]

Reaching that stage in the negotiations, Viry added, the two
countries could exchange plenipotentiaries. He also asserted
that he was sure that that way of negotiation would be "très
gouté ici par les Ministres qui souhaitent sincèrement la Paix".[4]

In answer to the previous three letters of Viry, which Fox,
son of the ex-Secretary of State, carried to Solar on January
4th, Solar wrote in his own handwriting a letter on the following day.[5] He made it clear in this letter that, as the French
were the first to make offers for peace during the last
negotiations and as these offers were rejected, they were not
likely to make others which might share the same fate; and
that he did not believe that they were prepared to accept the
same terms that they would have accepted during the previous
negotiations. However, he pointed out that the modifications
for which they were likely to ask were neither "considérables,
ni déraisonnables." Indicating that the declaration of war by

[1] *Ibid.*, 9, ff.18-26, Viry to Solar, December 15th 1761.

[2] *Ibid.*, 9, f.20.

[3] *Ibid.*, 9, f.22.

[4] *Ibid.*, 9, f.23.

[5] *Ibid.*, 9, ff.29-34, Solar to Viry, January 5th 1762. (Viry answered this letter only
on January 26th, Viry to Solar, February 9th; *ibid.*, 9, f.43).

Spain might have changed the attitude of the English towards peace, he asked Viry to tell him whether they still had the same attitude towards peace. Solar[1] seemed alarmed at this new situation which he describes "beaucoup plus délicate et critique".[2] At the same time Viry, writing from the other side of the Channel,[3] expressed his friends' surprise at the rupture of relations between Spain and their country and added his own views that this rupture of relations between England and Spain should not in the least interfere with the separate negotiations between France and England. In another letter[4] which reached Solar at the same time as the previous one, Viry confirmed his views that the sudden rupture of relations between England and Spain ought not to have any affect on the negotiations for a separate peace between the two countries, except that arrangements and negotiations about the questions of logwood and prizes between England and Spain ought to take place at the same time as those which had already started between France and England. Solar seemed very impressed after receiving Viry's last letters, delivered by George Pitt, when he asserted to the Count of Choiseul that the then English ministry was:

> "beaucoup plus doux, plus poli et plus honnête qu'il ne l'étoit de tems de M. Pitt".

And when significantly added:

> "Enfin, Je suis d'avis que si vous voulez la Paix, ou pouvez la vouloir, vous l'aurez infailliblement".[5]

These letters, which seemed to make Solar so confident about the attitude of the English ministers, did not have the same effects on the Duke of Choiseul,[6] who considered that Viry's letters had "un air entortillé, qui nous jette dans la méfiance"

---

[1] *Ibid.*, 9, ff.31-32. This fear was soon dissipated by Viry's letter of January 5th which reached Solar on 22nd, and thus Solar was able to ease the Count of Choiseul's mind on this matter by his letter of January 23rd (*ibid.*, 9, ff.44-45).

[2] *Ibid.*, 9, f.32.

[3] *Ibid.*, 9, ff.36-37, Viry to Solar, January 5th 1762. This letter was carried by George Pitt on his way to his embassy at Turin.

[4] *Ibid.*, 9, ff.39-41, Viry to Solar, January 12th 1762 (also carried by George Pitt).

[5] *Ibid.*, 9, ff.44-45, Solar to Count of Choiseul, January 23rd 1762.

[6] *Ibid.*, 9, ff.46-49, Duke of Choiseul to Solar, January 23rd 1762, and in Albemarle, I, 97-99.

and expressed grave doubts about the sincerity of the overture. In his opinion, it could have but one of three objects: either it was intended to sow jealousy between France and her allies, or it was a necessity because of the overwhelming differences between the different ministers in the English cabinet or because the burden of war was intolerable. Two days later, in a confidential conference with the Duke and Count of Choiseul, Solar discussed these same letters of Viry as well as those of December of the previous year.[1] The Choiseuls complained that the English overtures were too vague and stated that they could not move in this matter without their ally Spain, and that therefore it was impossible for them to make the first proposals. They suggested that the English ministers should either send a disguised envoy to France[2] who should carry on secret negotiations with France and, if England and France seemed likely to agree upon honest and reasonable terms for peace, Spain should then be included in the negotiations, and the same secret envoy should negotiate with her as with France; or alternatively that the English ministers should provide Viry with a memoir of the terms of the peace they were willing to grant, and receive in return the French proposals. The two French ministers ended their conversation with Solar by saying:

"Si le Ministère de Londres veut effectivement la Paix, en adoptant les éxpédiens ci-dessus proposées, cette Affaire peut-être conclue en moins de six semaines".[3]

In order that these negotiations should succeed, Solar[4] urged that no one of the allies except Spain should be acquainted with them till the three countries had reached an agreement, for he believed that:

"si chaqu'un veut consulter ses Alliés la paix ne se fera jamais".

[1] B.M., Add. MSS., 32934, ff.121-124, Solar to Viry, February 1st 1762. It is the first document in the Correspondence of the Secret Negotiations, which appears in the Newcastle Papers, and in the Egremont Papers (P.R.O., G.D., 1). It is also in L.H. MSS., 9, ff.50-58.

[2] It must be remembered that the idea of sending a disguised Envoy to France was not new, that it was Viry's in the first place, see supra, p. 121.

[3] L.H. MSS, 9, ff.56-57.

[4] Ibid., 9, ff.58-60, another letter of February 1st 1762, Solar to Viry.

He thought that peace in Germany would easily follow on peace between France, Spain and England, but suggested that:

> "les deux Cours de Versailles et de Londres pourroient en faisant leur Paix particulière, établir des Conditions honnêtes et raisonnables pour chaqu'un de leurs Alliés, que ceux-ci seroient ensuite les Maîtres d'accépter ou de refuser sans que cela pût en rien déranger la Paix des trois Couronnes". [1]

These two letters of Solar written at the beginning of February as well as the Duke of Choiseul's "Billet" of January 23rd, all of which Solar mentioned in his letters of February 4th and 11th, sent by ordinary post, did not reach Viry before March 2nd. [2] Viry, when he wrote his letter of February 22nd[3], was impatiently waiting for Le Roux, who was to deliver these important letters. Neither was Solar less impatient for Viry to receive them when he wrote on February 25th: [4]

> "Je compte qu'à l'heure qu'il est le Roux sera arrivé; et que vous aurez vu les Dispositions, où sont mes Correspondans de Lyon [5] pour le débit des Articles des Marchandises détaillées dans l'Etat qui étoit joint à mes Lettres". [6]

In the same letter Solar asked Viry to tell him, as soon as he received those letters, what was the decision of his friends. Since he received no answer to his letter of February 1st until April 1st, Solar concluded that the English ministers entrusted with the secret disapproved of the Choiseuls' suggested plan for peace making and feared lest the affair was at a standstill. [7]

In England the Duke of Choiseul's "Billet" and Solar's letters

---

[1] Ibid., 9, f.59.

[2] Ibid., 9, f.74, Viry to Solar, March 2nd 1762.

[3] Ibid., 9, f.67, Viry to Solar, February 22nd 1762; by then Viry, having received Solar's letters of February 4th and 11th, knew about the three important papers carried by Le Roux.

[4] Ibid., 9, ff.71-74.

[5] This is one of the forms by which Viry and Solar referred to the Two Choiseuls in their correspondence sent by ordinary post. They were also referred to in some other letters as "Négocians de Lyon" (Ibid., 9, f.66, Solar to Viry, February 18th; and ibid., 9, f.67, Viry to Solar, February 22nd); and as "Messieurs de Lyon" (ibid., 9, f.73, Solar to Viry, February 25th). On the whole, however, in their correspondence sent by ordinary post, the two Sardinian Envoys used metaphors in order to disguise the real nature of their correspondence, namely the language of merchants and traders.

[6] Ibid., 9, f.73.

[7] Ibid., 9, ff.83-84, Solar to Viry, April 1st 1762.

disappointed those who had based their hopes on the pacific inclinations of the French ministers. Newcastle[1] thought that they were of a provocative nature especially those passages in Duke of Choiseul's note which related to his doubts as to the sincerity of the English Government's overtures. Nevertheless Newcastle could not avoid expressing to Bute, and afterwards to the King his opinion that: *"we should not put a final stop to this channel"*.

As soon as he was acquainted with these papers, Hardwicke, who had never, as he declared to Newcastle,[2] expected very much from this channel, was not disappointed, though very much concerned. He described the style as "certainly not pleasant," but added that he could not say that he was vastly provoked by it, when he considered Choiseul's "Billet" as "a familiar note to a third Person, and not avowed to be intended to be transmitted".[3] He was, however, of Newcastle's opinion that this channel should not be stopped. As to the two methods of procedure for secretly negotiating the peace, suggested by the Choiseuls, Hardwicke did not think that on the subject of peace any of the ministers was courageous enough to adopt either the one or the other. Devonshire[4] considered "The French Papers" as "not at all Satisfactory", and the note from the Duke of Choiseul mere verbiage, and "full of Impertinence". Nevertheless he agreed with Newcastle and Hardwicke that they should not lose sight of the negotiation. He thought it necessary that France should be made to understand that,

---

[1] See Albemarle, 1, 99, Note from Newcastle to Hardwicke, most unlikely of January 27th, as Corbett thought it was (11, 286, footnote 1), for these French letters did not reach Viry till March 2nd, Newcastle's note must have been written on the same date or on the following day, because Hardwicke's answer to it is dated March 3rd. This note dated Wednesday was thus of March 3rd (for Sunday was February 28th (B.M., Add. MSS., 32835, 197r) and March 12th was a Friday (*Ibid.*, 32935, f.330r).) Besides, Newcastle's comments on these answers are indicated in his Memorandum of March 3rd, *ibid.*, 32999, f.418r.

[2] *Ibid.*, 32935, ff.160-161, Hardwicke to Newcastle, March 3rd 1762.

[3] *Ibid.*, 32935, f.160r. In his first letter of February 1st 1762, Solar pointed out also as regards the Duke of Choiseul's "Billet" that "il faut le regarder comme un Billet, confidential que M. le Duc écrit à son Ami qui n'en doit faire aucun usage" and added: "et je crois cette réflexion très nécessaire dans le cas que vous jugiez à propos de le communiquer très confidemment à vos Amis de Londres," L.H. MSS., 9, ff. 52-53.

[4] B.M., Add. MSS., 32935, ff.172-175, Devonshire to Bute, March 4th 1762.

though England was not obliged to sue for peace, yet she desired it. Devonshire seemed to believe also that the Choiseuls mean and wish peace. He suggested that the French ministers should meet them half-way, and if France declared that she would like to make some alterations in the terms for peace which she presented on the eve of the rupture of the previous year's negotiations, she should be asked to indicate them. As to Bute these answers puzzled him extremely; and he thought that the English ministers in the secret should not "lie down and submit", in fact that they should not continue the negotiations. But he soon changed his attitude and he told Egremont to write a letter to the Count of Viry complaining of the answers of the French ministers.[1] Moreover this answer of Egremont's was discussed in several meetings of the *"Kings' Ministers"*.[2] Apparently these ministers would not agree to despatch a secret envoy to negotiate with the Choiseuls, and the other alternative suggested by the Choiseuls was adopted, namely to set forth the terms of peace which they would be willing to offer.

This important matter necessitated two meetings which took place at Devonshire House on March 9th, and later at Egremont House on March 18th. The same members were present at the two meetings.[3] They discussed the answer to be sent to Viry and the terms of peace which they could offer to France. In the second meeting (of March 18th), the final answer was unanimously agreed upon.[4] The ministers concerned decided that it should be sent to Viry in order that he

---

[1] Albemarle, 1, 99-100, Newcastle to Hardwicke (March 3rd? 1762).

[2] As Newcastle referred to them when he differentiated them from those of the *Council*, B.M., Add. MSS., 32936, f.9r. (Observations upon Egremont, Draft of . . .) These meetings were private ones, which took place between those ministers only who were acquainted with these negotiations, which had been kept a profound secret from some ministers till they were for the first time discussed in a full Cabinet Meeting on March 29th, as will be explained later.

[3] Devonshire, Bute, Egremont, Newcastle, Hardwicke, Grenville, P.R.O., G.D., 21.

[4] Although it was stated in Egremont's Minute of 19th that the Ministers present agreed unanimously on the answer, yet it is indicated in Newcastle's Memorandum of the same date that Grenville was "Against Entering into any Particulars; And Demanding to know Whether the Duc de Choiseul adhered to His last Ultimatum", B.M., Add. MSS., 32999, f.427r.

might send it to Solar, who should be asked to show it to both
the Duke and Count of Choiseul[1]. It was agreed to allow the
French the right of fishing in the gulf of St. Lawrence and off
Newfoundland, and they were to be permitted to hold the
islands of Miquelon and St. Pierre. They also granted a French
police post of fifty men in the latter island. Goree was to be
surrendered to France. Of the Neutral Islands France was to
keep St. Lucia and St. Vincent, and England those of Dominca
and Tobago.[2] The English Engineers were to inspect the
"Cunette" in Dunkirk and its fate was left to their decision.
Moreover, it was stipulated that in Germany neither power
was to continue to aid her allies after the conclusion of peace,
except by granting financial assistance.[3]

There is no evidence that this letter was ever sent to Solar[4],
as was decided in the secret meeting at Egremont House of
March 18th. Another letter of March 27th, sent by Viry to
Solar provided the answer to Solar's two letters of February 1st
and of Duke of Choiseul's "Billet" of January 23rd.[5] This letter
though inspired by Egremont's letter to Viry of March 21st,
was by no means as important and as definite, for although it
defended strongly the sincerity of the English ministers in
their efforts for peace and made it clear that they were prepared to settle their grievances with Spain at the same time
as with France, yet it made no mention at all of the terms

[1] P.R.O., G.D., 21, Minute of Cabinet Council meeting of March 18th, written
on 19th.

[2] As regards the Neutral Islands, in this letter, Corbett states the reverse of what is
stated in the B.M., referred to in the following footnote, Corbett, 11, 286.

[3] B.M., Add. MSS., 32936, ff.1-8, Egremont to Viry, March 21st 1762.

[4] This letter which was supposed to answer Solar's letters of February 1st and
Duke of Choiseul's "Billet" of January 23rd is not in the Viry-Solar Correspondence
(L.H. MSS., 9-11) which contains a complete copy of the secret correspondence
which led to the peace. A minute examination of the following period's correspondence in the same collection reveals no trace of it. Neither does this letter appear
in the "Correspondance Politique", Angleterre (Ministère des Affaires Etrangères,
Paris). In the Egremont Papers (P.R.O., G.D., 3) there are apparently two drafts
of this letter dated March 1762, of which the first is marked as never having been
sent. The second draft is different from the first, and nearer to Viry's letter of
March 27th (L.H. MSS., 9, ff.88-96).

[5] L.H. MSS., 9, ff.88-96.

which England was prepared to offer to France and which were
indicated in Egremont's letter of March 21st, and in one of
its drafts in the Egremont Papers. What were the reasons
which induced the English Ministers, who were privy to the
negotiations, not to send these articles to France after dis-
cussing them and agreeing to send them to Solar? If we compare the date on which this letter was written (March 21st)
and that of the first cabinet council meeting, in which the
question of negotiation with France was for the first time
discussed openly (March 29th), we might find out an important
reason which must have had some effect on this change. If the
few ministers acquainted with the secret of the negotiations
decided to throw off the mask, and to have the matter of peace
discussed in a cabinet meeting[1], they must have found it wiser
not to precipitate the dispatch of these terms which might
commit them, especially since the news of the conquest
of Martinique, which arrived in England on March 22nd[2],
must have made it awkward for the ministers to stick to the
same terms stated by Egremont in his letter to Viry written on
the day before the news had reached England. Also was not
the question of Martinique one of the major points afterwards
discussed by the ministers in their meetings about the terms
of peace with France? After all, Hardwicke's predictions that
there was not enough courage among the English ministers
to follow either of the ways suggested by the Choiseuls[3]
proved to be right.

In another letter of the same date (March 27th),[4] in which

---

[1] Already on March 12th, on his Remarks on Egremont's Draft to Viry, Hardwicke
wondered whether it would be better to repeat to *"les autres Ministres du Roi"* the
discussion which they had before on this matter (most likely he meant the meeting of
March 9th), B.M., Add. MSS., 32935, f.330r.

[2] *Walpole's letters*, III, 496, Walpole announces the news to Horace Mann,
March 22nd 1762; *Memoirs of George III*, 1, 113; B.M., Add. MSS., 32936, f.42r.
Newcastle announcing this news to Rockingham, on March 22nd wrote: "This great
News coming *at this Time* will give weight to *all Our Operations*". Newcastle in his
Memorandum of the same date, questioned whether Egremont's letter to Viry has
been sent, and "Whether any Notice should be taken of the Success at Martinico",
B.M., Add. MSS., 32999, f.429r.

[3] See *supra*, p. 125.

[4] L.H. MSS., 9, ff.96-99.

THE NEGOTIATIONS OF 1762

he was answering Solar's second letter of February 1st, Viry
assured Solar that the request of the Duke of Choiseul to keep
the negotiations between the two countries a profound secret
was to be respected. He assured him again in this letter that
the English ministers were well disposed to peace, which, he
added, would be proved as soon as Egremont's health[1] enabled
him to attend a cabinet council which was to be held on the
question of peace.

Up to this point the negotiation with France had been kept
a profound secret. Only a few ministers were acquainted with
what was going on and the question had never been discussed
at a full cabinet council.[2] It was only discussed in what Newcastle called in his Memoranda the meetings of the *King's
ministers*,[3] namely those of March 9th and 18th, at Devonshire
House and Egremont House respectively. If the minutes of
these meetings [4] helped to indicate the different ministers
who were acquainted on the secret negotiations [5] some
questions still remained unanswered. When were these
different ministers acquainted with the secret? Was it from
the very beginning when Viry wrote his first letter of November 17th? Or did Bute wait until he received the answer of
the Duke of Choiseul agreeing to use the two Sardinian
Envoys? Were these ministers all acquainted at the same time?
However, there is a document which throws some direct
light on this affair. It is a letter in the Newcastle Papers,
written on February 28th,[6] where it was stated that Viry,
at the request of Bute and Egremont, had the honour to show

---

[1] Egremont took ill suddenly about the middle of March, Viry to Solar, March
16th 1762, *ibid.*, 9, f.82.

[2] B.M., Add. MSS., 32935, f.330r, Remarks on Egremont's Draft, March 12th
1762.

[3] *Ibid.*, 32936, f.9r, Observations on Egremont's Draft of . . .

[4] P.R.O., G.D., 21 (only in the Egremont Papers, Newcastle's minute of the
meeting of March 18th, the only one to be found in his papers about these very first
and secret meetings did not state the members present at the meeting, B.M., Add.
MSS., 32999, f.427r, Memoranda of March 19th 1762).

[5] Bute, Egremont, Newcastle, Hardwicke, Devonshire, Grenville, and (Mansfield)
later.

[6] B.M., Add. MSS., 32935, f.107r.

Newcastle the letter from Paris of February 11th.[1] In this letter Solar told Viry that, in his two letters of February 1st, he answered his letters of January 5th, 8th and 12th. It is obvious that Newcastle must have known then, or perhaps earlier,[2] that the negotiations had been proceeding secretly between England and France. Whether he was acquainted with the letters before they were dispatched to France, we do not know. Hardwicke seems to be also one of the earliest of those entrusted with the secret. His letter of March 3rd[3] proves that he knew before that date something about the negotiations, when he declared that he had never felt very hopeful about the channel of communication, namely the Viry-Solar channel. Devonshire, by March 4th,[4] if not earlier, knew about these negotiations, when he wrote to Bute commenting on the French papers. However uncertain we might be about the exact date when Bute acquainted the other ministers with his first secret overtures to France, it is most likely that Egremont, the Secretary of State concerned, and known for his pacific tendencies,[5] Newcastle and Hardwicke, as earnest advocates of peace, had been allowed to know all and had played an active part in the secret councils which met to debate the question. Devonshire must also be included as a member of these councils. Grenville's name was mentioned in connection with these secret negotiations for the first time in the list of ministers who attended the secret meeting of March 9th.[6] Mansfield was acquainted with the secret a few

---

[1] This letter was answered by Viry on February 23rd, L.H. MSS., 9, f.71. On the same date, in his memorandum, Newcastle pointed to "My Conversation with My Lord Bute". Whether it was on this answer we could not tell.

[2] The first time "the Secret Negotiations" appear in Newcastle's Papers, is in his memorandum of January 28th 1762, B.M., Add. MSS., 32999, f.380r.

[3] Ibid., 32935, ff.160-161; see supra, p. 125.

[4] Ibid., 32935, ff.172-175; see supra, pp. 125-126.

[5] On November 17th Fuentes acquainted Grimaldi with his conversation with Egremont, who told him that His Britannic Majesty was prepared to accept the last Ultimatum of France which had been rejected by Pitt, if only France made overtures for a renewal of the negotiations, A.E., C.P., Espagne, 534, f.184r.

[6] P.R.O., G.D., 21.

days after the meeting previously mentioned[1] ; however, his name did not appear with the others at the following secret meeting which took place on March 18th. There might be an explanation in the fact that when Mansfield was acquainted with the state of the secret negotiations and of Egremont's letter, his opinion and proposals for the methods to be followed were contrary to the other ministers' decisions and were more likely to put an end to the negotiations.[2]

It was on March 29th, however, that the cabinet council met, and, as though no previous steps had been taken, agreed to renew the negotiations with France.[3] It was decided in this meeting that the Secretary of State Egremont[4] should write to the Count of Choiseul suggesting that the two countries exchange ministers and that:

"the two last Ultimatums should be the Basis, upon which the Ministers are to treat; subject to such Variations as may naturally, and reasonably arise from the Alteration of Circumstances on either Side".[5]

This letter was to be conveyed to the Count of Choiseul by Solar, the Sardinian Minister. It was decided also that:

"the like Proposal should be made to Spain, through the Channel of the Sardinian Minister, at Madrid".[6]

In another cabinet meeting held on April 5th,[7] the form of the declaration of His Britannic Majesty [8] as well as that of Egre-

---

[1] B.M., Add. MSS., 32935, ff.390-393, Memorandum of Newcastle House of March 14th 1762 (on March 13th 1762 apparently).

[2] Ibid., 32935, f.390v, Newcastle stated that Mansfield's opinion and proposed methods ". . . must, at Once, put an End to This Negotiation; And, in My Humble Opinion, in the worst Manner; That is, upon Principles, which would make it impossible almost to Renew This Negotiation again".

[3] Ibid., 32999, ff.454-455, Minute of St. James's March 29th 1762; see also P.R.O., G.D., 21. The English Ministers found in the Declaration made by the Czar to the Courts of Vienna, France and Sweden recommending peace in the strongest manner, a good opportunity for making openly overtures for peace to France, B.M., Add. MSS., 32999, f.437r, Memoranda of March 27th 1762.

[4] Egremont was not present at the meeting (most likely because of his illness); members present were: The Chancellor, Devonshire, Bedford, Newcastle, Hardwicke, Bute, Mansfield, Ligonier, Grenville.

[5] B.M., Add. MSS., 32999, ff.454v-455r.

[6] Ibid., 32999, f.455r.

[7] P.R.O., G.D., 21, Minute of Cabinet Council at Egremont House, April 5th, 1762.

[8] L.H. MSS., 9, ff.105-107.

mont's letter to the Duke of Choiseul[1] were decided. They
were sent accompanied by a letter from Viry to Solar on April
8th [2]; he was to convey them to the Choiseuls. In another
letter of the same date,[3] Viry pointed out to Solar that France
was to decide whether or not the appointments of Ministers
to negotiate should be official. In order to prove to him the
sincerity of the English ministers, Viry sent him at the same
time a letter received by him from Bute,[4] in which the latter
expressed his joy at the steps taken by Egremont for the peace
negotiation. He expressed his feelings by stating that:

"Je serois charmé de voir la Paix rétablie entre nous, la France et
l'Espagne".

It was not long before the Count of Choiseul returned a
favourable reply to Egremont. Though he stated that France
could not make peace without Spain, yet he seemed hopeful
that the latter country would be willing to come to terms.
Although the Count of Choiseul approved of the idea of
exchanging ministers, he thought it better to exchange
memoirs first in order to draw up the preliminaries: after
that, Ministers could be exchanged. He was also of opinion
that peace with Germany should be left till an agreement was
reached between the three countries.[5] The Duke of Choiseul

[1] *Ibid.*, 9, ff.102-105. In this letter Egremont acquainted the Duke of Choiseul that
Count of Estaing was given his freedom unconditionally. Estaing, an officer captured
by the English in the Indies, was released; but having broken his promise by committing aggressive deeds against England, he was imprisoned again. Through Solar he
got his freedom. Estaing's release was used by France as a pretext for the overtures
of peace with England (as France told Spain later).

[2] *Ibid.*, 9, ff.100-102.

[3] *Ibid.*, 9, ff.107-110; also in A.E., C.P., Angleterre, 446, ff.42-43.

[4] L.H. MSS., 9, ff.110-112; a copy of the same letter is also in A.E., C.P.,
Angleterre, 446, ff.45-46.

[5] L.H. MSS., 9, ff.128-134, Count of Choiseul to Egremont, April 16th 1762.
The original letter is in P.R.O., G.D., 1. The spelling of some of the words and the
use of capital letters differs in the two texts.

It is worth pointing out how the engagements between Spain and France made it
impossible for the latter to answer formally in a counter-declaration to the declaration
of His Britannic Majesty, as the Count of Choiseul declared in a note of the same date
L.H. MSS., 9, ff.127-128.

"Je me serois expliqué plus ouvertement sans la nécessite où Je suis d'attendre la
Réponse d'Espagne, et cette même considération, ne m'a pas permis de répondre en
forme à la déclaration, c'est à dire par une autre déclaration, mais au titre près, ma
Lettre est la même Chose, et doit en tenir lieu puisqu'elle contient tout ce que
J'aurois pû mettre dans la contre Déclaration".

did not seem to care much for his promises to Spain, when, even before sending her a letter [1] to acquaint her with the overtures of His Britannic Majesty for peace and to ask her to accept them, in a long confidential letter to Solar,[2] he not only sketched out the terms of peace which he would be willing to accept, but also those which Spain was likely to accept in making peace with England. It was very natural, therefore, that he asked Solar to request Viry to maintain the utmost secrecy about this letter, which was to be shown only to Egremont and to Bute. In addition to what England had agreed to surrender in her last memoir during the Stanley-Bussy negotiations, in the previous year, the Duke of Choiseul demanded the cession of Martinique, whose recent conquest had been a serious blow to the French power in the West Indies and a corresponding gain to England. Taking upon himself to explain the three points of dispute between England and Spain, he pointed out that, as long as England's right of cutting and carrying logwood from Honduras Bay was confirmed, and the Spanish claim conceded, by which the British might not build any settlements on the Bay of Honduras, everything else would be easy to settle. Thus the Duke of Choiseul indicated the terms upon which he would accept peace and also the procedure for negotiating; the two Sardinian Envoys were to continue to act as go-betweens till the three Countries reached preliminary agreement, and then ministers would be exchanged publicly.

Negotiations for peace had been going on for about five months between France and England without the knowledge of Spain. As early as January 10th 1762, after the conversations had been going on for nearly two months, and one day before Spain declared war against England,[3] the Duke of Choiseul disingenuously intimated to Grimaldi that he had

---

[1] A memoir given to Grimaldi only on April 17th announced the news of this declaration taking Estaing's liberation as a pretext for the correspondence between France and England, A.E., C.P., Espagne, 536, ff.62-69.

[2] B.M., Add. MSS., 32937, ff.111-117, also in L.H. MSS., 9, ff.118-127, Duke of Choiseul to Solar, April 15th 1762.

[3] England declared war against Spain on January 2nd, the latter country declared war against England on January 11th.

K

received vague hints of England's anxiety to make peace but that

> ". . . he had replied to all these indirect hints that France could now neither hear nor enter into the slightest discussion without the concurrence of His Catholic Majesty, that he was persuaded that the two monarchs had no desire to perpetuate the war, but in case England found herself disposed to end it in a reasonable manner, he did not believe she should work for it by indirect methods, emissaries, or even words. England ought to make her propositions clearly to both courts, as France had when she thought peace was necessary". [1]

It was only on April 17th that the Duke of Choiseul informed Ossun [2] that England had asked for a renewal of the negotiations for peace. Although he asserted that His Christian Majesty could not make any decision without the consent of His Catholic Majesty, yet he acknowledged that "Nos pertes multipliées demandent quelque tems de repos". Only twelve days before the dispatch of this letter, and a week before receiving the Declaration of His Britannic Majesty, the Duke of Choiseul sent an enthusiastic letter to Ossun [3] in which he was considering everything "en beau". [4] Did he not also declare, in the same letter, that the forces of France and Spain could destroy England in thirty years' time?

> "Si J'étois le maître, nous ferions vis-à-vis de l'Angleterre, comme l'Espagne vis-à-vis des Maures, et si l'on prenoit bien véritablement ce parti, l'Angleterre seroit réduite et détruite d'icy à 30 ans. Le Roy Catholique a des forces respectables; notre marine est en mauvais état, mais elle se rétablira, tout ne se fait pas dans un jour, mais le courage est de tous les moments". [5]

It must be noticed here also that it was not long since France had been urging His Catholic Majesty to advance his declaration of war against England; embittering his feelings against England and raising his hopes in the event of a war against

[1] Aiton, "The Diplomacy of The Louisiana Cession", *A.H.R.*, XXXVI, 712, Grimaldi to Wall, January 11th 1762.

[2] A.E., C.P., Espagne, 536, ff.60-61, Duke of Choiseul to Ossun, April 17th 1762.

[3] *Ibid.*, Espagne, 536, ff.28-33, Duke of Choiseul to Ossun, April 5th 1762. "On peut me reprocher", he wrote to Ossun, "de voire en beau, cela est vray, mais cette maniere augmente mon courage", *ibid.*, Espagne, 536, f.32r.

[4] *Ibid.*, Espagne 536, 32r.

[5] *Ibid.*, Espagne 536, ff.32r-32v.

her; also, that, when the French ministry completely changed its attitude and begged Ossun to persuade His Catholic Majesty to accept the renewal of the negotiation asked for by England, Spain had not yet commenced her campaign in Portugal.[1] How could the sudden change in the French cabinet's policy be explained? Why was she so eager to negotiate peace with England? It is true that her losses were increasing and that her maritime war was growing more and more disadvantageous.[2] Nevertheless, the overwhelming factor in the change of her policy and in her earnest desire for peace with England, in spite of the fact that Spain had not yet started her military operations, was the change in the policy of Russia. By the death of the Tzarina, and the accession of Peter III to the Russian throne,[3] the balance of power was disturbed, for, as soon as the new Czar acceded to the throne, he declared his friendship to the King of Prussia, Frederick the Great, with whom he entered into negotiations for peace.[4] He also sent a declaration to the Empress Queen, to France and to Sweden strongly recommending peace, and acquainting them that he had resolved for the sake of peace, to surrender all his conquests in that war.[5] Sweden proposed to Prussia that negotiations for peace should be entered into.[6] Austria was also, therefore, very likely to make a decision for peace

---

[1] Ibid., Espagne, 536, f.84r, Ossun to Duke of Choiseul, April 19th 1762 (acquainting Choiseul that the attack on Portugal would not take place before April 23rd or 24th).

[2] Ibid., Espagne, 536, f.68r, Memoir delivered to Grimaldi on April 17th 1762; the effects of the loss of Martinique are stated in this memoir.

[3] Elizabeth, the Empress of Russia, died on January 5th 1762, Recueil des Instructions (Russie, 11), IX, 182. Although the Revolution in Russia took place early in January, France was not unduly alarmed until later when the actual effect of the pacific views of the new Czar were felt when France's ally Sweden proposed to Prussia entering into negotiations for peace, and when France felt threatened with losing Austria who might conclude her peace before her.

[4] The treaty of peace between Russia and Prussia was signed on May 5th 1762, Recueil des Instructions, Russie, 11, IX, 194, and was proclaimed at Breslaw, on 21st instant, Memoirs and Papers of Sir Andrew Mitchell, 11, 292, Mitchell (the British ambassador in Prussia) to Bute, May 23rd 1762.

[5] B.M., Add. MSS., 32999, f.437r, Newcastle's Memoranda of March 27th 1762.

[6] Peace between Prussia and Sweden was signed at Hamburgh on May 22nd 1762, Memoirs and Papers of Sir Andrew Mitchell, 11, 303, Mitchell to Bute, May 30th 1762.

with Germany.[1] Several factors were to hasten her decision. Not only was she deserted by her ally Russia, discouraged by her losses in Silesia, but also she was suffering from financial disorders, differences and disunion within her councils.[2] Even if Austria did not want to make peace without the consent of her ally France, the Czar might join the King of Prussia, in order to compel her to make peace. This idea as Chatelet, the French ambassador to the Court of Vienna, declared, "fait frémir".[3] The French ministers were, therefore threatened by the fact that peace might be concluded on the continent before that between France and England. The Duke of Choiseul's alarm was revealed, when he wrote to Ossun [4] explaining the reasons for which France was in favour of accepting the renewal of the negotiations for peace with England:

" . . . . définitivement la paix d'Allemagne se fera sous nos yeux et sans notre participation, tout au plus avec notre consentement forcé. . . . Il est donc essentiel, pour sauver notre considération dans l'Empire, tant pour le présent qu'à l'avenir, et pour tirer parti, en compensation, des possessions conquises par les armes du Roi, que la paix de mer précède la paix de terre; c'est ce qui détermine le désir du Roi sur l'accéptation de la négociation proposée par les Anglois".[6]

Not only was this peace on the continent likely to weaken France's situation in the Empire, and prevent her bargaining with the successes which her arms had gained for Maria Theresa on the Continent, but also it was likely to strengthen England's position in her maritime war against France and Spain, as the Duke of Choiseul declared:

"Les Anglois, débarrassés de la guerre du Continent, seront assés puissans pour nous empêcher de reprendre nos colonies et de reparer la perte affreuse de la Martinique, mais même pour entamer avec succès les possessions Espagnoles en Amérique".[5]

[1] A.E., C.P., Espagne, 536, f.60r, Duke of Choiseul to Ossun, April 17th 1762.
[2] Ibid., Autriche, 288, ff.37v-39r, Count of Chatelet to Count of Choiseul, April 21st 1762. Chatelet describes, in his letter, the state of affairs in Austria, see ibid., Autriche, 288, ff.26-40.
[3] Ibid., Autriche, 288, 37v.
[4] Ibid., Espagne, 536, ff.60-61, Duke of Choiseul to Ossun, April 17th 1762.
[5] Ibid., Espagne, 536, ff.60r-60v.
[6] Ibid., Espagne, 536, f.60v.

What was therefore the policy of the French Government in the new circumstances? This policy was indicated by the French Government as soon as the news of the accession of Peter III on the Russian throne reached Paris.[1] In his instructions to Breteuil, then French Ambassador in Russia, the Count of Choiseul stated that:

"Notre object véritable et principal, c'est la continuation de la guerre et le maintien du systeme, quant à present. En partant de ce principe, nous devons chercher à entretenir l'union avec les deux cours impériales. Mais, si elles entroient dans des vues opposées, nous devons faire valoir avec force et sans ménagement leurs engagements avec nous, qui ne leur permettent pas de traiter sans notre consentement. Ce n'est pas, Monsieur, que nous soyons éloignés de la paix ; mais nous ne croyons pas qu'elle puisse nous être avantageuse si elle vient par le canal de la Russie".[2]

Similarly the French foreign minister informed Chatelet at Vienna that France could not tolerate a peace forced on her by her allies but that she must take the lead in the peace-negotiations.[3] He therefore asked to be made acquainted with even the slightest rumour of such a move.[4] Thus while trying to hasten the negotiation with England, and to obtain the consent of Spain to join in the negotiations, France's policy towards Austria was:

"de gagner du tems, d'encourager et de retenir autant qu'il sera possible, la Cour de Vienne".[5]

In a long memoir of April 17th, drawn up by the Duke of Choiseul[6] the release of Count of Estaing, held a prisoner by the British, furnished a good pretext for bringing the negotiation with Spain into daylight. A letter joined to this memoir, from Egremont to the French government, dated February

---

[1] In his letter to Breteuil of January 31st 1762, Count of Choiseul said that the news reached him "last Thursday", which corresponded to January 28th (since Monday was 25th). The letter is in *Recueil des Instructions, Russie*, 11, IX, 183-192.

[2] *Ibid.*, 190-191.

[3] A.E., C.P., Autriche, 286, f.287v, Count of Choiseul to Chatelet, February 14th 1762.

[4] *Ibid.*, Autriche, 287, f.228r, Count of Choiseul to Chatelet, March 30th 1762.

[5] *Ibid.*, Autriche, 288, ff.39r-39v, Chatelet to Count of Choiseul, April 21st 1762.

[6] *Ibid.*, Espagne, 536, ff.62-69, Memoir given to Grimaldi on April 17th 1762.

22nd 1762,[1] concerning the return of that prisoner, enabled the Duke of Choiseul (after having received His Britannic Majesty's declaration) to direct Spanish attention to these peace overtures as something new.[2] His Catholic Majesty was recommended in this memoir, not to communicate the overtures to the Court of Vienna, giving as one of the reasons, that, eager as that Court then was for concluding peace, it was most likely , as soon as Vienna heard of these negotiations she would hasten her own with Germany and thus peace with Germany might be concluded before peace with England and France, and Spain. He explained the consequences of such a situation:

"nous perdrions beaucoup vis-à-vis de l'Angleterre, si la paix d'Allemagne où nous jouerions un rôle fort médiocre, étoit faite ou près d'être avant que les préliminaires de la paix de mer fussent signés".[3]

When he was acquainted with the memoir of the Duke of Choiseul and with his desire to negotiate peace with England, Charles III, whilst recalling that he had entered the war mainly to extricate France from her difficult situation,[4] did not object to the renewal of these negotiations, and to taking part in them, provided that France obtained honourable and reasonable terms and that His Catholic Majesty could obtain for Spain:

" les conditions les plus avantageuses qu'il seroit possible[5] "

This spirit shown by Charles foreshadowed that the French government was to be confronted with "d'assés grandes difficultés".[6] Besides he did not approve of concealing from Austria this renewal of the negotiations.[7] A few days later, in

---

[1] L.H. MSS., 9, ff.69-71, Egremont to Duke of Choiseul, February 22nd, this letter was given to Grimaldi at the same time as the memoir.

[2] A.E., C.P., Espagne, 536, f.63r.

[3] Ibid., Espagne, 536, f.68v.

[4] Ibid., Espagne, 536, ff.94v-95r, Ossun to Duke of Choiseul, April 26th 1762.

[5] Ibid., Espagne, 536, 95v.

[6] Ibid., Espagne, 536, 98r.

[7] Since the accession of Peter III on the Russian throne, His Catholic Majesty was for drawing nearer to the Court of Vienna and advising France to do the same, ibid., Espagne, 536, f.127r, Ossun to Duke of Choiseul, May 2nd 1762.

his remarks on the instructions sent to Grimaldi on this occasion, Ossun stated openly that:

"S.M.C. inclinoit plus à la continuation de la guerre qu'à une paix prochaine avec l'Angleterre; qu'en se prêtant, néanmoins, à entrer en négociation avec cette Puissance, ce Monarque vouloit s'assurer d'une entière indépendance dans la discussion et sur l'ajustment des griefs particuliers de l'Espagne, et que pour y mieux réussir, il évitoit de lier sa négociation particulière avec celle de la France". [1]

It is obvious, therefore, that the Duke of Choiseul was faced with great difficulties with regard to his ally Spain and that Charles III was not by any means a docile ally, easy to manage, he was not either, as Blart wrote:

"Disposée à prendre les armes et à les déposer au premier signe et selon les intérêts de la France". [2]

It was not so easy, after having excited all the war-like desires of the Spanish Sovereign, and after having encouraged his ambitions for military greatness and glory, to persuade him to lay down his arms. Sautreau well understood the difficulty of the task when he wrote:

"Il fallut tout l'art, toutes les cajoleries du ministère françois et de l'Ambassadeur, pour le rapprocher des vues nouvelles qu'on adoptoit". [3]

Charles III had his reasons for not yet being in favour of a policy of peace with England. He had his ambitions about Minorca, which according to the Secret Convention was to be his own possession, if the war was successful; about Gibraltar which he hoped to recover, [4] and about Portugal, [5] which he was expecting to conquer. Charles III, who had only just entered the conflict, and was therefore unable to realise the

---

[1] *Ibid.*, Espagne, 536, f.121r, Ossun to Duke of Choiseul, May 2nd 1762.

[2] Blart, 27.

[3] A.E., M.D., Espagne, 189, f.49v. The French were aware of this difficulty, Solar, in his 2nd letter of April 16th 1762, wrote to Viry: "Je vous fais encore cette Lettre très confidentielle pour vous marquer mes Inquiétudes sur les Dispositions de l'Espagne: C'est une Cour haute, difficile", L.H. MSS., 9, f.144.

[4] Blart, 27, Ossun to Duke of Choiseul, April 26th 1762.

[5] Already by the end of May the conquest of Portugal seemed to His Catholic Majesty certain, Ossun to Duke of Choiseul, May 31st 1762. Aware that His Catholic Majesty's successes in the conquest of Portugal was to encourage his desire for the continuation of war against England, Solar, already on April 16th, in a confidential letter wrote to Viry: "ce que Je désirerois pour faciliter la Paix, ce seroit que l'on n'épargnat rien pour secourir le Portugal, et le mettre en état de se bien déffendre", L.H. MSS., 9, f.144. (The same letter mentioned *supra*, footnote 3).

truth about his weakness did not think then that any of those acquisitions was beyond his strength.[1] Beside these dreams, stronger motives still determined Charles III to be in favour of continuing war. He thought that Austria, having lost Silesia in a disadvantageous peace, would look to Italy, with the support of Prussia,[2] for a compensation which would be to the detriment of the Infanta. A successful war would therefore assure the safety of the interests of his family in Italy; in these interests his weakness lay:

"le moindre risque que pourroient courir les états du Roi son fils le toucheroit plus que la perte des Indes".[3]

However, His Catholic Majesty did not waste much time in answering the Duke of Choiseul's communication about the English Peace overtures. In his letter, which was to be communicated to England, Grimaldi[4] expressed his King's request for a declaration of these overtures from England, similar to that addressed to France. Three days later his letter was dispatched to London.[5] By the same courier, Solar sent a letter to Viry in which he stated that the Choiseuls believed that, if they had been alone in their negotiations with England, namely without Spain, whose haughtiness greatly annoyed them, peace between France and England would have been concluded in less than three weeks.[6]

Meanwhile the negotiations between France and England were progressing favourably. The French letters dispatched on April 17th reached Viry on 21st.[7] He communicated them immediately to Bute and Egremont who displayed much satisfaction with their contents. Egremont seemed to Viry "transporté de joie".[8] On the recommendation of Bute, Viry was

---

[1] In the same letter of April 16th, Solar wrote to Viry: "les Espagnols ont une Idée chimerique de leur Puissance, qui, selon moi, n'est pas fort redoutable", *Ibid.*, 9, f.144.

[2] Prussia's support would mean Russia's and England's.

[3] A.E., C.P., Espagne, 536, f.122v, Ossun to Duke of Choiseul, May 2nd 1762.

[4] L.H. MSS., 9, ff.192-195, Grimaldi to Duke of Choiseul, May 9th 1762.

[5] *Ibid.*, 9, f.203, 1st letter Solar to Viry, May 12th 1762. This letter is also in B.M., Add. MSS., 32938, ff.174-177.

[6] L.H. MSS., 9, f.205.

[7] *Ibid.*, 9, f.179, Viry to Solar, May 4th 1762.

[8] *Ibid.*, 9, f.155-156, 157, Viry to Solar, May 4th 1762.

to communicate to the rest of the Ministers these letters and particularly the one from the Duke of Choiseul to Solar concerning the terms of peace which France was willing to accept.[1] Several meetings took place between the English ministers in order to frame a reply to Choiseul's letter. On April 23rd,[2] the Cabinet met, and the discussion, as might be expected, centred round the demand for the cession of Martinique. If the ministers consented to the surrender of the Island, they might lay themselves open to the charge of being very lenient towards France and encouraging the French government to press further concessions; it was therefore agreed that Martinique could be given back to the French only if the English were allowed to retain either Guadeloupe or Louisiana.[3] Newcastle feared that Choiseul might regard the price demanded for Martinique as excessive.[4] However, when the cabinet met again a week later to come to a final decision,[5] Bute argued that to ask for Guadeloupe or Louisiana in return for Martinique was to ask too much; and succeeded in inducing the cabinet council to consent to the restoration of Martinique in return for the neutral Islands [6] and Grenada.[7] Even Bedford, though acknowledging that the French Ministry would not have agreed entirely to the terms agreed upon in the first meeting, thought that the offer erred on the side of generosity.[8] However, on May 1st, the English proposals[9] were dispatched to France. They conceded to her the right of fishing

---

[1] Ibid., 9, f.157, These letters were communicated to Newcastle by Viry on April 22nd, Newcastle was recommended to keep the utmost secrecy about them, B.M., Add. MSS., 32937, f.294r, Viry to Newcastle, April 22nd 1762 (see supra, p. 133).

[2] L.H. MSS., 9, f.157, Viry to Solar, May 4th 1762.

[3] Winstanley, 117.

[4] B.M., Add. MSS., 32937, f.349r, Newcastle to Hardwicke, April 25th 1762. "We have once lost The Peace, by asking too much, and not departing from it soon enough", Ibid., 32937, f.349r.

[5] Grenville was too ill to attend this meeting, Grenville Papers, 1, 442, Grenville to Bute, April 19th 1762.

[6] Tobago, St. Lucia, Dominica and St. Vincent.

[7] Bedford Correspondence, 111, 76, Bute to Bedford, May 1st 1762.

[8] Ibid., 111, 77-78, Bedford to Bute, May 4th 1762.

[9] L.H. MSS., 9, ff.169-179, Egremont to Viry, May 1st 1762.

off the coast of Newfoundland, and in the Gulf of St. Lawrence, and the possession of the little islands of St. Pierre and Miquelon and also Goree. In the West Indies England claimed the neutral islands,[1] Grenada and the Grenadines[2]; Belleisle was to be exchanged for Minorca; in India, France was asked to propose the trading settlements which she would like.[3] In America the Mississippi was to form the boundary between the English and the French possessions.[4] As regards the evacuation of Germany, the restoration of the Prussian territories to their Lord, considered as certain after the conclusion of peace, was not expressly insisted upon.[5] Examining these proposals, it may be easily noticed that in three matters Bute went beyond Pitt's utmost concessions. He conceded a second island at the mouth of the St. Lawrence, restored Goree, and indicated possible concessions relative to the evacuation of Westphalia. But on the other hand, the influence of England's latest successes was felt in the demand for all neutral islands, Grenada and Grenadines, and a part of Louisiana including New Orleans. Bute evidently only intended to ask for easy concessions and to give way where French resistance was likely to be greatest.[6]

This was the last communication to France which Newcastle was to assist in framing, for he resigned his office on May 26th.[7] The time had then come for him to retire from the

[1] Dominica, and St. Lucia, were already in the possession of the British, Ibid., 9., f.173.

[2] The news of Grenada and Grenadines' acquisition reached Egremont while writing his letter to Viry, Ibid., 9, f.173.

[3] In his letter of April 15th to Solar, the Duke of Choiseul asked from the English Government "un Plan pour la Côte de Coromandel", Ibid., 9, f.124.

[4] The Duke of Choiseul had already expressed his readiness to grant England a concession on that article, in order to obtain better terms particularly as regards the West Indies. In his letter of April 15th, he wrote to Solar on that subject: "Je ne crois donc pas qu'il y ait de Difficulté sur la Cession entière du Canada à l'Angleterre, même avec les Limites, de la Détermination desquels il sera aisé de convenir rélativement à la Louisiane", Ibid., 9, f.123. A special note about these boundaries was joined to Viry's letter of May 4th to Solar, Ibid., 9, f.183.

[5] By that time, the subsidy treaty with Prussia, concluded in 1758, had not been renewed, hence it was no longer valid, Ruville, 111, 74.

[6] Ibid., 111, 74.

[7] See Yorke, 111, 302.

administration, in which his influence, since the accession of
George III, had been waning, and in which he had already
submitted to opposition to his policy, namely the declaration
of war against Spain, and the refusal of the Prussian subsidy.[1]
He was determined not to give way to Bute's interference in
the Treasury which "he had come to regard as his own pre-
serve".[2] The Duke of Newcastle insisted that the House of
Commons should be requested to vote two million pounds,
one half of which was to be allotted to the assistance of Portugal, and the other half to be devoted to the war in Germany.
This proposition being opposed by Bute and the majority of
his colleagues who thought that one million would be sufficient
for both purposes, Newcastle resigned.[3] Bute replaced him in
the Treasury, G. Grenville was appointed Secretary of State,
and Sir Francis Dashwood Chancellor of the Exchequer.[4] Newcastle's withdrawal from the administration left Bute far more
dependent upon the support of Grenville and Egremont[5] ;
and thus the difficulties of his task were accentuated.   Much
might happen to hinder him in his course. The Choiseuls
might prove themselves unconciliatory; and Bute's attempts
to placate them by concession might be thwarted by the two
Secretaries of State. The future of the administration was full
of uncertainties.

The proposals of the English ministers were greeted with
satisfaction by the Choiseuls. They were impressed by the
sincerity of the pacific intentions of these ministers, and though
both hoped to obtain more, yet they found these proposals
honest and reasonable.[6] In the opinion of the Count of Choiseul
they were:

[1] For Bute's conduct with regard to this question (withdrawal of the Prussian
Subsidy) and for overtures for peace which Bute was accused of having made to the
Court of Vienna without the knowledge of Prussia, Bute had often been charged with
bad faith. See on this question, Conclusion, pp. 205-206.

[2] Winstanley, 110.

[3] For more details on the circumstances and causes of Newcastle's resignation, see
ibid., 108-111.

[4] Memoirs of George III, 1, 135.

[5] It must be remembered that "Since the resignation of Newcastle, Hardwicke had
ceased to be summoned and Devonshire had refused to attend. Mansfield, still
recalcitrant, had gone on circuit to be out of the way", Corbett, 11, 349.

[6] L.H. MSS., 9, f. 209, 2nd letter Solar to Viry, May 12th 1762.

"à peu près conformes à Notre dernier Ultimatum, mais un peu plus avantageuses, malgré la perte de la Martinique et la défection du Czar". [1]

The Duke of Choiseul thought that:

"en y changeant quelques articles, étoient infiniment plus avantageuses que celles de l'année passée". [2]

However, before returning an answer to these proposals, France procured the consent of the Austrian Court, and obtained from Spain a provisional agreement to these negotiations till the latter could answer Britain officially after receiving His Britannic Majesty's declaration. [3]

In May, [4] it was necessary to inform the Court of Vienna and to acquire her consent to the separate negotiations between France and England, not only because Spain laid stress on this point, but also because the news had been already communicated to the Prussian and Russian ambassadors in London. [5] When Kaunitz heard of the English overtures and of his ally's desire for peace, he could not hide his surprise at the change in French policy and declared:

"je vous avouerai que je trouve que vous allés bien vite et que votre politique se prete avec une grande facilité aux circumstances; Car vous ne pouvés oublier qu'il y a deux jours que vous ne nous préchiés que la continuation de la guerre et maintenant vous ne voyés que des raisons de souhaiter la Paix". [6]

As soon as the Count of Choiseul received this letter, he made a point of defending the stability of French policy by indicating the reasons which made it necessary for France to wish for peace. [7] However, the Court of Vienna did not make any

[1] A.E., C.P., Autriche, 288, f.239r, Count of Choiseul to Chatelet, May 17th 1762.

[2] Ibid., Espagne, 536, f.205v, Duke of Choiseul to Ossun, May 16th 1762; see also Bedford Correspondence, 111, 81, Duke of Choiseul to Solar, May 13th 1762. The courier of London of May 4th reached Solar, May 11th 1762, L.H. MSS., 9, f.208.

[3] This declaration was communicated to Grimaldi about the end of May, A.E., C.P., Espagne, 536, f.259r, Duke of Choiseul to Ossun, May 29th 1762.

[4] It was on May 12th that the Choiseuls acquainted Starhemberg with the English overtures for peace, L.H. MSS., 9, f.210, Solar to Viry, May 12th 1762.

[5] Ibid., 9, f.210.

[6] A.E., C.P., Autriche, 288, ff.295r-295v, Chatelet to Count of Choiseul, May 24th 1762.

[7] A very good account of all the reasons which made France at that time so desirous for peace is given in ibid., Autriche, 288, ff.343r-344r, Count of Choiseul to Chatelet, May 31st 1762.

difficulties in giving her consent. The Duke of Choiseul announced it to Ossun in the following words:

> "La Cour de Vienne est enchantés des ouvertures de paix de la Cour de Londres. Elle nous a marqué toute satisfaction". [1]

As to Spain, the Duke of Choiseul, with an acceptable peace in sight, used every artifice to get that power's consent to cease hostilities, [2] as he had done previously in urging Spain's entry into the war. At any moment the war party, namely Pitt, might return to power in England, [3] and the change of the Continental war against Prussia [4] was not much encouragement to continue the fighting. Threatened with irremediable Russian disaffection the Duke of Choiseul instructed his ambassador in Spain to urge Charles III to agree to an immediate peace for the sake of France. He expressed his fears to Ossun by indicating that there could be no delay for he feared lest the English might ally with the Czar with unpredictable results. [5] He was impatiently awaiting the reply of His Catholic Majesty, for it seemed to him that in the uncertainty between concluding peace and continuing war:

> "nous marchons pour ainsy dire sur la lame d'un couteau et dans le doute de conclure la paix ou de continuer la guerre, il faut eviter dans les propos de donner par la suite des armes contre nous". [6]

However, the Choiseuls were not left long in this uncertainty. In his reply, though Charles stated that for him the war had just begun and that he expected to conquer Portugal, yet, for the sake of his ally, he expressed his consent to immediate

---

[1] *Ibid.*, Espagne 536, f.301r, Duke of Choiseul to Ossun, June 9th 1762.

[2] "Nous ne perdrons pas une Minute pour faire consentir l'Espagne à Nos Vues", Billet of the Duke of Choiseul to Solar, May 12th 1762, L.H. MSS., 9, f.308.

[3] "Nous avons eû une Peur effroïable du Changement du Ministère en Angleterre; et Je vous préviens bien positivement que je me désisterois de toutes Négociation pacifique, si Je cessois de traiter avec Milords Egremont et Bute", Billet Duke of Choiseul to Solar, May 25th 1762, *ibid.*, 9, ff.258-259; in another letter two days eariler to the same, the Duke of Choiseul declared that, "J'aimerois mieux d'aller ramer aux Galères que d'avoir rien de pacifique à démêler avec M. Pitt", *ibid.*, 9, f.252, Billet Duke of Choiseul to Solar, May 23rd 1762.

[4] For this change, see *supra*, pp. 135-137.

[5] A.E., C.P., Espagne, 536, f.221v, Duke of Choiseul to Ossun, May 17th 1762 (a confidential letter, a copy of a holograph).

[6] *Ibid.*, Autriche, 288, ff.345-346r, Count of Choiseul to Chatelet, May 31st 1762.

formal peace negotiations.[1] England was not less anxious in acquiring the consent of His Catholic Majesty to the negotiations. She therefore hastened to send a Declaration [2] for the overtures of peace, as requested by His Catholic Majesty, which declaration reached Paris on May 25th.[3] Anxious to save time, Bute and Egremont [4] also prepared a note on the settlement of grievances which they were willing to accept in their peace with Spain.[5] This note was sent at the same time as the declaration to Solar. The Duke of Choiseul was asked to get these terms adopted by Spain; pretending that they were his own views on the settlement of the grievances between his ally Spain and England.[6] To the other three conditions of peace mentioned in this note, about the prizes, the fisheries, and the cutting of logwood at Honduras Bay, another article was added. This article concerned the renewal of all the treaties which existed between England and Spain before the war.[7] On May 29th, after paraphrasing this note in his own words, the Duke of Choiseul hastened to send it, as well as the declaration of England to Spain, for as he declared:

"rien n'est si pressé; Je crains que la tête ne s'échauffe dans cette Partie sur les Conquêtes Portugaises",[8]

and because he hoped that by the time the English ministers would answer his counter proposals, Madrid might have been able to send her answer.[9]

It was not before May 30th that the Choiseuls sent their answer to the English terms. It reached Viry early in June.[10]

[1] See *ibid.*, Espagne, 536, ff.274-280, Ossun to Duke of Choiseul, May 31st 1762.

[2] Dated May 19th, L.H. MSS., 9, ff.217-218 (sent to France on May 22nd 1762, *ibid.*, 9, f.233, Viry to Solar, May 22nd 1762).

[3] *Ibid.*, 9, f.280, Solar to Viry, May 26th 1762.

[4] *Ibid.*, 9, f.235, Viry to Solar, May 22nd 1762.

[5] *Ibid.*, 9, ff.237-239.

[6] *Ibid.*, 9, f.239.

[7] *Ibid.*, 9, f.238.

[8] *Ibid.*, 9, f.285, Duke of Choiseul to Solar, May 28th 1762 (a long and an important letter, ff.284-297).

[9] *Ibid.*, 9, f.284.

[10] *Ibid.*, 9, ff.261-279, Memoire joined to Duke of Choiseul's Billet of May 23rd. Viry received it on June 3rd, *Ibid.*, 10, f.1, Viry to Solar, June 4th.

Accepting nearly all that had been conceded, the Choiseuls refused to surrender St. Lucia. It was stated in the French Memoir that:

"La Guadeloupe, Mariegalante, la Martinique, Ste. Lucie sont indispensables pour le soutient du Commerce des François". [1]

They asked also for Isle Royale; [2] and in India for the Comptoirs of Karikals, Pondicheri, Masulipatan, Devi, Chandamagor, and Mahé. [3] In Germany, the army of Ferdinand of Brunswick was not to give any help to the Prussian King; and the occupation of the Prussian territories, either by French or Austrian troops, was to be continued until the general peace, when they would be assigned to the rightful owner. [4] The importance and the advantages of granting to England the Mississippi as boundary between the possessions of the two countries, and the possession of The Port of Mobile were indicated plainly. It was stated that not only was the new boundary giving England 1,400 miles more, but also:

"elle met la Louisianne et la Floride dans la dépendance absolue des Colonies Angloises". [5]

The Duke of Choiseul claimed that the terms of peace which he was offering England then were more advantageous to her than those of the previous year, [6] and asserted:

"Jamais nous n'aurions consenti l'Année passée à la cession de la Mobille et à l'arrête des Limites de la Louisianne, tel que nous l'offrons . . . nous sentons le Prix de cette Cession, qui entraine la perte de notre Colonie". [7]

He also foresaw the difficulties which Spain was likely to raise

---

[1] *Ibid.*, 9, 272; in his letter of May 28th 1762, the Duke of Choiseul declared to Solar: "Il ne nous est pas possible de cédar Ste. Lucie, et Je vous déclare franchement, mon cher Ambassadeur si l'Angleterre persiste à la vouloir, que mon avis dans le Conseil sera de rompre la Négociation : Je crois que sans Ste. Lucie, la France n'aura pas les Possessions de première nécessité qui lui sont indispensables en Amérique." (*Ibid.*, 9, f.289.)

[2] *Ibid.*, 9, f.268.

[3] *Ibid.*, 9, ff.274-275.

[4] *Ibid.*, 9, ff.276-277.

[5] *Ibid.*, 9, f.273; for the importance of the situation of the Mobile see map, appendix 6.

[6] *Ibid.*, 9, f.286.

[7] *Ibid.*, 9, ff.288-289.

because of her colony Florida. Although expecting difficulties
from Spain, the Duke of Choiseul believed he could overcome
them.[1] The memoir, which reached England on June 3rd,
was not favourably received by the English ministers. It was
only Bute, according to Newcastle's account of what the
former told him, who thought that the terms offered by France
were favourable and talked of peace with France as certain.[2]
A few days later his conversation with Hardwicke did not give
the same impression, for, though he did not say anything
directly in connection with the peace negotiation with France
he complained that she was similar to other countries in her
desire to take advantage of the rumours about divisions in
the English cabinet.[3] As to the two Secretaries of State,
Egremont and Grenville, they were displeased with the
French proposals.[4] Egremont declared that this answer was
unreasonable and captious and his opinion was echoed by
Mansfield.[5] Even Bedford, to the surprise of Viry, was not
pleased and expressed his surprise at the fact that France did
not accept the terms which England had offered her.[6] The
illness of George III having retarded the meeting of a cabinet
council, it only met on June 21st,[7] in order to discuss these
proposals and the answer to be sent to France. At this meeting
Bute delivered himself with reserve. He agreed that a firm
but polite answer should be given to France. The meeting
adjourned after a long debate. Three days later the ministers
reassembled to decide the final answer to the French memoir,
and to approve Egremont's letter.[8] The ministers were against

---

[1] Ibid., 9, f.294.

[2] B.M., Add. MSS., 32939, f.264v, Newcastle to Devonshire, June 10th 1762

[3] Ibid., 32939, ff.418v-419r, Hardwicke to Newcastle June 19th 1762.

[4] L.H. MSS., 10, f.73, Viry to Solar, June 27th 1762.

[5] Winstanley, 119.

[6] L.H. MSS., 10, ff.73-74, Viry to Solar, June 27th 1762.

[7] Ibid., 10, f.86, Viry to Solar, June 27th 1762; see also B.M., Add. MSS., 32940, f.6r, Barrington to Newcastle, June 21st 1762 (Members present in the meeting were Lord Chancellor, Bute, Egremont, Grenville, Bedford, Halifax, Mansfield, Melcombe, Ligonier, B.M., Add. MSS., 32940, ff.24r-24v, Hardwicke to Newcastle June 22nd 1762).

[8] L.H. MSS., 10, f.90, Viry to Solar, June 27th 1762.

any further concessions to France and all agreed with Egremont's answer which tended rather to insist upon the former
answer sent from England on May 1st.[1] Viry explained the
reasons for the attitude of the ministers, who though sincerely
desirous of peace were dubious whether it was a practical
measure:

> "de pouvoir faire à la France de plus grandes Concessions, ni de pouvoir
> rien retrancher des demandes qu'on avoit faites, sans que les Secrétaires
> d'Etat s'exposâssent à avoir immanquablement un procès et que touts
> ceux qui y auroient part à des autres concessions . . . puissent se
> garantir d'être vivement attaqués dans la Chambre des Communes, et
> principalement lui Milord Bute qui sûrement n'éviteroit pas en pareil
> cas des recherches encore plus dangereuses que celles qu'on pourroit
> faire contre les Secrétaires d'Etat".[2]

However, the Choiseuls were assured of a cession of St.
Lucia, if they agreed with the rest of the English proposals.
Only His Britannic Majesty, Bute and Egremont knew of this
concession which Viry, after having recommended the French
ministers to keep the utmost secrecy about it, announced to
the Choiseuls in the following words:

> "la Cession de l'Isle de Ste. Lucie à la France n'arrêtera pas la Signature
> des Préliminaires, si la Réponse de la Cour de Versailles au Mémoire
> que J'envois donne une entière satisfaction dans tous les autres Points".[3]

On the other side of the Channel, in France, the Choiseuls
were waiting impatiently for the answer of the English
ministers to their proposals. The Duke of Choiseul thought
that once they had adjusted their own terms with England
"les autres Parties s'ajusteront Sûrement".[4] Solar considered

---

[1] B.M., Add. MSS., 32940, f.113v, Newcastle to Hardwicke, June 28th 1762

[2] L.H. MSS., 10, ff.83-84, Viry to Solar, June 27th 1762.

[3] *Ibid.*, 10, f.193, Viry to Solar, June 28th 1762. It must be pointed out here an
important differentiation between these two negotiations of 1761 and 1762, made by
Professor B. Williams, in vol. 11, 139-140.

> "On the English side there is a remarkable contrast between the conduct of these
> negotiations and Pitt's in the previous year. In spite of his arbitrary temper and
> his differences with his colleagues Pitt had never gone a step without fully con-
> sulting the Cabinet. Bute on the other hand treated the foreign intriguer Viry
> with more confidence than his English Colleagues".

[4] L.H. MSS., 10, f.18, Billet Duke of Choiseul to Solar, June 12th (wrongly
dated July 12th).

peace as concluded if the answers to the French proposals were favourable, and especially with regard to the cession of St. Lucia;[1] and suggested that, as soon as preliminary articles were agreed upon, and the reply of Spain to His Britannic Majesty's declaration sent, the three countries should exchange ministers in order to stop Spain from hindering the peace through taking advantage of the negotiations being secret.[2] The earnestness of the Choiseuls for peace then went so far as to make Solar divulge some of the military secrets of Spain's campaign in Portugal. Thus in a very confidential letter Solar indicated that:

> "il est décidé que l'Armée Espaňole va marcher tout droit à Lisbonne, sans s'arrêter pour les Sièges qui seront faits par un Détachement de la même Armée".[3]

The Duke of Choiseul feared that once Spain succeeded in the conquest of Lisbon, she would increase her pretentions; he therefore urged the English ministers, if they desired the conclusion of peace, to send all troops available to Portugal in order to hinder the attempts of Spain to that effect.[4] Though Viry indicated to Solar that the illness of His Britannic Majesty was delaying the meeting of the cabinet [5] and consequently the answer to the French proposals, the Choiseuls were surprised at the long silence of the English ministers, and the delay in the answer caused them great uneasiness,[6] specially as they had received, meanwhile, the reply of Spain to His Britannic Majesty's declaration,[7] which reply they were only hoping to receive at about the same time as the answer of the English ministers to their proposals, and which they never

---

[1] *Ibid.*, 10, f.15. Solar to Viry, June 17th 1762.

[2] *Ibid.*, 10, ff. 15-16.

[3] *Ibid.*, 10, f. 21, Solar to Viry, June 17th 1762.

[4] *Ibid.*, 10, ff.20-21. Neither was Nivernais later on less anxious about the danger of the Portuguese campaign, when he wrote to Count of Choiseul "ce diable de Portugal me fait trembler. Si Madrid s'enivre de sa conquête comme Londres de la sienne, nous sommes perdus", Perey, 510, Nivernais to Count of Choiseul, October 28th 1762.

[5] L.H. MSS., 10, ff.9-10, Viry to Solar, June 11th 1762. *ibid.*, 10, ff.11-13, Viry to Solar, June 15th 1762.

[6] *Ibid.*, 10, f.26, Solar to Viry, June 24th 1762.

[7] *Ibid.*, 10, f.27.

THE NEGOTIATIONS OF 1762

expected to receive before the answer from England. They, therefore, deferred for a few days the sending of Spain's answer to England, hoping that they might meanwhile receive the answer from England. However, they could not wait any longer because they feared to be suspected by Grimaldi, who, aware of their impatience to receive the answer from Spain, might suspect what was going on between France and England behind his back, or might think that France's views on peace had changed and that she was no longer in earnest for peace.[1] Sending the Spanish papers, the Count of Choiseul sent also a letter to Egremont, in which he announced that His Catholic Majesty and the Empress Queen adopted sincerely the pacific views of the two courts.[2]

In the same letter, as though no previous memoirs had been exchanged between the two countries, the Count of Choiseul announced the dispatch of a memoir of the French proposals for peace as an answer to His Britannic Majesty's overtures of peace.[3] This memoir contained the proposals of France, which, though they were set forth in articles, and differed slightly in article five, relative to the boundaries of Louisiana, were the same as those already sent to England, without the knowledge of Spain, at the end of the previous month.[4] The alteration in article five was due to Grimaldi's objection to it as it stood previously. He considered it "préjudiciable aux Etablissemens de l'Espagne"; and demanded therefore the the omission of the Port of Mobile.[5] In spite of the fact that the Duke of Choiseul yielded to the Spanish ambassador's views on this point, he declared that he still held the same views on this article as stated in the previous memoir, and recommended the English ministers to insist on this article as formerly offered.[6] Although the Duke of Choiseul indicated

[1] *Ibid.*, 10, ff.132-134, Duke of Choiseul to Solar, June 29th 1762.

[2] *Ibid.*, 10, f.96, Count of Choiseul to Egremont, June 28th 1762.

[3] *Ibid.*, 10, f.98.

[4] *Ibid.*, 10, f.134, Duke of Choiseul to Solar, June 29th 1762.

[5] *Ibid.*, 10, f.143, Solar to Viry, June 30th 1762.

[6] *Ibid.*, 10, f.143-144.

that the Spanish proposals were general, yet he drew the attention of Solar to the fact that:

> "l'Ambassadeur a ordre de concérter toute sa Négociation avec nous, et je crois selon le dérnier Courier, que ce qui regarde cette Couronne ne souffrira pas de difficulté".

Nevertheless he requested that England should hasten her decision before anything could happen to endanger his prestige with His Catholic Majesty.[1] He also recommended Egremont and Bute [2] to insert, in the answer to Spain some personal reference which would flatter His Catholic Majesty.[3] The Duke of Choiseul added that although he did not mention it in his statement of the terms of Spain for peace,[4] that the latter country would give a guarantee to England to export all the logwood which she needed from Honduras, yet he assured England that Spain, who had always shown willingness to grant that right to England, did not object to it but did not at the same time want to appear as if she was forced to do it.[5]

The two Couriers: the one dispatched from England on June 28th [6] and for which the Choiseuls had been waiting nearly a month, and the other from France containing the Spanish papers sent on 30th of the same month,[7] were received in the respective countries at the same time, namely July 2nd.[8] These letters and memoirs were differently received in each of the two countries. The Choiseuls, though not satisfied with Egremont's answer, which they considered rigorous

[1] Ibid., 10, f.135.

[2] It is worth stating here that by comparing this letter of June 30th 1762 from Solar to Viry in L.H. MSS., 10, ff.139-147 with a copy of the same letter in the Egremont Papers (P.R.O., G.D., 1) it is noticed that the names of "Egremont and Bute" in the first letter ff.144, 145, 146, have been replaced in the copy of the Egremont Papers by "les ministres d'Angleterre". This little difference had its significant importance.

[3] L.H. MSS., 10, f.146.

[4] In his letter to Count of Choiseul of June 25th 1762, ibid., 10, ff.99-103.

[5] Ibid., 10, f.147, Solar to Viry, June 30th 1762 (very confidential as indicated in a copy of the same letter in P.R.O., G.D., 1).

[6] L.H. MSS., 10, f.166, Viry to Solar, June 28th 1762.

[7] Ibid., 10, f.140, Solar to Viry, June 20th 1762.

[8] Ibid., 10, f.232, Viry to Solar, July 12th 1762 (Egremont received them on the following day, Grenville Papers, 1, 462), L.H. MSS., 10, f.216, Solar to Viry, July 5th 1762.

and stern, were nevertheless persuaded by Viry's letter about
the possibility of a cession of St. Lucia in the case of an agreement on the other terms of peace, to take a more hopeful
view about the prospects of the negotiations.[1] At the same
time the Choiseuls asked for an important change in connection with the article on the boundaries of Louisiana, which
the English, in their proposals, had expanded to their advantage, so as to include New Orleans and a larger part of Louisiana. They asked therefore that New Orleans on the East bank
of the Mississippi should remain in the possession of France.[2]

If the Choiseuls asserted already their belief in reaching a
conciliation between the two courts, it was because of the
secret offer of Bute and Egremont about a cession of St.
Lucia,[3] the importance of which made the Duke of Choiseul
previously declare that he would rather continue the war
than lose it. This island was considered an important corner-
stone in the new colonial policy of the French Ministers not
only because it would secure the defence of the sugar islands
but also because it would provide a Windward fleet base in
the West Indies.[4] In order to retain this possession, the Duke
of Choiseul was willing to sacrifice Louisiana east of the
Mississippi and consequently he was sacrificing Spain's interest,
for the eastern Louisiana with the Mississippi boundary would
give England territory on the Gulf of Mexico.[5]

On the other hand, in England the last French memoir
(June 28th), reduced to formal articles and regularly signed
on behalf of France and Spain by Choiseul and Wall, did not
change anything in the attitude of Grenville and the rest of
the ministers, who, after Ferdinand's late victory on the
Diemal, became more determined than ever not to yield on

---

[1] *Ibid.*, 10, ff.218-220, in the same letter of July 5th 1762, Solar to Viry.

[2] *Ibid.*, 10, f.219.

[3] Solar assured Viry of this fact when he wrote that "après la Cession que l'Angleterre fait de l'Isle de Ste. Lucie, rien n'arrêtera plus ici ce Ministère de conclure
la Paix, étant très disposé à se prêter à l'Egard des autres Articles", *ibid.*, 10, f.231,
Solar to Viry, July 11th 1762.

[4] Corbett, 11, 339.

[5] See map, Appendix 6.

the St. Lucia question.[1] Furthermore, the reply of the Spanish government was considered to be insolent and over-bearing. Spain demanded full compensation for the Spanish prizes, the right of fishing off the shores of Newfoundland. As to the Bays of Honduras and Campeachy, she insisted that England should quit and demolish all her establishments there, without mentioning anything about the security of the British logwood trade.[2] Bute was in a delicate position, because of the secret step which he had taken jointly with Egremont, and his desire to cede St. Lucia to France, which was then the price of obtaining peace; he found making further resistance on the ceding of it in the new circumstances practically impossible. In order to keep the rest of the ministers quiet, Egremont was obliged to present to Viry formal observations on the French proposals, in which the original British attitude was firmly maintained.[3] Egremont repeated that it was impossible after sacrificing Martinique and Guadeloupe to give up St. Lucia too;[4] and that their loyalty to Prussia did not permit them to accept the proposals about Wesel and Gueldres without Frederick's consent.[5]

In the same despatch, Viry, annoyed with Grenville's attitude and objections, stated in his letter to Solar:

"Vous ne sauriez croire combien cet honnête Homme Nous gêne; Il peut être bien à la Cour, mais Il voudroit en même tems être populaire".

Alluding to his occasional influences on Egremont he went on to say:

"et le Pis est, c'est que Milord Egremont se met quelque fois en Tête la même Chose".[6]

In the same letter, Viry related to Solar that, since the last

[1] Corbett, 11, 346.

[2] L.H. MSS.; 10, ff. 99-103, Duke of Choiseul to Count of Choiseul, June 25th 1762, acquainting him with His Catholic Majesty's answer; Solar in a very confidential letter, assured Viry of this article (logwood cutting), ibid., 10, f.147, June 30th 1762 also in P.R.O., G.D., 1.

[3] L.H. MSS., 10, ff.271-287, Observations on the English Memoir by Egremont, July 10th 1762.

[4] Ibid., 10, f.276.

[5] Ibid., 10, f.281.

[6] Ibid., 10, f.291, Viry to Solar, July 12th, holograph.

dispatches from Paris contained Bute's secret concession, it was impossible to show them to Grenville. Nevertheless, Viry told him that they contained a definite declaration that, if the British claim to St. Lucia and New Orleans were not abandoned, the negotiations would be broken off. He had talked with Grenville for six hours but was sure that six hours more would not make him give up St. Lucia, and Egremont sided with him on New Orleans.[1] In another letter written at the same time, Viry expressed Bute's surprise at the objection of the Choiseuls to the Mississippi boundary as indicated by Egremont, stating that it was the Duke of Choiseul who had already fixed it in his memoir of May 29th, with which memoir the members of the Cabinet meeting were acquainted. Viry warned Solar, therefore, that France should be careful about this article in order not to raise more difficulties in the way of a cession of St. Lucia to France.[2] Moreover, Solar was to ask the Choiseuls to send an answer to the last British memoir without revealing anything of the secret of the offer of St. Lucia, which was only known to Egremont and Bute, so that it could be shown to the Cabinet, and discussed by its members. In this answer, St. Lucia should be insisted on as a *sine qua non*, and a new line excluding New Orleans should be proposed, but with the stipulation that navigation in the Mississippi should be common to the two nations.[3] It would also be well to suggest that Wesel and Gueldres should be occupied by joint Anglo-French troops till the general peace; nevertheless, it must at the same time be remembered that England must get Prussia's consent on this point before accepting it, which consultation was not at all to delay the signature of the Preliminaries.[4] As to Spain, Bute, depending on the Duke of Choiseul to bring her to accept these desirable terms of peace, agreed with all his views, and particularly was in favour of exchanging plenipotentiary ambassadors. At

[1] *Ibid.*, 10, ff.291-292.

[2] *Ibid.*, 10, ff.303-304, Viry to Solar, July 12th 1762.

[3] *Ibid.*, 10, ff.313-314.

[4] *Ibid.*, 10, ff.315-316.

the end of his letter, Viry related Bute's fears about the difficulties which the conquest of Cuba by British arms would put in the way of concluding peace.[1]

Receiving this courier on July 14th [2] Solar was so pleased with it that he declared to Viry that:

"la Paix est faite entre nous et l'Angleterre; j'espère qu'elle le sera de même avec l'Espagne".[3]

After two different conferences with the Choiseuls, an agreement was reached on the conditions to be sent to England, in answer to her last memoir, in spite of Grimaldi's "verbiages", which went on for two whole days,[4] and thus retarded the dispatch of the courier for that time. Grimaldi was against the idea of proposing the nomination of plenipotentiaries, and tried in vain to persuade Count of Choiseul to omit it from his letter to Egremont.[5] More important still was the Spanish ambassador's objection to article 6, relative to the Mississippi boundary, which objection compelled the Choiseuls to yield to his desire, and set forth the article in the way he wished, but at the same time the Count of Choiseul signed a separate article relative to the same question, but reduced, in the way desired by England.[6] At the same time Solar asserted that France was prepared to sign a peace even without Spain, as soon as the plenipotentiaries were appointed from both sides;[7] and added that, even if Spain proved to be difficult and could not come to terms with England, the latter country, having finished her struggle against France and her expensive war in

---

[1] Ibid., 10, ff.318-319.

[2] Ibid., 10, f.321, Solar to Viry, July 15th 1762.

[3] Ibid., 10, f.324, Solar to Viry, July 15th 1762 (another letter)

[4] Ibid., 10, f.327, Solar to Viry, July 20th 1762 (a very confidential letter as Solar stated at the end of it "cette Lettre est des plus confidentielles . . . vous ne pouvez tout au plus la confier qu'a Milord Bute seulement", ibid., 10, f.330).

[5] Ibid., 10, f.328, Grimaldi's objection on this matter was due, as he declared it himself, to the fact that "dès que les Ministres seroient nommés la Paix n'étoit plus douteuse".

[6] Ibid., 10, ff.361-362, Duke of Choiseul to Solar, July 21st 1762, The separate Note on Article 6 is in ibid., 10, ff.373-374.

[7] Ibid., 10, f.328.

Germany, could easily make Spain repent her "ridicule obstination".[1] In the same courier, the Duke of Choiseul gave his word
of honour that all obstacles about article 6 would be overcome.[2] The special note on this article was to be shown to the
Council of His Britannic Majesty as well as the preliminary
articles set forth by France, but the English Government was
recommended to keep the note absolutely secret till the
signature of the Preliminaries.[3]

When this courier arrived on July 24th,[4] Bute was reported
to have declared that peace was made.[5] Yet this was not the
opinion of the other ministers when on the 26th a cabinet meeting
was summoned to discuss the French answers. In this meeting,
Bute was reported to have begun by agreeing entirely to the
terms consented to by France; to have treated the peace as
made, and no longer insisted upon any explanation about
England's terms of peace with Spain; but the Lord President,
Granville, was reported to have told Bute that he thought
peace was farther off than ever, that he never could agree to
the peace with France without Spain, and pointed to the
Spanish memoir sent at the same time as "a very insolent"[6] one,
saying that Bute might be "The Dupe of France" if he pleased,
but that he (Granville) would not.

> "This ran so high", as Newcastle related, "That My Lord Bute was single
> in His Opinion; And the Council broke up, without coming to any
> Determination".

The meeting was adjourned, and was to meet two days later.[7]
In the interval Bute spoke to the members of the Cabinet
and the King summoned some of them to his cabinet,[8] with

[1] *Ibid.*, 10, ff.329-330.

[2] *Ibid.*, 10, f.363.

[3] *Ibid.*, 10, f.430, Solar to Viry, July 21st 1762.

[4] B.M., Add. MSS., 32941, f.48r, Jones to Newcastle, July 25th 1762.

[5] *Life and Letters of Lady Sarah Lennox*, 1, 69.

[6] Bute also was of the same opinion as regards the Spanish memoir, he considered
it "insolent" and written "in the haughty style of that court", Hardwicke to Newcastle,
July 28th 1762, Yorke III, 403.

[7] B.M., Add. MSS., 33000, ff.97r-97v: an account of Devonshire's Conversation
on July 31st 1762, sent to Newcastle on August 2nd by Hardwicke.

[8] L.H. MSS., 11, f.60, Viry to Solar, August 1st 1762.

the result that Bute's proposals in the second meeting [1] were agreed to by all the members: the terms of peace between England and France having been decided, Bedford was to be sent forthwith to negotiate with France and in particular to settle what related to Spain with the help of France. It was also indicated that France should endeavour to persuade Spain to be a party to the Treaty; but if her efforts were unsuccessful, she should pledge herself not to assist Spain in the war against England.[2] In his letter of July 31st to Count of Choiseul,[3] Egremont declared that His Britannic Majesty consented, though with deep regret, to give up St. Lucia and New Orleans. He would also proceed at once to exchange plenipotentiaries. As to the question of Gueldres and Wesel, Egremont had leave to say that the King had already gone as far as he could without breaking faith with his ally. Nevertheless, England agreed to the proposal that the occupied Prussian territories should merely be evacuated instead of being surrendered to King Frederick.[4] Slight alterations in the other terms of the preliminaries between France and England, were also asked by Egremont.

Obtaining thus the conditions he desired in his peace with England, the Duke of Choiseul's next task was to induce Spain to come to an agreement with England.

---

[1] This meeting took place on 28th (July). A third meeting took place on 30th where the letters of 31st to the Choiseuls and to Solar were put into their final form, P.R.O., G.D., 21, Minute of a Cabinet Council Meeting at the Lord President's House, July 30th 1762.

[2] B.M., Add. MSS., 33000, ff.97v-98r.

[3] L.H. MSS., 11, ff.8-16, Egremont to Count of Choiseul, July 31st 1762.

[4] Ibid., 11, f.22, "Mémoire tiré de la lettre d'Egremont à Viry, pour communiquer à Grimaldi".

CHAPTER V

THE NEGOTIATIONS OF 1762

Second Stage (The Preliminaries)

It was one thing to get Charles III to agree to consider preliminaries of peace, quite another to get him to sign them. As early as June 12th, 1762,[1] Ossun pointing to the points of difference between Spain and England, which were likely to delay the conclusion of an agreement between the two Courts, stated that the article relative to the logwood in the Campeachy and Honduras Bay was a great difficulty in the way of such an agreement. Spain, demanding that England abandon and demolish her illicit establishments on that bay, insisted on not granting the British the right of cutting the logwood they needed and importing it till they had evacuated the above-mentioned settlements.[2] Foreseeing also in the article concerning the renewal of the Commercial treaties between the two Courts another difficulty, Ossun summed up his considerations on this important affair in the following words:

> "Ainsi je regarde cet article et celui du Bois de Campêche comme les points qui pourront faire trainer, et peut-être manquer la paix de l'Espagne avec l'Angleterre, à moins que M. de Grimaldi ne parvienne à trouver un ajustement, qui satisfasse les deux Parties".[3]

With regard to the articles between France and England, the one about the Mississippi boundary [4] was another difficulty in the way of bringing Spain to an agreement with England. It had already, as indicated previously, caused Grimaldi to

---

[1] A.E., C.P., Espagne, 536, ff.314-326, Ossun to Duke of Choiseul, June 12th 1762.

[2] As Spain stated in her answer to His Britannic Majesty's declaration, see chapter V, p. 152, Duke of Choiseul to Count of Choiseul, June 25th 1762.

[3] A.E., C.P., Espagne, 536, ff.324v-325r.

[4] *Ibid.*, Espagne, 536, ff.381r-381v, Duke of Choiseul to Ossun, June 29th 1762.

object; and he so strenuously opposed it that the Duke of Choiseul was compelled, in order to please both Grimaldi and England, to agree with him temporarily and set forth that article in the way the Spanish ambassador had demanded, and at the same time to draft a secret note on the same article according to England's desire, which article was added to the French Memoir sent to England.[1] This article, as desired by England and accepted by France, yielded to England Eastern Louisiana, thus giving her territory on the Gulf of Mexico, an arrangement disadvantageous to Spain.   Also Ossun found Wall on this article very difficult to persuade.[2] Neither was the Duke of Choiseul less conscious of Spain's objection to this new boundary. Early in the previous year, when he was trying to persuade Spain to join France in her struggle against England, he had warned her of the danger to which the Spanish possessions in America were exposed after France's loss of Canada.[3]   It was in order to obtain St. Lucia that the Duke of Choiseul was, thus, shutting his eyes to that danger, and sacrificing his ally's interests. These last two articles (renewal of the commercial treaties and the Mississippi boundary) were to prove real obstacles to the conclusion of peace between the three Courts, as will be indicated in this final stage of the negotiations.

Almost sure that his country's interests were secured in her peace negotiations with England, the Duke of Choiseul exerted all his efforts to persuade Spain to accept the terms offered by England. In a letter of July 22nd,[4] in which he explained to Ossun the reasons for which he desired so earnestly the conclusion of peace as soon as possible, he complained of Grimaldi's objections to the article about the Mississippi boundary. Having received early in August, from England, a favourable answer to his proposals for peace, in which

[1] See Chapter IV, p. 156.

[2] A.E., C.P., Espagne, 536, f.450v, Ossun to Duke of Choiseul, June 12th 1762.

[3] Aiton, "The Diplomacy of the Louisiana Cession", *A.H.R.*, XXXVI, 704, footnote 10, Duke of Choiseul to Ossun, January 27th 1761.

[4] A.E., C.P., Espagne, 536, ff.491-499, Duke of Choiseul to Ossun.

England ceded St. Lucia and New Orleans to France [1] the Duke declared to Ossun that:

> "la France et l'Angleterre sont d'accord sur leurs conditions de paix personnelles, de sorte que si nous étions seuls en guerre dans les mêmes circonstances où nous nous trouvons, il est évident que la paix seroit faite. Ce n'est donc pas ce qui regarde les conditions de la France qu'il faut examiner, puisqu'Elle est contente, et que de plus Elle en est convenue";
>
> "c'est la marche du Roy", he continued, "relativement à l'Espagne pour la confection de la paix vis-à-vis de l'Angleterre, et celle de l'Angleterre avec l'Espagne, qui mérite toute notre attention et tous nos soins". [2]

In the same letter, he urged Ossun to indicate to His Catholic Majesty how much France needed his help on that occasion, saying that the conclusion of peace depended on him, to whom the French were already indebted for the very overtures of peace made by England to them. He drew Ossun's attention to the best way of accelerating the conclusion of peace, which was, in his opinion, that His Catholic Majesty should allow the exchange of plenipotentiaries between England and France, and authorise Grimaldi to negotiate with the Duke of Bedford, the English plenipotentiary who was to be dispatched to Paris, the terms of conciliation between his country Spain and England. [3] In order to obtain the immediate consent of Charles III to that measure, His Christian Majesty wrote a personal letter to his cousin, the King of Spain, which letter the Duke considered so important that he proposed to carry it himself to the King of Spain. It was, however, sent with O'Dunne, [4] the late French minister in Portugal. In his letter, Louis XV informed Charles III of the latest results of the negotiations

---

[1] This answer of August 1st with other letters was received by Solar on August 4th, L.H. MSS., 11, f.114, Solar to Viry, August 12th 1762. In the same letter, Solar declared that:
"nous convinmes que tout ce qui est relatif à la France est arrêté définitivement, et que nous pouvions regarder la Paix comme prête à être conclue entre la France et L'Angleterre", *Ibid.*, 11, f.119.

[2] A.E., C.P., Espagne, 537, ff.20r-20v., Duke of Choiseul to Ossun, August 8th 1762.

[3] *Ibid.*, Espagne, 537, ff.20v-21r.

[4] O'Dunne left on August 5th, Count of Choiseul to Egremont, August 10th 1762, L.H. MSS., 11, f.155.

with England and asked for his consent to the nomination of plenipotentiaries and for his authorisation to Grimaldi.[1] The dispatch of O'Dunne was also intended: "pour sauver . . . l'aigreur de l'Espagne contre l'Angleterre",[2] because, to the great surprise of the Choiseuls, as Solar indicated, England did not send an answer to Grimaldi's note on the Spanish proposals of peace;[3] this neglect on the part of England, the Choiseuls thought, was likely to cause ill feelings between England and Spain, which could only be prevented or at least softened by that special courier to Spain.[4] Neither did the Duke of Choiseul think then that such a neglect, on the part of England, was likely to help him in bringing Spain to an agreement with England about the conditions of their peace.[5] Three days after the departure of O'Dunne to Spain, and before he reached that country, an answer was received from Ossun,[6] in which he explained the terms upon which His Catholic Majesty was prepared to conclude peace with England. These terms were favourably received by the Choiseuls and were considered by Solar as very reasonable. At the same time Grimaldi received new instructions from Spain which also pleased the Choiseuls. It was reported that the two French ministers were so pleased with the contents of Ossun's answer, as well as with the instructions sent to Grimaldi, that they declared that, if England had sent some answer to the Spanish proposals and if O'Dunne had not left for Spain, they would have proceeded at once to nominate the plenipotentiaries.[7] The King of Spain requested that the question of the prizes

[1] L.H. MSS., 11, ff.121-122, Solar to Viry, August 12th 1762.

[2] Ibid., 11, f.104, Billet, Duke of Choiseul to Solar, August 12th 1762.

[3] Ibid., 11, f.115.

[4] Ibid., 11, ff.105-106.

[5] In the same billet the Duke of Choiseul wrote to Solar:
"Je répondois de la Cour de Madrid au fond pourvu que dans la forme on voulût bien à Londres lui marquer de la Considération; et c'est précisément à quoi l'on manque, en lui refusant même une réponse", ibid., 11, f.105.

[6] A.E., C.P., Espagne, 537, ff.4-12, Ossun to Duke of Choiseul, August 2nd 1762; this answer was received on August 8th 1762, Solar to Viry, August 12th 1762, L.H. MSS., 11, f.125.

[7] L.H. MSS., 11, f.127.

should be settled according to the treaties and not according to the particular laws of England; he still insisted that Spain should be given the right of fishing in the Newfoundland fisheries; he accorded the English a provisional right of cutting and importing the logwood they needed in the Bay of Honduras, until a firm and convenient arrangement would be concluded between the two courts on this point, provided that they demolished and evacuated the illicit establishments on that Bay; His Catholic Majesty consented that treaties of peace and commerce between the two Courts would continue to be valid for six months, starting from the day of the signature of the treaty of peace till they concluded a new treaty of commerce. As to Portugal, he declared that, though he did not intend to keep any of his conquests there, yet he might ask for slight alterations in the boundaries between the two countries; besides, His Catholic Majesty asked to be permitted to intervene as a contracting party in fixing the boundaries of Canada, which he was determined not to let reach the Gulf of Mexico.[1] These articles, though slightly better than those of July, were by no means satisfactory or likely to be admitted by England, who stated her views on these different points pending between the two countries in Egremont's letter of August 21st to the Count of Choiseul;[2] these views were altogether different from those of His Catholic Majesty, and if England did not answer Grimaldi's note of July it was because as Egremont indicated, it was impossible:

"de répondre à un Projet de Préliminaires, où l'on trouve à redire à tout autant sur le Fond que sur la Forme sans aigrir et indisposer les Esprits plutôt que les rapprocher, par les Remarques qu'on ne sauroit se dispenser de faire sans commettre la Dignité du Roy".[3]

It was therefore, as Egremont wrote to Count of Choiseul on the same day in which he wrote to Viry:

"par Délicatesse pour un Ministre [Grimaldi] que nous estimions trop pour avoir risqué de le rebuter au Commencement de notre Négociation".[4]

[1] A.E., C.P., Espagne, 537, ff.4-12.   [2] L.H. MSS., 11, ff.183-188.
[3] Ibid., 11, f.205, Egremont to Viry, August 21st 1762.
[4] Ibid., 11, f.196, Egremont to Count of Choiseul, August 21st 1762.

However O'Dunne, who reached St. Ildephonse on August 18th, and met General Wall and His Catholic Majesty on the very day of his arrival, did not find any difficulty in the mission for which he was dispatched; he also hastened to write on the same day to the Duke of Choiseul to assure him that His Catholic Majesty was well disposed to satisfy his cousin Louis XV. O'Dunne stated that he told him that:

" . . . il venoit de faire et qu'il fairoit toujours tout ce qui dépendra de luy pour la satisfaction et le bien de son cousin".[1]

In a letter of the same date, Ossun assuring the Duke of Choiseul of the good dispositions of Charles III, wrote to him:

"qu'au surplus Sa Majesté Catholique s'étoit non seulement prêtée à tout ce que desiroit le Roy, mais qu'il le laisseroit en quelque façon le maître de régler les conditions de la Paix particulière de l'Espagne".[2]

The Court of Madrid, therefore, gave its consent to an exchange of plenipotentiaries between England and France, and authorised Grimaldi to come if possible to an agreement regarding the questions at issue between his court and England. But this authorisation by no means implied that he had really been ordered to pursue a conciliatory policy.

Early in September, the Duke of Bedford [3] proceeded to Paris and the Duke of Nivernais to London,[4] in order to settle the preliminaries between the three courts on the basis of the agreements already reached. As far as England and France were concerned, apart from some details and a few small points, the two courts were practically in agreement about most of the articles. Nevertheless the task of the two plenipotentiaries was not as easy as it might appear to be: Bedford, in particular, besides adjusting details with the French court, had also to settle with Grimaldi the points of disagreement between England and Spain. These particular negotiations between

[1] A.E., C.P., Espagne, 537, ff.62v-63r, O'Dunne to Duke of Choiseul, August 18th 1762.

[2] Ibid., Espagne, 537, f.55v, Ossun to Duke of Choiseul, August 18th 1762.

[3] On Bedford, see Viry's letter to Solar, September 4th 1762, L.H. MSS., 11, ff.349-358.

[4] On Nivernais, see Albemarle, 1, 119-121; Bedford Correspondence, 111, 99 (footnote); Memoirs of George III, 1, 151-152.

Spain and England, upon which nothing was yet agreed, and about which there did not seem to exist any spirit of concession or compromise from either side, were very important for the conclusion of the preliminaries between England and France. The success of these negotiations depended, then, very much on the settlement of the different terms between England and Spain, for the Choiseuls, who previously declared that they were willing to abandon Spain, if she would not come to reasonable terms with England, were no longer prepared to do so.[1] The Duke of Nivernais was also strongly recommended in his instructions:

"de publier en toute occasion l'amitié intime qui l'unit au Roy d'Espagne et la volenté décidée qu'ont ces deux Souverains de résserrer de plus en plus les liens qu'ils ont contractés pour le bien de leur Monarchie et par une inclination naturelle qui les attache l'un à l'autre".[2]

In these same instructions, foreseeing the objections and the difficulties that the Spanish ambassador, Grimaldi, would make about the article relative to the Louisiana boundary, Nivernais was instructed to settle first the rest of the articles with France and leave that article, which it was stated, was the only difficult one, to the last.[3] Moreover, Nivernais' attention was drawn to the importance of hastening the signature of the preliminaries in order to assure the cessation of hostilities and the conclusion of peace, which assurances could only be secured if the preliminaries were signed in time, namely, before the opening of the parliamentary session in England, and announced in the King'[4] speech at the opening of the session.[2]

A cabinet meeting of September 3rd decided on Bedford's instructions.[5] He was first of all to be guided in his negotiations

---

[1] L.H. MSS., 11. ff.175-176, Solar to Viry, August 22nd 1762 (neither was England likely to accept the conclusion of peace without the inclusion of Spain, see infra, p. 168).

[2] A.E., C.P., Angleterre, 447, f.20v, "Memoire pour servir d'Instructions au Duc de Nivernais . . . ", September 2nd 1762.

[3] Ibid., Angleterre, 447, ff.14r-14v.

[4] Ibid., Angleterre, 447, ff.26v-27r.

[5] P.R.O., C.D., 21, Minute of a Cabinet Meeting at St. James's, September 3rd 1762.

M

with France by the *Projet d'Articles Préliminaires arrêtés entre la France et l'Angleterre*, dated, *Versailles le 21 Juillet, 1762.*[1] He was to use this project as the basis of his negotiations with France, provided that France could agree to the several alterations and explanations indicated in the instructions. Great stress was laid upon certain articles of these instructions. The Mississippi boundary was one of these. Bedford was recommended to be most careful in defining the boundaries between the possessions of the two countries in America. A map [2] was joined to his instructions in order to help him in fixing these boundaries easily. This boundary as stated in this article and as shown by the map was to:

" . . . be drawn from the source of the Mississippi to the Sea, dividing that River, longitudinally, in equal Parts, from Its Source to the River Iberville, from the branching of which Last from the Mississippi, the said Line of Limits is to be continued dividing in the same manner, the River Iberville, and the Lakes Maurepas and Pontchartrain to the sea".[3]

In connection with the same article, Bedford was strongly recommended also to see that:

"the Navigation, as far as the said coloured Line extends, is to be in common to Both Nations".[4]

As to article 12, relative to Germany, Bedford was requested to make it clear that Wesel and Gueldres should be evacuated by His Christian Majesty; he was also to stipulate that no succours either in men or money should be given by either of the contracting powers to any of their repsective allies. Bedford's attention 'was also drawn in particular to the great importance of ensuring security for Portugal, in the following words:

" . . . should Spain refuse to come to an Accommodation upon reasonable terms, Our Will and Pleasure is, that you do make it a condition *sine qua non*, of Our Separate Peace with France that That Crown do not take part with Spain, in the present war, either as Principal, or Auxiliary, against Us, or Portugal".

[1] P.R.O., S.P., F., France, 253, Instructions to Bedford, September 4th 1762.

[2] See Appendix 5.

[3] This boundary may be followed better on the map of Appendix 6, where River Iberville can be seen.

[4] The coloured line does not exist on the map, see Appendix 5.

Separate instructions of a secret nature, [1] were also given to Bedford to guide him in the negotiations with Spain. In these instructions great stress was laid upon the article relating to Amglo-Spanish commercial relations:

"You are to take Care, that all the Treaties, as well of Peace as of Commerce, which existed at the time of the Rupture between the Two Crowns, are renewed in all their Parts, except what shall be derogated from by the future Treaty; And This without any exception, notwithstanding anything which may have been stipulated to the contrary". [2]

The appointment of Bedford was open to adverse criticism. Being so biased in favour of peace, he was expected to concede too easily much to the enemy. [3] Neither were his temperament and disposition suited for the delicate work of peace. [4] Hardwicke, who knew him well, thought that, despite his passion for peace, nobody was so likely to take offence on some immaterial point, and break off the negotiations.

"In another light," stated Hardwicke, "No Man is more likely to take a disgust at Instructions, that may be sent to Him; or at the Ministers here differing in opinion from Him; or not agreeing to Everything His Grace Shall propose. I am sure I should not wish to be the Secretary of State to have the Correspondence with Him". [5]

It is not surprising to realise that many of Hardwicke's predictions were realised. Neither of the secretaries of State had any confidence in him. Viry, when relating to Solar Bedford's relations with them, wrote:

"Il n'est pas mal avec Milord Egremont . . . Pour M. George Grenville, il le méprise et ne le croit point propre pour le Poste qu'il remplit". [6]

They were not long in giving him a practical illustration of

[1] P.R.O., S.P., F., France, 17, Instructions to Bedford, September 4th 1762.

[2] *Ibid*., France, 253, Draft of Separate Instructions for Bedford, September 4th 1762.

[3] B.M., Add. MSS., 32941, f.127r; Newcastle to Hardwicke, July 31st 1762: "I doubt there is scarce any Peace His Grace would reject". Newcastle added also that "The sending My Friend the Duke of Bedford to negotiate and settle The Terms of Peace, I think, a most fatal Step both for His Grace and The Public", *ibid*., 32941, f.126v; see also Riker, 11, 241.

[4] Temperley, 497, considered Bedford's appointment not a wholly fortunate choice.

[5] B.M., Add. MSS., 32941, f.123r, Hardwicke to Newcastle, July 31st 1762.

[6] L.H. MSS., 11, f.351, Viry to Solar, 6th letter of September 4th 1762; see also *Bedford Correspondence*, 111, f.128, Rigby to Bedford, September 29th 1762.

their hostility. Immediately after Bedford left England, on the day after he sailed from Dover, Egremont wrote him a letter in which, limiting his independent authority, he informed Bedford that the preliminaries of peace must be approved by the king before being signed. In order to pacify Bedford, who naturally resented such a restriction of his authority,[1] he was informed that this decision had been inspired by a desire to lighten the weight of his responsibility.[2] In the same letter, which was to reach Bedford before he had conversed with the French ministers and the Spanish ambassador,[3] other instructions were forwarded to Bedford. He was to ". . . insist upon signing the Preliminaries with France and Spain at the same time"[4] Egremont made his reason for the above-mentioned decision clear when he asserted that:

" . . . by the Signature of both Crowns at the same time, the Security of Portugal can be more easily and effectually provided for, an Object of such high Importance, and which his Majesty has so much at heart, that Your Grace cannot be too cautious against all Attempts to elude giving that perfect Satisfaction on this head".[5]

He was also recommended with regard the article on the Mississippi boundary, to take "particular Care in the wording" of that article,". . . and to avoid, above all Things, the tedious and unsatisfactory Method of leaving any Thing to the Discussion of Commissaries."[6]

[1] In his letter to Bute of September 20th, Bedford expressed a strong remonstrance to Bute, *Bedford Correspondence*, 111, 116.

[2] L.H. MSS., 12, f.35, Egremont to Bedford, September 7th 1762. Count of Choiseul confirmed that Bedford's authority was restricted on the following day of his departure from England:
"il est extrêmement offensé des restrictions qu'on a mis à ses instructions dès le lendemain de son départ de Londres", A.E., C.P., Angleterre 447, ff.311r-311v, Count of Choiseul to Nivernais, October 16th 1762.

[3] L.H., MSS., 12, ff.29-30. It is interesting to know that although Bedford received this letter (Egremont's of September 7th) yet he did not, in his answer of 12th, mention anything about restricting his authority, P.R.O., S.P., F., France, 253, Bedford to Egremont, September 12th and 13th 1762. This silence on the side of Bedford, made Egremont insist on the same point in his following letter of 16th of the same month, *ibid.*, France 253; the first time Bedford mentioned anything about this point, was in his letter to Egremont of September 19th 1762, see *Bedford Correspondence*, 111, 113.

[4] L.H. MSS., 12, f.31.

[5] *Ibid.*, 12, f.32.

[6] *Ibid.*, 12, f.33.

However, Egremont's letter added that, in the event of an absolute refusal of Spain to proceed in the negotiations, and consequently of the making of a separate peace with France (which event was considered as very improbable), Bedford was to make it an essential condition that France would not take part in the war either against England or Portugal.[1]

However, Bedford sailing from Dover on September 6th, reached Paris on the 12th. Nivernais arrived in England a few days after Bedford had quitted it, and on the 13th he had his first interview with Egremont.[2] But the main negotiation was carried on in Paris because of Bedford's double responsibility of negotiating both with the French ministers and with Grimaldi, the Spanish ambassador.

On September 14th, Bedford had a conversation with the Count of Choiseul which lasted above four hours. They went through nearly all the preliminaries. Their discussion was chiefly confined to the points in which France was interested apart from Spain. This was preparatory to the more decisive interview which he was to have with the Duke of Choiseul who had reserved the most delicate points of the negotiation to be settled by Bedford and himself.[3] This interview with the Duke of Choiseul took place on the following day and Bedford had nine hours conversation,[4] first tête-à-tête with the Duke of Choiseul and then with the two Choiseuls and Grimaldi. With the Duke, they conferred on the Spanish business, as Bedford stated. Bedford was assured that His Most Christian Majesty would be able to remove all difficulties concerning Portugal, provided that the English were prepared to give satisfaction to Spain on other points. However, he found that the Choiseuls had not yet ventured to own to Grimaldi all that had passed between the two Courts in relation to Mobile, in other words the boundary between the French and the English possessions in America, nor about the navigation down the

[1] Ibid., 12, f.34.

[2] Bedford Correspondence, III, 98-99.

[3] Ibid., 111, 100.

[4] Ibid., 111, 101-113, Bedford to Egremont, September 19th 1762. In the same letter, Bedford relates to Egremont his conference with the Choiseuls and Grimaldi.

Mississippi to the sea. The Duke of Choiseul even requested the English Plenipotentiary to conceal this agreement between the two courts from Grimaldi till they had again talked to him about it. Bedford wrote home

> "I find they are much embarrassed with regard to that Court, and very apprehensive of M. Grimaldi being informed of the Note they had sent about the *Mobile*, and the Navigation, They have offered to Us, thro' the River *Iberville*, and the Lakes, into the Gulph of Mexico".[1]

The Duke two days before told him that at the bare mention of the possibility of the English on the Gulf, Grimaldi

> "had already *monté sur ses grands Chevaux*",

that the only difficulty he perceived in concluding peace immediately, arose from Grimaldi himself, for the King of Spain had left to His Cousin the King of France "*Carte Blanche*".[2] Bedford and the Duke also conferred on the three points of dispute between England and Spain. They were practically of the same opinion on these points, apart from the fishery, about which the Duke of Choiseul seemed to know very little of the intentions of Spain, except that it had put them much out of humour. When Bedford asked the Duke how far France could answer for Spain, the latter answered that His Catholic Majesty declared that he was ready to make peace with England whenever France should desire it, and that he had given His Christian Majesty all freedom to order Grimaldi to sign, but that he believed that the Spanish ambassador was so ill-intentioned to the peace, that he feared it might be frustrated through him. In the afternoon of the same day, Bedford had another conversation with the two Choiseuls and Grimaldi who, he found, as he declared to Egremont:

> " . . . by the difficulties he started upon every article, even the most trifling one, that of the prizes, which he disputed with me to the utmost . . . could not be in any degree relied on".[3]

[1] L.H. MSS., 12, ff.45-46, Bedford to Egremont, September 12th 1762.

[2] *Ibid.*, 12, ff.48-49. As a matter of fact, Grimaldi, in his objection, had the firm backing of his Court. As early as June 18th 1762, he had rejected the idea that the cession of Mobile to England would not harm Spanish interests, and until September 5th, this boundary was not approved by Wall, see Aiton, "The Diplomacy of the Louisiana Cession", *A.H.R.*, XXXVI, 716-717.

[3] *Bedford Correspondence*, 111, 105-106.

Nevertheless they agreed after an hour's discussion upon the logwood article. As to the right of fishing at the banks of Newfoundland, Grimaldi declared that he would by no means hear of any proposal that did not absolutely ensure this right to the Biscayans and Guipuscoans. More vigorous still was Grimaldi's objection to the article relative to the renewal of the commercial treaties between England and Spain. Grimaldi was insistent that England should engage herself to make a new treaty of commerce and limit the duration of former treaties to the conclusion of the new agreement, namely for no longer term than half, or at the most, a whole year; and described the treaties of commerce which subsisted before the war to be "so contradictory to each other, and so burthensome to Spain" that M. Arriaga, then principal minister of finance, had written to him that the King would no longer endure it.[1] He concluded by saying:

" . . . that no force on earth should prevail with him to exceed his instructions in this point, and that he would rather lose his right arm than sign it".[2]

The Duke of Choiseul intervened then, in order to reconcile all differences on this point. He drew up an article on this question in which he only added after the term year (the duration of the previous commercial treaties between Spain and England till a new one is concluded) "plus, ou moins".[3] Whereas Grimaldi after a long debate assented to it, Bedford only took it *ad referendum*. In the following day (17th September), the Sardinian Envoy Solar tried to persuade Bedford to accept the Duke of Choiseul's article about renewing the treaties of commerce with Spain, in order, as he told him, to prevent Grimaldi from frustrating the conclusion of the preliminaries. But Bedford, who had been strictly requested not to yield on this important point, still held the same

[1] It is of importance to remember here that one of the main motives which had decided the policy of Charles III against England was his belief that war with the British would enable him to get rid of the British treaties etc. . . ., see Chapter II, p. 43.

[2] *Bedford Correspondence*, 111, 107.

[3] L.H. MSS., 12, f.77, Paper marked D. sent to Egremont in Bedford's letter of September 19th 1762.

opinion.[1] The article on Portugal seemed also to be another difficult point to settle between England and Spain. Grimaldi declared that, if the English were determined to ask compensation for Havannah, should it be taken, Spain had undoubtedly "more than an equal right" to ask compensations for what she had actually gained in Portugal.[2]

Relating to Nivernais the results of these different conversations which took place with Bedford, the Count of Choiseul wrote:

"les différences qui se trouvent entre nous sont si peu considérables que nous aurions pu conclure et signer sans envoyer de nouveaux Courriers, s'il, n'y avoit pas de difficultés plus considérables, mais nous en éprouvons de très grandes de la part de l'Espagne, sur les objets qui l'intéressent et sur notre article 6".

Acquainting him with the difficulties existing in the negotiations between Spain and England, apart from the Spanish claim for a share in the Newfoundland fisheries, and from the English claim for the complete evacuation of Portugal, the Count of Choiseul ascertained that:

"le 4er Article qui stipule le renouvellement des traités de paix et de Commerce, souffre beaucoup de difficultés à Madrid; le ministère de Madrid pretend que le dernier traité de commerce fait par M. Keene est si désavantageux à l'Espagne qu'il n'est pas possible de le laisser subsister".[3]

In England, Egremont was growing anxious: it was about a fortnight since Bedford had reached Paris and not a word on his conferences there had come from him. He wrote to Grenville

"Pray come to town soon; I fear you will be much wanted".[4]

Two days later the long dispatch in which Bedford had related his first conferences in Paris, arrived. Egremont, displeased with it, sent it on immediately to meet his colleague on his

---

[1] *Bedford Correspondence*, III, 107-108, 110-111 (for fuller details on Bedford's first conversations in Paris see his long letter in *ibid.*, III, 101-113).

[2] *Ibid.*, III, 108-109.

[3] A.E., C.P., Angleterre, 447, f.95v, Count of Choiseul to Nivernais, September 19th 1762.

[4] *Grenville Papers*, I, 474, Egremont to Grenville, September 24th 1762.

way to London, in order that Grenville would be fully informed of the state of the negotiations in Paris before he
arrived in London.

> "You will see" Egremont wrote to him "that that headstrong silly wretch
> has already given up two or three points in his conversation with
> Choiseul, and that his design was to have signed without any
> communication here". [1]

The points which Bedford had let go were of little importance. They concerned the inspection of the fishery stations, [2]
Dunkirk, and the status of the factories to be restored to
France in India. [3] His next dispatches which contained a project of the preliminaries between England and France and
Spain, [4] and which followed close on the heels of the others, [5]
caused still greater dissatisfaction. Egremont declaimed against
the "falsehood, inconsistency, insolence" of these papers and
doubted whether the negotiation could proceed. He complained of the project of the Preliminaries:

> "that every article almost is altered in a *projet* sent from the Duke de
> Choiseul to the Duke of Bedford; and all points *tant grands que petits*
> varied from what was settled and agreed as to France. As to Spain, the
> *Havannah*, by name proposed to be delivered up, without any compensa-
> tion to England; and the old treaties to continue in force till a new
> treaty of commerce is to be made, and stipulated to be concluded in
> the space of one year". [6]

The terms offered, however, were in many points identical
with the preliminaries approved by parliament. The territory
of the Prussian king was to be evacuated by the French, who on

---

[1] *Ibid.*, 1, 475, Egremont to Grenville, September 26th 1762; Viry also declared
to Solar that "L'on n'est point satisfait de l'expédition que le Courier du Duc de
Bedford a apporté". L.H. MSS., 11, f.396, September 27th 1762.

[2] In his letter of September 19th 1762 to Nivernais, Count of Choiseul asked him
"de débattre cet article en représentant aux Ministres Anglois que cette clause intéresse
la dignité de la Couronne et n'est d'aucune conséquence pour l'Angleterre", A.E.,
C.P., Angleterre, 447, f.33r.

[3] See *Bedford Correspondence*, 111, 127, Rigby to Bedford, September 29th 1762.

[4] On September 25th 1762, Count of Choiseul wrote to Nivernais relating to him
that the French ministers had settled their preliminaries with Bedford: those between
England and France and those between England and Spain, but without the consent of
Spain, from whom an answer was expected on October 6th, A.E., C.P., Angleterre,
447, f.155r.

[5] They reached England on September 28th, *Bedford Correspondence*, 111, 125,
Rigby to Bedford, September 29th.

[6] *Grenville Papers*, 1, 476, Egremont to Grenville, October (2nd?) 1762.

account of their engagements with the Court of Vienna, as they declared to Bedford, were not able to enter into the stipulation about withdrawing the financial assistance from the allies.[1] But in three particulars there was a fundamental difference between these terms and the Preliminaries. There was no guarnatee that the French fishing boats would keep at a certain distance from the English coasts; there was a stipulation of one year for the conclusion of a future commercial treaty between England and Spain; and there was no compensation offered for the surrender of the important possession of Havannah (which conquest was known in England on September 29th). Bute on the contrary was satisfied with the terms offered by the French government and was even prepared to give up Havannah without compensation, and thus found himself in direct conflict with the two Secretaries of State.[2]

Meanwhile the Duke of Choiseul was endeavouring to overcome the objections of Spain, as represented by her ambassador Grimaldi and as already indicated in the course of relating the conversations with Bedford. On September 20th,[3] soon after the first conversations with Bedford took place, the Duke of Choiseul wrote to Ossun. He told him that France had settled her preliminaries with England and that the conclusion of peace thus depended on His Catholic Majesty's decisions. Sending him at the same time a project of preliminary articles about the different points of dispute between Spain and England, the Duke assured him that they were all *sine qua non* conditions, and that

> "l'univers entier auroit beau se relayer pour conférer avec M. de Bedford, que je doute que ce même univers reussit à faire changer un mot".[4]
> " . . . La réponse à ce courier" he added "sera la décision finale de la paix ou de la guerre, et par conséquent la décision du bonheur ou du Malheur de la France et de l'Europe".

He recommended Ossun to send the answer to this letter as

[1] L.H. MSS., 12, ff.93-94, Bedford to Egremont, September 24th 1762.

[2] See Albemarle, 1, 128-132, Fox to Cumberland, September 29th 1762.

[3] A.E., C.P., Espagne, 537, ff.160-168, Duke of Choiseul to Ossun, September 20th 1762.

[4] Ibid., Espagne, 537, ff.160v-161r.

soon as possible and expressed his hopes that Ossun would succeed "a émouvoir de façon la sensibilité du Roi d'Espagne pour le Roi et la Royaume" so that that sovereign would decide in comformity with the wishes of His Christian Majesty.[1] In a private letter of the same date, the Duke of Choiseul expressed himself more openly to Ossun:

"Je vous préviens aussi que nous ne souffrirons pas que le Paix soit manquée pour l'article 6. La Louisianne nous appartient en toute souveraineté, et le Roi n'entend point que les dispositions qu'il fait relativement à son bien puissent être contrariées au point de détruire un ouvrage aussi utile à son Royaume".

Ossun was to exert every effort to make His Catholic Majesty adopt those articles without causing any ill-feeling between the two Courts. He finished his private letter by telling Ossun that:

"je vous confie que j'abjurerois la politique pour ma vie si cette paix est manquée; il ne me seroit pas possible de me mêler de cette besogne pour la troisième fois".[2]

Understanding that he could no longer resist the persistent requests of France for adhering to peace, and realising the difficulties with which he might be faced alone if France decided to conclude peace without him, and especially with his unsuccessful military operations in Portugal and America, Charles III asked Ossun on September 28th to relieve his government from its anxiety, by announcing to her that His Catholic Majesty was not going to make her miss the peace which she wanted. Nevertheless he laid stress upon the fact that if he was adhering to peace, it was only in order to please his ally France, and made clear all the sacrifices which he had made for her when he spoke to Ossun in the following words:

"Je n'ai entrepris la guerre que pour procurer la paix au Roi mon cousin; puisqu'il est content des conditions que lui offre l'Angleterre, je ne ferai pas manquer la paix de la France pour mes intérêts personnels; je les remets absolument entre les mains du Roi mon cousin . . . Vous savez bien . . . que mon objet principal en entrant en guerre a été de servir et d'obliger le Roi mon Cousin".

In the same letter Charles authorised His Christian Majesty to

[1] *Ibid.*, Espagne, 537, f.167v.

[2] *Ibid.*, Espagne, 537, ff.185r-185v. Duke of Choiseul to Ossun, September 20th 1762 (copy of a holograph).

sign the peace for him, taking upon himself to ratify whatever was agreed with England.[1]

Before Spain's reply of September 29th was received,
positive news of the capitulation of Havannah changed the
entire complexion of the negotiations. It had been thought
that this important position was impregnable and rumours
of the English successes had been scoffed at by Spain.[2] England would now demand better terms and the elation which
swept the nation made it a difficult task for the English peace
party to avoid a continuation of war. Bute thought that the
Spanish concession regarding the logwood would be a sufficient compensation for Havannah.[3] Bedford not only sustained him, but expressed his fears that, if the point were
insisted upon, the negotiations might be broken off.[4] Within
an hour of the news being told, it was reported that Egremont
and Grenville both declared that they would not sign a peace
which did not allow of compensation being given for the surrender of Havannah.[5] Bute's opponents were stronger than
he was. In asking for compensation for the restoration of
Havannah, they were certain of popular support. Bute found
himself in a very critical situation: universally unpopular with
the nation and opposed by influential colleagues, he seemed
likely to forfeit all results of his efforts at peace-making.

At this crisis Bute decided to summon a meeting of the
cabinet on October 4th[6], in which he intended to propose

[1] *Ibid.*, Espagne, 537, ff.203v-204r. Ossun to Duke of Choiseul, September 29th
1762.

[2] Aiton, "The Diplomacy of the Louisiana Cession", *A.H.R.*, XXXVI, 717.

[3] Riker, 11, 241-242, see also Fitzmaurice, 1, 145. It was reported in a most
secret conversation with Cumberland at Clermont on October 1st 1762, that Bute
adhered to an opinion of agreeing to the preliminaries sent by Bedford, by which the
Havannah was to be restored without any equivalent or compensation, B.M., Add.
MSS., 32943, f.30r.

[4] L.H. MSS., 12, ff.101-102, Bedford to Egremont, October 11th 1762.

[5] Corbett, 11, 360.

[6] In his letter to Solar, Viry could not hide his fears about Bute's decision to
summon a meeting when he wrote: "cette Affaire se trouve aujourd'hui dans une
Situation où Milord Bute ne croit pas pouvoir se dispenser, quoique je lui soutienne
le contraire, d'assembler le Conseil, pour envoier au Duc de Bedford des Instructions
sur ce nouveau Projet de Preliminaires et que je ne suis sans de fortes inquiétudes sur
le résultat de ce Conseil", Viry to Solar, September 28th 1762, L.H. MSS., 11, ff.408-
409. However, this cabinet meeting never met, see Winstanley, 127, footnote 6.

renewing Bedford's full powers to sign with both Courts
after restricting him to the material terms stipulated by
England and France before his departure. He depended on the
royal authority to overcome the two Secretaries of State.[1]
That last hope faded, when the King failed to make either
Egremont or Grenville abandon their convictions.[2] They still
persisted in their demand for compensation for the restoration
of Havannah. Bute came to the conclusion that nobody would
consent to surrendering Havannah to Spain without a compensation.[3] Bute was in a desperate situation. His entire
political salvation depended upon the conclusion of peace. No
amount of royal favour could restore his position if his
colleagues further obstructed his peace policy and Parliament
finally rejected it. Some changes in the administration were,
therefore, needed before a cabinet meeting took place about
the important affair of peace,[4] not only in order to provide
for Bute some support in the cabinet, but also because he was
in need of someone who could guide the Peace through
Parliament and guarantee its success. George Grenville, who
since the resignation of Newcastle had led the opposition in
the cabinet, and who was far abler and far more dangerous
than Egremont,[5] "was forced to go to the Admiralty, and
Halifax took his place as Foreign Secretary for the North".[6]
Grenville's previous oppositions to Bute were not the only
reason he was dismissed from his post; he had also violently
disagreed with Bute on a question of the first importance.
Whereas Bute wished the preliminaries to be signed before
they were submitted to Parliament, a device for avoiding

[1] See *Bedford Correspondence*, 111, 128, Rigby to Bedford, September 29th 1762.

[2] *Ibid.*, 111, 132-133, Rigby to Bedford, September 30th 1762.

[3] *Ibid*, 111, 133; see also Hardwicke to Newcastle, October 17th 1762, Yorke,
111, 422-423.

[4] Bute wrote to Bedford, October 14th 1762, explaining the reasons for his long
silence: "the strange situation of things here, and the necessity of some alteration,
made me delay writing, till I could inform you of the remedy that has been applied to
the weakness under which the Government laboured", *Bedford Correspondence*, 111, 135.

[5] Winstanley, 127-128.

[6] Corbett, 11, 361.

what Bute said would "create confusion",[1] Grenville insisted that they should be submitted to Parliament before anything was done,[2] which opinion

> "spread such rumours over the city, and sunk the Cabinet so extremely in the eyes of even well-meaning people, that some change was unavoidable".[3]

The promotion of Halifax[4] was not the only one which occurred at this time. Henry Fox, who had been asked to receive the Seals as well as the leadership of the Commons, rejected the first and accepted the second and on October 13th, he was declared "a Cabinet Councillor and His Majesty's Minister in the House of Commons".[5] From this point events progressed smoothly. Even before these changes had officially taken place, Viry secretly acquainted Nivernais with them, pointing out at the same time their importance for the progress of the negotiations. Still more important, he informed him that it had been decided in principle that Florida or Porto Rico should be demanded for Havannah, and that no variation of the material points would be permitted.[6]

On October 22nd, the cabinet met to consider the final terms of the preliminaries of peace. The ministers discussed in that meeting the Counter-project of preliminary articles, prepared by Egremont in answer to the Project of preliminary articles, sent by the Duke of Bedford in his letter of September 24th, as well as the observations on it. After having made some alterations in these two papers, they agreed unanimously

[1] Riker, 11, 254.

[2] Corbett, 11, 359.

[3] *Bedford Correspondence*, 111, 135, Bute to Bedford, October 14th 1762.

[4] Riker described Halifax as "a man of talent and enterprise, although of an exceedingly factious disposition", 11, 254.

[5] *Ibid.*, 11, 253; Riker considered Fox the fittest for guiding peace through Parliament, 11, 248-249. See also Winstanley, 129. Viry in his letter of October 24th assured Solar that Bute would not have succeeded in the negotiations for peace without introducing this change in the ministry, L.H. MSS., 11, ff.422-423.

[6] A.E., C.P., Angleterre, 447, ff.279-281, Nivernais to Count of Choiseul, October 11th 1762 (received in Paris on 15th October); the letter was marked "Pour Vous Seul".

about their contents.[1] Describing this meeting, Bute wrote
to Bedford:

> "I do assure you, I never was present at a more unanimous cabinet than
> the one held on Friday".[2]

However, the importance of the matter made it necessary for
the ministers to meet again. Three days later, on October
25th, another meeting was held. The same ministers who
attended the first meeting except Ligonier and Mansfield,
who were out of town, met at the Lord President's House.
They agreed finally on the Counter-project, the Observations,
and Egremont's letters to Bedford.[3] When these different
papers were despatched to Bedford on October 26th, his
attention was drawn to the important fact that the articles
sent to him were the "real ultimatum" to present to France,
informing him that:

> "notwithstanding all the disadvantage and perplexities that attend the
> continuation of the war, even these difficulties are preferred to ceding
> an iota more than is done in the articles now sent".

In the conditions regarding France, nothing was altered from
the project they had agreed to before Bedford's departure to
Paris.[4] A reasonable inspection was asked for in respect of
the French fishery station.[5] Although a distance was also to
be observed with regard the fishing regions of the French,
a distance of Thirty leagues from the South East Coast of
Cape Breton, within which the French were not allowed to
fish, Bedford was instructed in case he met with any objection
to it, to reduce that distance as little as he possibly could.[6]

---

[1] P.R.O., G.D., 21, minute of a Cabinet Council at St. James's, October 22nd
1762; also in L.H. MSS., 12, ff.139-140 (ten members were present at the Council:
The Chancellor, the President, Bute, Halifax, Gower, Ligonier, Mansfield, George
Grenville, Fox, Egremont); see also B.M., Add. MSS., 32943, ff.286-387, Jones to
Newcastle, October 23rd 1762.

[2] Bedford Correspondence, 111, 137, Bute to Bedford, October 24th 1762.

[3] Apart from Egremont's Secret and Confidential letter of October 26th to Bedford
in which he related to him the above-mentioned details about the second meeting
of the ministers, L.H. MSS., 12, ff.135-137.

[4] Bedford Correspondence, 111, 138.

[5] Bedford was for ceding on this point and even agreed with the French to omit
the clause about this inspection, Count of Choiseul to Nivernais October 30th,
A.E., C.P., Angleterre, 447, f.389r.

[6] L.H. MSS., 12, ff.108-109, Egremont to Bedford, October 26th 1762.

From Spain some sacrifices were demanded. She was to concede the claim of England to cut and import logwood and to
erect settlements in connection with the timber trade in
certain parts of her territory, on the understanding that no
fortifications were to be built.   She was to surrender her
claim to the Newfoundland fisheries in their entirety; the
prize claims were to be decided in the English Courts of Law;
either Florida or Porto Rico was to be ceded in return for
Havana;[1] but any conquests which came to the knowledge
of the governments after the delivery of the ultimatum were
to be restored without compensation.[2] The treaties of commerce between the two Courts were to be renewed unconditionally.[3] On October 26th, Rigby and a messenger left
for France, carrying with them the English answer with Bedford's authority for giving his formal consent to the terms of
peace as indicated in the Counter-project.[4]

Now that agreement was reached between the English
ministers about the preliminary articles of peace, and that
they were prepared to sign with France and Spain, it is important to find out what were the effects of the surrender of
Havannah on the Courts of Paris and Madrid. The news of the
fall of Havannah, which was only known in Paris on October
2nd, was a serious blow to the Duke of Choiseul, who on the
following day, wrote to Ossun:

> "Je ne vous parlerai pas ici de l'extraordinaire sécurité de la Cour de
> Madrid sur Cet événement . . . Je ne vous détaillerai pas les fautes
> politiques que cette sécurité nous a fait faire relativement à la paix,
> non plus que les conséquences terribles pour la Monarchie d'Espagne
> et pour la France que l'on peut prévoir de cette perte. Il est question à
> présent de partir du point où nous sommes et de savoir les intentions
> du roi d'Espagne. Les nôtres sont qu'il faut se presser de faire la paix à
> quelque prix que ce soit".[5]

[1] On this point in particular, Egremont wrote to Bedford: "It is the King's Pleasure
that you do peremptorily insist upon one of the Two Cessions . . . as it is of indispensable Necessity, that a proper Compensation should be obtained for the important
Restitution of the Havana: The manifest Inferiority, in Value of either of the Two,
compared with the Conquest which is to be given up, will afford your Grace irresistible Arguments upon this Occasion", ibid., 12, ff.110-111.

[2] Ruville, III, 79-80.

[3] L.H. MSS., 12, f.127, "Observations sur le Contre Projet".

[4] B.M., Add. MSS., 32944, f.93r, Jones to Newcastle, October 27th 1762.

[5] Blart, 38.

In order to avoid more difficulties from that side, or in other words to facilitate Spain's accession to the peace, and in order to render the Family Compact less unpopular in Spain,[1] Louis XV again wrote a personal letter to his cousin, in which he deplored the loss of Havannah and offered Louisiana to Charles III so that his ally would lose nothing in the peace. Louisiana could be used, he explained, in exchange for the restitution of Havannah or kept to offset the loss of other Spanish territory which the English might demand for the restoration of that conquest.[2] In an accompanying letter, the Duke of Choiseul instructed Ossun to play up the value of this cession as a sacrifice in acknowledgement for French gratitude to Spain for her aid in the war and for her assent to an immediate peace.[3] As a matter of fact, by this cession of Louisiana to Spain, the Duke of Choiseul aimed not only at accelerating Spain's accession to peace, but, more important still, at strengthening the union of the two countries, which he had so much at heart, that he was prepared to do anything to maintain it. Explaining the importance of this union and its value to France as well as to Spain he wrote in a private letter to Ossun:

"je regarde cette union bien ménagée plus utile pour les deux Régnes que la Louisianne et beaucoup de possessions Americaines".[4]

He declared in another private letter of the same date that:

[1] *Ibid.*, 39. In his article on "The Diplomacy of the Louisiana Cession", Aiton came to the conclusion that the cession of Louisiana was: "A peace bribe proffered by France in order to win the consent of the king of Spain to an immediate signing of preliminaries of a peace that promised all that France could hope for under the circumstances. The little island of St. Lucia was the pivotal point of the peace. To secure it Choiseul was willing to give up Louisiana east of the Mississippi . . . Louisiana was viewed as not too great a price to pay for the return of the sugar islands, St. Lucia, and the continuance of a close alliance between the two Bourbon Courts. The cession was given all the appearance of an impulsive, generous, even quixotic gesture, but it was a calculated move of a selfish national policy, carefully staged by a statesman intent on deriving every ounce of advantage for his own Country", *A.H.R.*, XXXVI, 719-720.

[2] A.E., C.P., Espagne, 537, f.222r, Louis XV to Charles III, October 9th 1762.

[3] Later on Béliardi, the French Consul General, was also recommended to initiate propaganda among the Spanish merchants with a view to magnifying the generosity of France, Duke of Choiseul to Ossun, November 3rd 1762, Blart, 41-42.

[4] A.E., C.P., Espagne, 537, f.223v, Duke of Choiseul to Ossun, October 9th 1762.

N

"Nous désirons que dans le bonheur et dans le malheur, la cour d'Espagne soit contente de nous. Je n'ai point de peine à soutenir ce sistème . . . je le soutiendrai aux dépens de ma Vie tant que je serai dans le ministère".[1]

In Madrid the disaster of Havannah neither discouraged His Catholic Majesty, nor made him more inclined to peace. He expressed an admirable courage when he told Ossun:

"Vous savez la nouvelle. J'en ai pris mon parti sans peine; quand on fait la guerre, il faut s'attendre aux bons et aux mauvais succès. Mes troupes se sont bien defendues, c'est ce qui me console, et je n'ai jamais dormi plus tranquillement que la nuit dernière".[2]

Charles III and Wall pretended not to understand Choiseul's difficulties. It is true that Ossun unskilfully announced this defeat to Charles III and showed him the Duke of Choiseul's letter of October 3rd announcing to Ossun the unhappy news, which letter the Duke never thought that Ossun was likely to show to His Catholic Majesty. This letter, the Duke said, had been written:

"dans la chaleur et l'abbatement de la première connoissance d'un événement fâcheux".[3]

It was natural, therefore, that His Catholic Majesty, hurt by the untactful manner of Ossun, should declare to the latter:

"J'ai de grands moyens à employer, et lorsqu'on a des ressources et du courage, on ne cède pas et l'on ne plie pas si facilement"

and that Wall should also inform Ossun that Charles III would continue the war regardless of its results. This belligerent attitude of the King of Spain frightened the Duke of Choiseul, who was anxious lest the English Parliament should meet before the preliminaries could be signed. He blamed Ossun for his hasty communication about that disaster to Charles III, and considered it the main reason why the King of Spain remained determined to continue the war.[4]

Fortunately for the Duke of Choiseul, he received from

---

[1] *Ibid.*, Espagne, 537, f.225r, Duke of Choiseul to Ossun, October 9th 1762 (another letter).

[2] Rousseau, 1, 100.

[3] *Ibid.*, Espagne, 537, f.256r, Duke of Choiseul to Ossun, October 20th 1762.

[4] See Rousseau, 1, 100-102.

Nivernais an important and confidential letter with news of his confidential conversation with Viry about what the English ministers had agreed in principle as compensation for Havannah. Florida, Porto Rico, or a part of Yucatan was to be demanded in exchange for the restoration of Havannah to Spain. The Duke of Choiseul hastened to acquaint Ossun with this important information.[1] In a private letter to Ossun, he advised that Spain should cede Florida.[2] Nevertheless he asked Ossun not to insist upon that particular cession, for more important was Spain's consent to accept any of these three as compensation for the restoration of Havannah.[3]

A decision was soon reached in Madrid. Spain regarded Florida as the least valuable of these possessions and its loss as decidedly less harmful than English acquisition of Louisiana, with its danger of smuggling into Mexico and its threat of an advance by the English into the treasures of overseas Spain. On October 23rd, 1762, Grimaldi was ordered to sign the preliminaries of peace, and at the same time, to accept Louisiana as just recompense for Spanish aid in the war.[4] This cession of Louisiana, besides contributing to His Catholic Majesty's agreement to sign the preliminaries, had served some other purposes of the Duke of Choiseul. This is best explained by Ossun, who wrote to the Duke from a very reliable source he heard that:

"la lettre du Roi avoit causé à Sa Majesté Catholique la satisfaction la plus complette et avoit entièrement fermé la bouche à des personnes qui, à ce qu'on m'a assuré, travailloient à faire envisager à ce Monarque la France comme ne pensant qu'à ses intérêts personnels et comme s'embarrassent fort peu de ceux de l'Espagne; ainsi j'ose dire que cette lettre . . . est venue fort à propos".[5]

[1] The Duke sent Ossun on October 15th a copy of Nivernais letter of October 12th (it is dated in the original A.E., C.P., Angleterre, 447, ff.279-281, October 11th, see supra, p. 178) to Count of Choiseul, A.E., C.P., Espagne, 537, ff.235-237.

[2] Ibid., Espagne, 537, f.250r, Duke of Choiseul to Ossun, October 15th 1762.

[3] Ibid., Espagne, 537, f.259r, Duke of Choiseul to Ossun, October 20th 1762.

[4] Aiton, "The Diplomacy of the Louisiana Cession", A.H.R., XXXVI, 718. In his letter of October 23rd, Wall ordered Grimaldi to sign and to accept Louisiana as Spain's just due, ibid., 718, footnote 48.

[5] A.E., C.P., Espagne, 537, ff.269r-269v, Ossun to Duke of Choiseul, October 22nd 1762.

Spain thus ceased to be an obstacle to the peace, and the Choiseuls, who were not satisfied with the terms of the English Counter-project,[1] henceforth concentrated all their efforts on getting better terms, if they could, from Bedford. They thought it more beneficial to their cause not to announce His Catholic Majesty's orders to Grimaldi for the conclusion of peace,[2] in order that, by persuading Bedford of the importance of their endeavours to make Spain consent to the terms wanted by England,[3] they might be able to persuade him to yield a few points to their advantage in the preliminaries. Here too they succeeded and Bedford made some further concessions. However, it must be noted that there was a very important fact, which helped the French ministers to obtain those few alterations to their advantage. After the first meeting of October 22nd, in which the answer to the project of the Preliminaries to France was decided, Bute confided to Viry its decisions, in order to communicate them to Nivernais, who was, in his turn, to send them to his court.[4] Not only did Bute acquaint him with the articles of the preliminaries which were then England's ultimatum, but also drew his attention to the few points on which Bedford had some latitude and freedom of action. More important still was Bute's information that Bedford could also omit the "inspection raisonnable" with regard to the French fishery stations, a point which was not even mentioned in the actual instructions sent at that juncture to Bedford. It is evident therefore that Bute's eagerness to facilitate the adherence of the French ministers to that

[1] *Ibid.*, Angleterre 447, ff.388r-388v, Count of Choiseul to Nivernais, October 30th 1762.

[2] *Ibid.*, Angleterre, 447, f.392v, Count of Choiseul to Nivernais, October 31st 1762, see also Perey, 513, Count of Choiseul wrote to Nivernais, October 31st 1762: "Le roi d'Espagne consent à cédar la Floride ; mais je vous prie de ne confier à personne ce secret. J'espère que ce sacrifice nous fera faire la paix".

[3] Bedford, in his letter announcing the signature of the Preliminaries to Egremont, alluded this deviation of the limits of his instructions with regard France to the latter's help to make Spain accept favourable terms for England, *Bedford Correspondence*, III, 144,147, November 3rd 1762.

[4] A.E., C.P., Angleterre, 447, ff.351-353, Nivernais to Count of Choiseul, October 24th 1762. In his letter, Nivernais related all the valuable information Viry had given him.

ultimatum, made him indicate not only what had been decided in the way of concessions to France, but also what was likely to be accepted by the other ministers. There is no evidence that Bedford was acquainted with that important step taken by Bute. Moreover, Nivernais' important letter reached the Count of Choiseul before Bedford received his instructions.[1] The French ministers were thus well prepared when they conferred with Bedford on the final articles of the preliminaries. This preparation helped them in obtaining some concessions from Bedford. With regard to the French fishery, the distance off any of the British coasts both mainland and of the islands in the Gulf of Saint Lawrence, within which the French were not allowed to fish, was reduced from six to three leagues, and that from the coast of Cape Breton, from thirty to fifteen leagues. Moreover, Bedford took the liberty of giving up the *inspection raisonnable*, with regard to the fisheries' stations and was satisfied instead with the insertion of the French King's *parole royale*. In the article about Germany, Bedford also ventured to accept the payment by the French of the arrears of the subsidies then due to the Court of Vienna.[2] As to the articles concerning Spain, Bedford proved to be inexorable. The Count of Choiseul also declared to Nivernais:

> "il faut avouer que cette couronne [Spain] est traitée d'une manière bien humiliante. Ses instructions ne lui donnoient aucune marge à cet êgard".[3]

These preliminaries of peace, signed by Count of Choiseul, created Duke of Praslin on that occasion,[4] Grimaldi and Bed-

---

[1] In his letter of October 30th, Count of Choiseul commented on Nivernais' information without mentioning that Bedford had received his instructions, *ibid.*, Angleterre, 447, ff.388-389; on the following day, October 31st, Count of Choiseul acquainted Nivernais that Bedford had at last received his instructions, *ibid.*, Angleterre, 447, ff.391-392.

[2] See *Bedford Correspondence*, 111, 147-148, Bedford to Egremont, November 3rd 1762.

[3] A.E., C.P., Angleterre, 448, f.10r, Count of Choiseul to Nivernais, November 3rd 1762.

[4] *Bedford Correspondence*, 111, 149.

ford on November 3rd between France, Spain, and England,[1] were differently received by each of the three contracting parties. On the same day that these preliminaries were signed, Louis XV fulfilled his earlier promise about a cession to Charles III of Louisiana, which now became the new Western boundary of the British Colonies. In the letter enclosing the instrument for that cession, he described the peace as bad but necessary. Nevertheless he added that:

"la considération des pertes que nous avons faites en Amérique, et des dangers que nous y courons pour l'avenir m'a déterminé à encourager l'Ambassadeur de Votre Majesté à signer conjointement avec mes Ministres des conditions qui m'affligent, mais que je crois dans les circonstances où nous nous trouvons plus utiles pour nous, que celles que nous aurions à espérer dans la suite".[2]

Announcing the signature of the preliminaries to Nivernais, the Count of Choiseul made the following true and just comments on the peace:

"la paix n'est pas bonne, mais elle est nécessaire, et je crois que, dans la situation présente on ne pouvoit pas se flatter d'en faire une meilleure".[3]

Moreover as the Duke of Choiseul explained in his official letter to Ossun of November 3rd:

"Nous sentons parfaitement ici que la paix ne sera ni glorieuse ni utile pour la France et pour l'Espagne; mais malheuresement les circonstances ne nous ont pas permis d'obtenir de meilleures Conditions".[4]

He communicated to him in a private letter of the same date a truer statement of his views on these preliminaries as far as France and Spain were concerned:

"L'Espagne est traitée un peu durement, Quant à nous, les conditions sont meilleures que celles de l'année passée et celles que nous pouvions espérer l'année prochaine".[5]

To Spain, who only fought for six months, the preliminaries

[1] A translation of these Preliminaries is in *Parliamentary History of England*, XV, 1241-1251.

[2] A.E., C.P., Espagne, 537, ff.292r-292v, His Christian Majesty to His Catholic Majesty, November 3rd 1762.

[3] *Ibid.*, Angleterre, 448, f.11v, November 3rd 1762.

[4] *Ibid.*, Espagne, 537, f.290r.

[5] *Ibid.*, Espagne, 537, f.307r.

were by no means satisfactory. Grimaldi was persuaded that he had signed a bad peace for his country but had kept a good union with France.[1] It was hard for Spain to renounce the different claims about which she had been so long negotiating. She lost Florida,[2] but was compensated for it by Louisiana.

In England, the signed preliminaries which arrived on November 8th,[3] were agreed upon by the different ministers in a cabinet meeting on 10th.[4] Acquainting him with the satisfaction of the other members of the cabinet with the preliminaries, Bute congratulated Bedford,

> "on the noblest and most essential service ever performed by a subject for his King and Country".

His Britannic Majesty he added

> "expressed the highest approbation of your conduct".

However, Bute asked him not to expect too sudden a change in many people "deluded by the blackest art of faction"; he told him that, one day before his courier arrived, the city had intelligence that the preliminaries were signed and that Porto Rico had been ceded, whereupon it was asserted that Florida would have been infinitely better, as Porto Rico was "a useless barren isle", but as soon as the opposite proved to be the real arrangement, the same people immediately disparaged Florida.[5]

There was every reason for Bute to be delighted with the signature of the preliminaries. To reach that important stage in the completion of the work for peace was indeed a triumph for Bute, who, throughout these negotiations, had to overcome the division in the cabinet and the opposition of his

[1] Aiton, "The Diplomacy of the Louisiana Cession", *A.H.R.*, XXVI, 719.

[2] In England, Florida was not considered as a fair compensation for the restoration of Havannah to Spain, see conclusion, pp. 202-203.

[3] *Memoirs of George III*, 1, 162.

[4] P.R.O., C.D., 21, Minute of Cabinet Council at Arlington Street, November 10th 1762. Members present were: The Archbishop of Canterbury, Lord Chancellor, Lord President, Bute, Halifax, Egremont, Gower, Ligonier, Mansfield, Grenville, Fox.

[5] *Bedford Correspondence*, 111, 152, Bute to Bedford, November 10th 1762.

colleagues, as well as the difficulties of the diplomatic struggle with Spain. With the support of France, which he gained by some concessions, this struggle was won and consequently Spain, defeated in the war, accepted the terms desired by England. Although the struggle thus ended in a complete victory for him, the danger was not yet over. The preliminaries of peace had been signed, but they were to be submitted to parliament for approval; and no one could predict what might happen then. Bute had, with the help of Fox, to prepare to meet parliament. The ministers were certain to be attacked,[1] and it was necessary to strengthen the cabinet. The next question to be settled was the proper formula in which the peace should be made public,[2] a question which had been already at issue between Bute and Grenville, and which had long remained undecided. Should the preliminaries be submitted to Parliament before being confirmed by the definitive treaty itself, or should the Peace be finally concluded before the Houses were given the right to discuss it? The final solution was very ingenious: the preliminaries were to be brought to Parliament, but His Britannic Majesty was first to ratify them under the great seal. When this solution was decided upon, Hardwicke told Newcastle that the national faith was then pledged, for it would be both useless to attack the preliminaries and impossible to break them.[3] Fortunately for the Bute Ministry and the credit of His Britannic Majesty, Fox took the responsibility of the peace upon himself. Without his aid one could easily imagine what the result might have been.[4] Fox fulfilled his task by the most discreditable means, by open bribery and ruthless proscription, so that when Parliament met both Houses had been "purged and poisoned to the core."[5]

[1] *Ibid.*, 111, 154, Fox to Bedford, November 12th 1762: "We are loudly threatened".

[2] "Bute was also much perplexed as to the best method of bringing the peace before Parliament", Fitzmaurice, 1, 146.

[3] Riker, 11, 264-265.

[4] *Ibid.*, 11, 257.

[5] Corbett, 11, 363.

Pointing to the large amounts of money used in bribery, Walpole asserted that:

"Twenty-five thousand pounds, as Martin, Secretary of the Treasury, afterwards owned, were issued in one morning; and in a single fortnight a vast majority was purchased to approve the peace !"[1]

Riker accepted Walpole's statement when he indicated that the Court grudged no amount of money to accomplish its end and that unlimited credit and confidence were given to Fox.[2]

On December 9th, that "memorable day", as Walpole called it, the two Houses debated the Preliminaries. In the House of Lords, many objections were made and some severe reflections were thrown out againt Bute who defended his conduct:

"in a well-connected speech, delivered with great propriety, to the surprise of many, who did not think him so well qualified in the art and faculty of elocution".

It was reported that not only did he avow himself a warm promoter of the peace, but even expressed a desire that his having contributed to the cessation of hostilities should be engraved on his tomb.[3] Even the Duke of Cumberland, his enemy, was obliged to confess that Bute's speech was one of the finest he ever heard in his life.[4] Hardwicke, in his speech [5] disapproved of giving in to France "in several very material points", in spite of the fact that all the French sugar islands except St. Domingo had been taken; that most of the dominions of His Britannic Majesty and his allies in Germany had been recovered; that Havannah, the "key and barrier of Spanish West Indies", had fallen. He objected to the cession of St. Lucia to France, the omission of the inspection of St. Pierre,

---

[1] *Memoirs of George III*, 1, 157.

[2] Riker, 11, 269-270.

[3] *Parliamentary History of England*, XV, 1252.

[4] *Bedford Correspondence*, 111, 170, Rigby to Bedford, December 13th 1762.

[5] See *Parliamentary History of England*, XV, 1251-1258 (footnote), Notes of Hardwicke's Speech in the House of Lords, on the Preliminaries of Peace, December 9th 1762.

which was even accepted by France; to the restoration of the French East India trade to the same state as before the war. He considered the Spanish part of the preliminaries "perhaps the best".[1] More important still was Hardwicke's general observation:

> "This is the first instance that I know of wherein preliminaries, signed and ratified,[2] have been laid before a House of Parliament, and their general approbation demanded to them".[3]

In spite of these objections and others, the Preliminaries passed through the House of Lords without a division. Of more importance were the proceedings in the House of Commons, where Pitt appeared at last "swathed in flannel", and gave his speech which lasted for three and a half hours.[4] He began by stating that:

> "Unattached to any party, I am, and wish to be, entirely single. My sole reason for coming here to-night is to give the House an account of my personal and individual opinion, to which I feel in honour bound, after the part I have taken in affairs".[5]

In his speech,[6] he examined the terms of the Preliminaries in detail. He started with his objections to the concessions made to France on the fisheries and in the West Indies, insisting all the time on the strategic and economic value both to France.[7] He objected also to the concessions made to France in the East Indies where France had no conquests to return. He reprobated in the strongest terms the article about the King of Prussia whom he styled the most magnanimous ally England

---

[1] Ibid., XV, 1253-1254.

[2] The ratifications of the Preliminaries arrived in London on November 26th 1762, Bedford Correspondence, 111, 159, Rigby to Bedford, November 26th 1762; on 29th, the preliminary articles of peace with France and Spain were laid before both Houses; on December 9th, they were taken into consideration, Thackeray, 11, 13.

[3] Parliamentary History of England, XV, 1255-1256; (for information on the other speeches which took place in the House of Lords on the preliminaries, see Memoirs of George III, 1, 175-176).

[4] Corbett, 11, 363.

[5] Williams, 11, 146.

[6] See Parliamentary History of England, XV, 1259-1271.

[7] See on this point Chapter III, pp. 102-105.

ever had. He called it insidious, tricking, base and treacherous.

"Upon the whole, the terms of the proposed treaty met with his most hearty disapprobation. He saw in them the seeds of a future war. The peace was insecure, because it restored the enemy to her former greatness. The peace was inadequate, because the places gained were no equivalent for the places surrendered".[1]

Commenting on Pitt's speech, Walpole asserted that it contained considerable matter, much reason and some passages of great beauty, but that the faintness of his voice and the prolixity with which he dwelt on the articles of the fisheries wearied the House and made the courtiers represent it as "unmeasurably dull, tedious, and uninteresting".[2] After listening to one more speech, Pitt left without voting, as Fox rose to answer him. However, the preliminaries were approved in that House by an overwhelming majority of 319 to 65. The administration had thus won a substantial victory. "It was a great and marvellous triumph," Riker stated, "for the Court, the Bute Ministry, and Henry Fox".[3] It was, indeed, Bute's hour of triumph. The work which he had set out to do was almost accomplished. By the help of Fox, he had carried the preliminaries through Parliament. Walpole reported that George III had told Lady Holland that he would never forget his obligations to her husband for his work for the Peace.[4]

[1] *Parliamentary History of England*, XV, 1270.
[2] *Memoirs of George III*, 1, 178.
[3] Riker, 11, 273.
[4] *Memoirs of George III*, 1, 231.

CHAPTER VI

THE DEFINITIVE TREATY

The preliminary articles of peace settled most of the questions pending between England, France and Spain, and apart from the article about Dunkirk, only a few points remained to be worded in their final form. However, there were two other important articles, besides that of Dunkirk, on which England and France negotiated throughout the interval between the signature of the preliminaries and that of the definitive treaty. These articles concerned the East Indies, and the Mississippi boundary. Differences between France and England on the latter article were not so serious as those in respect of the other two articles about Dunkirk and the East Indies, which differences endangered the conclusion of the definitive treaty. As to Spain and England, there was not, apart from a few immaterial alterations in the wording of the articles concerning them, any serious differences. As a matter of fact, Grimaldi showed eagerness to sign the definitive treaty in order to restore Cuba to his country as soon as possible.[1]

As to the Mississippi boundary, in order to make certain of freedom of navigation in the Mississippi river to the sea,[2] the English insisted on the omission of a certain clause:

> "jusques à la rivière Iberville et de là par une ligne tirée au milieu de cette rivière et des lacs Maurepas et Pontchartrain".[3]

The omission of these words had its importance in facilitating British trade with the Spanish Colonies, as can be easily seen from a map;[4] it allowed them to navigate in the Mississippi

---

[1] A.E., C.P., Angleterre, 449, f.110r; Praslin to Nivernais, January 14th 1763.

[2] See ibid., Angleterre, 449, ff.34v-35r, Nivernais to Praslin, January 5th 1763.

[3] Bedford Correspondence, 111, 178-179, Bedford to Egremont, December 24th 1762.

[4] See Appendix 5, the map joined to Bedford's Instructions of September 4th 1762.

from its source to the sea directly without being restricted to following the Mississippi course to a certain point, and then the river Iberville and the two Lakes of Maurepas and Pont-chartrain. Praslin could not hide his surprise at the new demands of England about an article to which she had already adhered in the preliminaries and which occupied an important place in the negotiations:

"C'est ce fameux article," Praslin wrote, "sur lequel nous avions donné une note secrète et qui nous embarassoit beaucoup à cause de l'Espagne".[1]

In spite of Bedford's persistent endeavours to bring them to accept the omission desired by England in that article, the two French Foreign Ministers "would in no sort consent to"[2] it. Grimaldi took a great part in arguing against Bedford. This interference of the Spanish ambassador "I own, increases my suspicion" declared Bedford "that the report I have heard that France intended to cede New Orleans, Etc. to Spain has some foundation".[3]

As Bedford proved obdurate on that question, Praslin wrote to Nivernais recommending him not to yield on that point, and at the same time indicated to him that it was only "par honeur et par egard pour la Cour de Madrid", that he could not yield on that clause so contrary to what had been decided in the preliminaries.[4] However in a cabinet meeting of January 17th, where Bedford's letters of December 23rd and 24th,

---

[1] A.E., C.P., Angleterre, 448, f.426v, Praslin to Nivernais, December 26th 1762.

[2] *Bedford Correspondence*, III, 179.

[3] *Ibid.*, III, 180. The French tried to keep, for a while, the cession of Louisiana to Spain a secret from England, A.E., C.P., Angleterre, 448, f.75v, Duke of Choiseul to Nivernais, November 20th 1762, also *ibid.*, Angleterre, 448, f.197r, Nivernais to Praslin, December 1st 1762. When this news transpired in London and Nivernais was asked whether it was true he answered that he did not know anything about that matter and asked for instructions about what he should say if such a question was repeated to him, *ibid.*, Angleterre, 449, f.11v, Nivernais to Praslin January 1st 1763. A week later he received the following instructions: "vous pouvés répondre qu'en effet le Roy l'a offerte à Sa Majesté Catholique comme une possession qui est à la convenance de l'Espagne et qui nous devient plus à charge qu'utile après le démembrement qui vient d'en être fait en faveur de l'Angleterre", *ibid.*, Angleterre, 449, f.72v, January 8th 1763.

[4] *Ibid.*, Angleterre, 449, f.72r, Praslin to Nivernais, January 8th 1763.

and the project of the definitive treaty were discussed,[1] Bute, taking the preliminaries as a basis of all his arguments, succeeded in winning over the members of the cabinet,[2] and it was decided with regard to the Mississippi boundary article [3]

"not to insist on anything new; but to stand upon the Preliminary Article, which gives us an equal Right to the Navigation of Mississippi; and all obstructions to the free Navigation of That River will be Infractions of the Treaty".[4]

As to the article relative to Dunkirk, it was stipulated, in the preliminaries, that Dunkirk should be reduced to the state fixed by the Treaty of Aix-la-Chapelle; the Cunette was to remain as it was then, provided that the English engineers, named by His Britannic Majesty, verified that this "Cunette" was only of use to keep the air wholesome and the inhabitants healthy.[5] Thus the fate of the Cunette depended on the report of the English engineer, who, authorised on December 11th to proceed to France for "the Inspection and Examination of the Cunette agreeably to the 5th Article of the Preliminaries",[6] late in the same month was already at Dunkirk inspecting it.[7] Praslin, not very impressed by the English engineer, feared the results of his inspection for he described him to Nivernais as:

"un homme vieux, sourd et taciturne, qui a fait sa visite sans s'expliquer et sans se laisser pênêtrer".[8]

Praslin's fears were soon realised when Desmaretz declared

---

[1] P.R.O., G.D., 21, Minutes of a Cabinet Council at Duke of Cumberland's Lodging, January 17th 1763.

[2] L.H. MSS., ff.437-438, Billet Bute to Viry, January 21st 1763.

[3] An examination of this article in the Preliminaries (Article 6), (in *Parliamentary History of England*, XV, 1244) and the same in the Definitive Treaty (Article 7), (in Appendix 1, 217-218) proves that no alteration was made in this article.

[4] P.R.O., G.D., 21 (meeting of January 17th).

[5] *Parliamentary History of England*, XV, 1243-1244.

[6] P.R.O., S.P., F., France, 255, Egremont to Desmarétz, December 11th 1762.

[7] A.E., C.P., Angleterre, 448, f.426v. Praslin to Nivernais, December 26th, 1762.

[8] *Ibid.*, Angleterre, 449, f.27v, January 3rd 1763.

that "La Cunette" ought to be destroyed; [1] nevertheless Nivernais advised Praslin to "sonder à fond" what instructions Bedford had been given on that question. [2] In another letter of the same date Nivernais expressed his doubts about the English yielding on that point. [3] Four days later, he related to Praslin, that without committing him, and only as an individual, he had shown his indignation at Desmaretz's report. He described it as "impertinent, absurde et injuste"; and declared that the demolition of the "Cunette" was not only inadmissible, but also impracticable. [4] Nivernais was deceived when he thought then that the anger he affected had had its effect and was likely to change the English views about the fate of the "Cunette". When Praslin was acquainted with that decision, he was furious, and described the Engineer as "dificile, Bouau, sauvage, sourd, peu éclairé dans son art". Neither was his disappointment less, for as he declared to Nivernais, he was relying on Bute to choose for the inspection an intelligent and well-intentioned engineer. [5] A week later Nivernais was sure that nothing could be done to save the "Cunette" from being destroyed. He asserted his views in the following words:

"Il n'y a effort humain qui puisse sauver notre Cunette, si ce n'est la rupture du Traité et la continuation de la guerre. On tient ici avec une tenacité invincible au raport de l'Ingénieur Desmarèts".

He also made it clear to him that the demolition of the Cunette was seriously considered a *sine qua non* condition. [6]

At the same time the article relating to the East Indies was proving to be another difficult question, though not as important as the previous one, on which neither Court showed any

[1] Colonel Desmaretz declared that "La Cunette" contributed to the wholesomeness of the air but had as a principal object the uses of a channel, St. Leger, 332; for the fate of the Cunette and post treaty discussions about it, see *ibid.*, 332-337.

[2] A.E., C.P., Angleterre, 449, f.50v, Nivernais to Praslin, January 8th 1763.

[3] *Ibid.*, Angleterre, 449, f.67v.

[4] *Ibid.*, Angleterre, 449, ff.92v-93r, Nivernais to Praslin, January 12th 1763.

[5] *Ibid.*, Angleterre, 449, f.109r, Praslin to Nivernais, January 14th 1763.

[6] *Ibid.*, Angleterre, 449, ff.169r, 170r, Nivernais to Praslin, January 21st 1763.

sign of compromising. Whereas England insisted that both
countries should be in the same position as they were at the
beginning of 1749, France insisted that the date should be
the beginning of July of that year and not the beginning of
that year. This insistence on the part of France was due to
the fact that in that interval she had gained some important
positions on the coast of Cormandel and therefore insisted
on that date in order to maintain those advantageous posts
to her trade there. France was asking for too much, while
her losses during the war against England in that field did not
allow her to have such pretentions. Nivernais was aware of that
fact, when pointing to that article, he wrote to Praslin:

> "Je ne sais comment on le trouvera à notre compagnie des Indes, mais
> soyés assuré ,Monsieur le Duc, qu'il est Phisiquement impossible de le
> faire tourner d'une manière plus avantageuse pour nous, et que c'est
> de ce côté-ci un *ultimatum* dans toute la force du mot. Il est bon même
> que vous sachiés que cet article tel qu'on vous le propose à signer déplait
> ici à un grand nombre de gens, et est fort au dessous des prétensions et
> des désirs de La Compagnie Angloise".[1]

Bute's Billet of January 21st to Viry, which was sent to
Choiseul, proved that Nivernais was right in his conception
that these two articles, as desired by the English were *sine
qua non* conditions. In that note, Bute indicated clearly that
Bedford was instructed to ask the French ministers for a
decisive answer in connection with the two articles about
Dunkirk and the East Indies which were, as presented by the
English, *sine qua non* conditions.[2] In order to make light of
the effects of yielding to England on the article of Dunkirk,
Nivernais drew Praslin's attention to the fact that Dunkirk
was only reduced to the state fixed by the treaty of Aix-la-
Chapelle and not by that of Utrecht, and that it was hinted to
him, that as long as France could change the direction of the
"Cunette", nobody was likely to annoy France on that point.[3]

---

[1] *Ibid.*, Angleterre, 449, ff.171r-171v, Nivernais to Praslin, January 21st 1763.
On the role played by the East India Company on this article, see Sutherland, "The
East India Company and the Peace of Paris", *E.H.R.*, LXII, 179-190.

[2] L.H. MSS., 11, f.446, Billet Bute to Viry, January 21st 1763.

[3] A.E., C.P., Angleterre, 449, ff.214r-214v, Nivernais to Praslin, January 27th
1763.

Realising the impossibility of resisting any longer in connection with Dunkirk, the French gave way on that article,[1] as well as on that of the East Indies. In the same letter, Praslin with a sigh of relief stated to Nivernais that:

"notre grande affaire est enfin terminée tant bien que mal".[2]

Whereas the article relating to the Mississippi boundary remained unchanged in the definitive treaty, those of Dunkirk and the East Indies were altered to the advantage of England. The East Indian article partly differed in the greater precision of its definition and also in the date at which possessions of "comptoirs" by the French justified their restoration under the definitive treaty and in recognition of the rulers of the Carnatic and Deccan.[3] As to the article about Dunkirk, the "Cunette" was to be destroyed immediately after the exchange of the ratifications.[4]

Portugal, who acceded to the definitive treaty, did not take any active part in the negotiations between England, France and Spain. Only acquainted with these negotiations on August 31st, Portugal had good reason to complain about several things. Not only had her ally, England, left her in the dark about these negotiations for five months, since they officially started, but also it was not till the preliminaries were almost on the eve of being signed, that she was acquainted with any of the results of the conference in Paris and London.[5] Neither was she asked to send a minister to negotiate with the three other countries when Plenipotentiaries had been exchanged between England and France.[6] When His Faithful Majesty

---

[1] *Ibid.*, Angleterre, 449, f.257r, Praslin to Nivernais, February 8th 1763.

[2] *Ibid.*, Angleterre, 449, f.255r.

[3] Sutherland "The East India Company and the Peace of Paris", *E.H.R.*, LXII, 181.

[4] Compare article XIII of the Definitive Treaty, Appendix I, p. 221 with article V of the Preliminaries, *Parliamentary History of England*, XV, 1243-1244.

[5] See Portugal's complaints in a memoir of October 9th 1762, delivered by Mello (the Portuguese Ambassador in London), P.R.O., S.P., F., Portugal, 57.

[6] His Faithful Majesty was acquainted with that exchange of Plenipotentiaries between France and England about October 14th 1762, *ibid.*, Portugal, 57, Hay (British ambassador in Portugal) to Egremont, October 14th 1762.

O

complained of that, the British Ambassador assured him that
Bedford had strict orders to insist on the specific inclusion
of Portugal as a *sine qua non* condition in any peace between
the three countries, and this was but intended to pave the way
for the Portuguese minister. However, Mello, the Portuguese
minister in London, was appointed by his court Envoy Extra-
ordinary and plenipotentiary to sign the peace.[1] On October
30th, Egremont wrote to Bedford acquainting him with
Mello's appointment to sign either the preliminaries or the
accession of the Most Faithful King to the definitive treaty,
and asked him to acquaint the French Ministers with these
favourable intentions of the Court of Portugal.[2] However,
the preliminaries were signed before Mello left for Paris.
The British ministers differed in their views about the time of
his departure to Paris: whereas Egremont seemed to be in
favour of Mello's departure at once to Paris, Bute and Viry,
fearing any difficulties raised by him there which might hinder
the signature of peace, thought that he should not go to Paris
until His Faithful Majesty adhered to the Preliminaries.[3]
Nivernais was naturally of Bute's opinion, but when he
declared to Mello his fears about the latter's immediate
departure to Paris, Mello assured him that he understood
very well the importance of concluding the whole business
promptly and added that neither had he orders to ask for any
new clause in the negotiations nor had he any intention of
raising any difficulties, that all he desired was to express to
His Christian Majesty his master's earnest desire to live in
friendship with him.[4] However, it was not very long after
Mello's arrival in Paris (which took place on December
14th[5]), that the ratifications of the preliminaries were signed

[1] *Ibid.*, Portugal, 57.

[2] P.R.O., S.P., F., France, 253.

[3] A.E., C.P., Angleterre, 448, ff.38v-39r, Nivernais to Praslin, November 31st
1762.

[4] *Ibid.*, Angleterre, 448, f.64r, Nivernais to Praslin, November 18th 1762.

[5] P.R.O., S.P., F., France, 255, Bedford to Egremont, December 15th 1762.

by His Faithful Majesty and given to Hay, the British ambassador in Lisbon, who dispatched them on the same day to Bedford in Paris.[1] Portugal had thus no voice at all in the framing of the articles to which she adhered without any difficulty, as is usually the fate of small countries in a general peace. Although Mello was invited to take part in some of the conferences in Paris on the definitive treaty, yet there is no evidence at all that he had any influence on them. The only objections which he raised were when the ministers of France and Spain refused to alternate with his country.[2] This question of alternating was first raised with France. In a conference of December 21st,[3] where Grimaldi was present, the Duke of Choiseul objected to his country alternating with Portugal. He indicated to Mello that his court had never before alternated with that of Lisbon,[4] and that if he insisted on his request, the definitive treaty would be only delayed. Mello yielded soon to the Duke's arguments. Bedford following the example of the Duke of Choiseul and using the same arguments, showed to Mello the Treaty of 1703, the last made between England and Portugal and "signed upon separate Instruments". Mello readily assented to Bedford's request.[5] It was therefore agreed that neither France nor England was to alternate with Portugal. As to Spain Mello took it for granted that she would alternate with his country, procedure which had been followed since the peace of Utrecht. Six weeks elapsed, as Mello indicated in his complaints against that Court, without Grimaldi raising any objection to that

[1] *Ibid.*, Portugal, 57, Hay to Egremont, December 28th 1762 (the Preliminaries were signed and dispatched on December 25th).

[2] *Ibid.*, Portugal, 58, Hay to Egremont, January 12th 1763 (secret).

[3] Three days before this conference, Bedford writing to Egremont, informed him that the Duke of Choiseul told him that as France did not intend to alternate with Portugal, neither England nor Spain should alternate, that the three countries should recur in the definitive treaty to the same method adopted in the preliminaries namely that Portugal should acede to the Definitive Treaty after it had been signed by the three countries, *ibid.*, France 255, Bedford to Egremont, December 18th 1762.

[4] Count d'Oyeras, the Portuguese foreign minister also informed Hay that France has made the same objection of alternating with Portugal at the Treaty of Utrecht 1713, *ibid.*, Portugal, 58, Hay to Egremont, January 12th 1763 (secret).

[5] *Ibid.*, France, 255, Bedford to Egremont, December 23rd 1762.

arrangement. It was only when the articles of the definitive treaty were agreed upon that he showed a letter from his Court asking him not to alternate with the Court of Lisbon, if the other contracting powers were not to do so.[1] On the same day the Duke of Choiseul received this complaint, he answered Mello stating that:

"ni le Roy ni le Roy de la grande Bretagne n'ont rien à ce que je pense à démêler sur un diférend particulier de pur cérémonial, qui ne les concerne pas".[2]

However, Mello yielded again, and acceded to the definitive treaty of peace on the same day it was signed by England, France and Spain in Paris (on February 10th, 1763).[3]

---

[1] A.E., C.P., Portugal, 94, ff. 2r-2v, Mello to Duke of Choiseul, February 6th 1763.
[2] *Ibid.*, Portugal, 94, f. 5r, Duke of Choiseul to Mello, February 6th 1763.
[3] P.R.O., S.P., F., Portugal, 58, Egremont to Hay, February 22nd 1763.

CHAPTER VII

CONCLUSION

The time has come to consider, in the light of the negotiations discussed in their different stages in this thesis, to what extent the belligerent countries achieved their war aims at "The Peace of Paris", that long drawn-out diplomatic struggle which agitated the different countries of Europe and in particular England, France and Spain from the end of 1759 until February 1763, when the definitive treaty was signed and put an end to the war between England, France, Spain and Portugal. The Peace of Hubertsburg signed on February 15th, put an end to the war between the rest of the belligerent countries, Prussia, Austria, and Saxony-Poland,[1] who took part in the Seven Years' War in Europe.

In England contemporaries differed in their estimation of the peace, but they all agreed as to its importance. George III, very pleased with it, declared that Great Britain had never before concluded such a peace, and that no other European Power had ever concluded another similar to it.[2] Egremont spoke of the peace as glorious.[3] Gower considered it an advantageous peace for England.[4] Granville on his death-bed, according to Wood, Pitt's former under secretary, declared his approbation:

"on the most glorious war and most honourable peace this nation ever saw".[5]

On the other hand, to many the peace was not satisfactory. Hardwicke attacked it and considered it inadequate; many echoed his opinion and thought that incomplete advantage had been taken of the British victories. However, Pitt was the

[1] Prussia had concluded her peace individually with Russia and Sweden in May of the previous year, see chapter IV, p. 135, footnotes 4 and 6.

[2] *Bedford Correspondence*, 111, 199, Neville to Bedford, February 16th 1763.

[3] *Ibid.*, 111, 199-200.

[4] *Ibid.*, 111, 207, Gower to Bedford, February 16th 1763.

[1] Williams, 11, 141.

only one who opposed it sincerely and vehemently. He was also the only man in the first rank of politics, although it was a mercantilist age, who voiced his opposition for the peace, in economic and strategic terms. He condemned the peace which laid the foundation of the British Empire, a peace which is usually regarded as the result of his own successful policy, because he saw in the articles of the preliminaries the seeds of a future war: by restoring the enemy to her former greatness, peace, in his opinion was insecure. Furthermore, the peace was inadequate because the places gained were not equivalent to those surrendered. The only particulars which met with his approbation were the surrender of North America by the French, and the restitution of Minorca. Pitt's views expressed the opinion generally prevalent in England, that peace had sacrificed British interests, and that the continental colonies were the chief beneficiaries of the war. At the same time it was recognised that France, by receiving back a share in the fisheries and her West Indian colonies, would, in the near future, again be in a position to challenge British maritime supremacy.

English historians have echoed the opposition's opinion; yet although they agreed that England might have asked for more, they still maintained that the Peace of Paris was advantageous to England. They agreed that better terms might have been obtained and condemned the treaty because it ceded— so they believed—valuable conquests without adequate compensation: for instance, Florida was considered a poor exchange for Havannah; they blamed the terms of the treaty for rendering France a dangerous enemy to England.[1]

On reflection, it cannot be admitted that all the objections raised against the peace were well founded. In objecting to granting France the fisheries, it was assumed as a principle that England ought to monopolise all the fisheries for the purpose of preventing France from ever re-establishing her naval power, and thus from ever becoming a menace to England. Beside the impracticability of the attainment of such

---

[1] See Lecky, III, 213; Hunt, *Political History of England*, 41; Williams, 11, 142; see also Temperley, 505-506.

designs,[1] it is of importance to note that the concessions in regard to the fisheries, as stipulated by the peace, did not to any considerable degree tend to increase the naval power of France.

Some of the concessions made to France in the West Indies were the bait which was to gain France's support against the bellicose designs of Spain and her demands. The history of the negotiations in 1762 showed the importance which St. Lucia had particularly played in that respect. Besides, as declared by the Choiseuls, France was not prepared to make peace without this concession.[2]

As regards Florida, which was considered a poor equivalent for the extremely important conquest of Havannah, it is true that the English could have asked for better compensation,[3] but apart from Bute's policy of seeking peace at any price, the English statesmen were more interested in the settlement of their other articles with Spain, and in particular in those dealing with the renewal of the commercial treaties without any stipulations between England and Spain, and with keeping their rights to the logwood in the Gulf of Mexico. The first one proved to be one of the most difficult ones to be agreed upon. Even when it was fairly clear the war was lost, Charles III insisted on non-renewal of the commercial treaties as an essential condition of his willingness to make peace with England. To England this article was of vital importance to her economic life: Spain and her Empire were "The Darling and The Silver Mine of England." To the English success at Havannah and to the help of France (which England gained by other concessions) was due to Spain's readiness to accept the settlement of those articles to the advantage of England.

However, without such concessions peace would have been

[1] As already indicated in chapter III, 103-105; on the role which the fisheries had played in the negotiations of 1761, see chapter III.

[2] See Chapter IV, p. 153.

[3] Egremont was aware of the inferiority of value of the compensation asked by England for Havannah, but had his reasons, see *Bedford Correspondence*, 111, 139, Egremont to Bedford, October 26th 1762 (see chapter V, p. 180 footnote 1).

unattainable. Although France was in a disadvantageous position on account of her military disasters, she was still one of
the main powers of Europe and was not likely to submit to a
humiliating peace. Thus by making some concessions to France,
England secured great possessions and the prolongation of an
expensive war was prevented.

The fact that the peace in its final form was due more to
Bute's personal influence than to any clear colonial policy,
increased the clamour against it. If this peace had been carried
through in a different spirit, and by another statesman, it
might have been welcomed in England. However, there can
be no doubt that the terms of "The Peace of Paris" were
extremely advantageous to England. It established British
maritime supremacy, and placed England in the position of
the foremost colonial power in the world. England achieved
her primary war aim: the security of the American colonies
was obtained, France after resigning all pretentions to Nova
Scotia ceded Canada with all its dependencies, together with
Cape Breton and all other islands in the gulf and river of St.
Lawrence. The boundaries between the two countries'
possessions in America were clearly defined so as to prevent
the possibility of dispute, and so advantageously, that a large
part of the territory of Louisiana was added to England's possessions in America. Spain by ceding Florida to England, con-
solidated the British Empire in that part of the world. The
report of the Board of Trade made by Lord Shelburne (who
became the President of the Board of Trade in April 1763, in
the Grenville Ministry), in defence of the Government
assured these advantages: "The total exclusion of the French
from Canada and the Spaniards from Florida gives Great Britain
the universal empire of that extended coast". The English also
gained new fields of commerce with the Indians and supplied
English manufactured goods to 70,000 "Acadians". The British
exports to America had greatly increased. The concessions
made by France in the Newfoundland fisheries enabled the
British to maintain 4,000 more seamen than before. "Thus
the possessions of the whole continent of North America
assured us an abundance of population and commerce—and

therefore of sailors and of ships." [1] Senegal, Grenada and The Grenadines, Dominica, St. Vincent and Tobago became English possessions. Minorca had been restored to England. The English allies in Germany, with the exception of the King of Prussia, were to receive back those parts of their dominions in the possession of the French. Spain consented to abandon her claim to fish off the coasts of Newfoundland, and to cede Florida to England in return for the restoration of Havannah.

The most questionable arrangement in the preliminaries was that which concerned Prussia. Frederick accused the English Government, in the person of Lord Bute, of having concluded a separate peace with France without due regard to his country's interests. This accusation originated from Bedford's giving way in the Preliminaries on the article relative to the evacuation of Cleves, Wesel and Gueldres. Not only was France permitted merely to evacuate them "as soon as it can be done", but also there was a declaration that she was to be permitted to pay all arrears of her subsidy to Austria. However, Halifax, the Secretary of State for the Northern Department, was able jointly with France to reach a solution, which met with Frederick's approbation and which led to the conclusion of peace between Prussia and Austria. [2] On December 9th, when the Preliminaries of peace were discussed in both Houses, nothing was known of the arrangement made by Halifax. Nevertheless it was not fair to describe that particular article as faithless and treacherous, since according to the only treaty then valid between England and Prussia, that of Westminster, England had only to remove the French from German soil. This accusation was not the only one made against Bute; he was also accused of having secretly approached the Court of Vienna with an offer to guarantee Silesia to Austria if she would retire from the struggle, and of having attempted to deter the Emperor Peter III from his treaty of peace and alliance with Frederick, on the ground that the alliance of Russia would make him too extravagant in his

---

[1] Extracts of this report in Temperley, 505.

[2] See Corbett, 11, 362-365, and Ruville, 111, 93-94.

demands at the conclusion of the war. These charges were groundless.[1] As to the termination of the Prussian subsidy, it was fully justified. England was under no formal obligation to continue indefinitely her annual subsidy to Frederick. Besides, the complete change of the circumstances from those in which England's alliance with Frederick had been concluded was more than justifiable for Great Britain's action towards him. In May 1762, he concluded his peace with Russia and Sweden respectively and thus the great league against him was dissolved. However, acquitting Bute of these different charges does not, on any account, defend the sagacity of his diplomacy. His policy was to blame for sacrificing Great Britain's future international position for the sake of a momentary triumph in domestic politics. Dorn's assessment of Bute's policy in this respect is very sound:

"A great opportunity . . . of affecting an understanding with Prussia and Russia and of establishing a solid European system, with Great Britain as the predominating partner, which would have secured the peace, was deliberately sacrificed to petty domestic and personal interests".

The frequent efforts made by the British diplomats between 1763 and 1776 to combine with Russia and Prussia as a counterpoise to the Austro-Bourbon coalition failed each time because of the inflexible opposition of the embittered and resentful Frederick II of Prussia.[2] Further, the belief that England had deserted Frederick made a lasting impression in Germany. More than a century later Bismarck attributed his distrust of England to the desertion of Frederick in 1762.[3]

In France peace which was as necessary to the French people as "le manger et le boire" according to Voltaire's saying, met with great delight and satisfaction. The French Nation hastened to join willingly in the festivals held on that occasion.[4] The period from December 1762 to March 1763, namely, from

---

[1] W. L. Dorn proved, by his article "Frederic the Great and Lord Bute", based on original documents, that these charges against Bute were groundless, *J.M.H.*, I, 529-560; see also Temperley, 495.

[2] Dorn, "Frederic the Great and Lord Bute", *J.M.H.*, I, 560.

[3] Williams, II, 143.

[4] Jobez, V, 612.

the signature of the Preliminaries to the arrival of the ratification of the definitive treaty, as indicated in the *Journal
de Barbier*, is full of the news of public festivals and rejoicings,
also of the private balls held in Paris and Versailles on that
occasion.[1] Further, several poems [2] had been made on the
peace which expressed the joy and relief with which the
French nation received the news, in spite of the fact that
France had lost some valuable possessions by that peace.

In France contemporaries agreed that the peace, though
disadvantageous was necessary, and were convinced that,
taking into consideration the circumstances in which it was
concluded, a better peace was impossible to obtain. Louis
XV expressed these very views when he said:

"la paix que nous venons de faire n'est pas bonne ni glorieuse; *personne
ne le sent mieux que moi*; mais dans les circomstances malheureuses, elle
ne pouvoit être meilleure".[3]

The Count of Choiseul and the Duke of Choiseul agreed in
their views with Louis XV.[4]

However, both Soulange-Bodin and Jobez considered the
terms of the peace of Paris ruinous to France. Whereas the
first calls it "le déplorable traité de Paris",[5] the latter asserts
that France made a disastrous peace at Utrecht in 1713, in
1763 she concluded another "plus ruineuse encore et plus
honteuse".[6] Boutaric, on the other hand, admits that although
the peace was deplorable, yet he realised that France's position
at that time could not have allowed her a better peace.[7]
Flassan considered it adroit and necessary.[8]

It is true that the peace of Paris was not a glorious peace
for France yet considering the state of France when she concluded this peace, it is not by any means a disastrous one; and

[1] *Journal de Barbier*, VIII, 59-68.
[2] Chevalier de Viguier, *Ode sur la Paix*, Paris 1863 (read and approved December 30th 1762); J. A. Tricot, *Le Retour de la Paix*, Paris 1763 etc.
[3] Boutaric, I, 112.
[4] See Chapter V, p. 186.
[5] Soulange-Bodin, 229.
[6] Jobez, v, 611.
[7] Boutaric, I, 111.
[8] Flassan, VI, 482-483, see *infra*, p. 208.

Flassan's words on the peace are the best guide for its estimation.

Spain was responsible to a considerable extent for the failure of the negotiations in 1761,[1] and the Duke of Choiseul failed to obtain during the war even with the help of Spain any victories to help him in obtaining better terms for his country. But by taking upon himself, during the negotiations in 1762, the task of persuading Spain to submit to England's demands, the Duke of Choiseul succeeded in obtaining some concessions from England and in concluding an honourable peace for France. France's gains were therefore to some extent acquired at the expense of Spain. The French had been granted the right of fishing in the gulf of St. Lawrence, as well as off Newfoundland, and the islands of St. Pierre and Miquelon had been ceded to them as shelters for their fishing vessels. England restored her important conquests of Guadeloupe, Marie Galante, Desirade, Martinique, St. Lucia, Belleisle and Goree. In India, France had been given back the trade settlements which she held at the beginning of 1749. These valuable possessions in the West Indies, Goree with its command of the slave trade, and her important trade settlements in India and the share in the fisheries were sufficient to restore France, in the future, to her position among the maritime powers in Europe. France's aim was, therefore, attained; she had neither been deprived of all her colonies, nor had her maritime power been annihilated. With the exception of Russia, she had also conserved all her allies. Flassan's sound comments on the Peace of Paris as regards France are worth quoting in full:

"La Paix de 1763 était nécessaire et adroite, en la considérant par rapport aux malheureuses circonstances où on la fit, puisqu'elle ne privait pas la France de ses ressources essentielles, et de ce qui la constituait puissance maritime. Il convient même d'observer, comme caractère honorable et special, que La cour de Versailles conserva tous ses alliés, avant et après la guerre, à l'exception de la Russie; au lieu que l'Angleterre, après la guerre, resta près de dix ans, sans allié sur le continent".[2]

[1] See Chapter III, pp. 108-112.
[2] Flassan, VI, 482-483.

After the conclusion of the Peace of Paris, the Duke of Choiseul directed all his efforts to make France benefit from the Spanish trade. He attempted the execution of his plans for France's recovery, by trying to substitute France for England in the economic life of the Spanish peninsula, and welding together the French and Spanish nations in a great commercial system which Choiseul hoped would play a significant part in the duel with England for political power.[1] Choiseul's influence was directed, therefore, in all the crises which occurred in the relations between England, France and Spain, towards averting war, because it was only during peace that the Duke of Choiseul could successfully pursue his military and economic rehabilitation.[2] At the same time, Louis XV was preparing France for her next war against England: almost on the morrow of the peace, on April 7th, 1763, he ordered Broglie to make some secret investigations of the coasts of England, in preparation for a plan of invasion when the time came for France to attack her. La Rosière, an intelligent and capable officer, was chosen for the task. He spent a year in England and was successful in his investigations. Broglie, Tercier, Eon, and Durand alone were acquainted with the secret. However this plan, which was approved by the French Council in November 1770, when there was a question of war against England, was never used.[3]

As for Spain, this peace was by no means advantageous to her.[4] It is true that her military disasters during her short war did not entitle her to expect better terms than what she had obtained by that peace: Cuba and Manila were restored to her, Florida was ceded to England, but Spain received Louisiana from France in compensation. Nevertheless it must be noted that if her loss of Florida was compensated for by Louisiana, the rest of the terms of peace did not give her

[1] Brown, 50.

[2] Ramsey, 151.

[3] Boutaric, I, 112-114.

[4] Collado considered it very costly: it cost her great sacrifices in men, money and in territory, 11, 216.

any satisfaction for her grievances against England. Partly because of the disadvantageous military position of Spain and partly because of France's help to England in negotiating with Spain, all these questions were settled to the advantage of England. The prizes question was to be settled, according to England's wishes, by the British Court of Admiralty; Spain consented to relinquish her claim to fish off the banks of Newfoundland; and it was agreed that the fortifications erected in the Bay of Honduras should be demolished. The English were to be allowed to cut logwood and to carry it away, and also to build and occupy without interruption the houses and magazines necessary for themselves, their families and effects. Besides, Charles III was compelled to yield to England on the question of the renewal of the commercial treaties between the two Courts. Here again Charles III failed to get rid of the British treaties and recapture the Indies trade for the Spaniards and extinguish British contraband trade.[1] This failure meant also that France and Spain had failed in the economic objectives which they had set out at the beginning of 1762. They had failed to exclude any significant amount of British goods from their accustomed European market, and to break British commercial predominance in Spain.[2]

It is true that Charles III was responsible for drawing his country into this short and unsuccessful war against England; it is also true that this policy was dictated to him by the interests of his country and not by the French Foreign minister's persistent appeals for succour. The apparent threat of an English attack on his American colonies persuaded him that this policy was the wisest. It is true that Spain in her desperate situation on the eve of negotiating the peace was not in a position to obtain advantageous terms, yet it is also true that the Duke of Choiseul was responsible to a great extent for the unsatisfactory nature of the terms that Spain

---

[1] This aim was one of the main motives which induced Charles III to enter war against England.

[2] See Christelow, "Economic Background of the Anglo-Spanish War of 1762", J.M.H., XVIII, 34-35.

had to accept. Choiseul, in fact, played a very successful role in the latest stage of the negotiations and succeeded at the expense of Spain in gaining advantages for France. Throughout the negotiations Choiseul used Spain for his own purposes.[1]

Thus whereas England's victories during the Seven Years' War enabled her to obtain an advantageous peace, France's adroit diplomacy made it possible for her to obtain an honourable peace in spite of her military disasters, while Spain, without either victories or clever diplomacy, came out of war to her disadvantage and did not achieve her aims.

---

[1] *Supra*, pp. 151-152, and Chapter V, p. 159.

THE DEFINITIVE TREATY OF PEACE
CONCLUDED AT PARIS, FEBRUARY 10th, 1763[1]

Au Nom de la Très sainte et indivisible Trinité, Père, Fils, et saint Esprit, ainsi soit-il.

Soit notoire à tous Ceux qu'il appartiendra, ou peut appartenir, en Manière quelconque.

Il a plû au Tout Puissant de répandre l'Esprit d'Union et de Concorde, sur les Princes dont les Divisions avoient porté le Trouble dans les Quatre Parties du Monde, et de leur inspirer le Dessein de faire succéder les Douceurs de la Paix, aux Malheurs d'une longue et sanglante Guerre, qui, après s'être élevée entre l'Angleterre, et la France, pendant le Règne du Sérénissime et très Puissant Prince, George Second, par la Grâce de Dieu, Roy de la Grande Bretagne, de glorieuse Mémoire—a été continuée sous le Règne du Sérénissime et très Puissant Prince, George Trois, Son Successeur, et s'est communiquée dans ses Progrès, à l'Espagne, et au Portugal; En conséquence, Le Sérénissime et très Puissant Prince, GEORGE TROIS, par la Grâce de Dieu, Roy de la Grande Bretagne, de France et d'Irlande, Duc de Brunswick et de Lunebourg, Archi-Trésorier, et Electeur du Saint Empire Romain:—Le Sérénissime et Très Puissant Prince, CHARLES TROIS, par la Grâce de Dieu, Roy d'Espagne, et des Indes; Le Serenissime et très Puissant Prince, LOUIS QUINZE, par la Grâce de Dieu, Roy Très Chrétien, après avoir posé les Fondemens de la Paix dans les Préliminaires, signés le Trois Novembre dernier, à Fontainbleau, Et Le Sérénissime et très Puissant Prince Don Joseph Premier, par la Grâce de Dieu, Roy de Portugal et des Algavues, après y avoir accédé, ont résolu de consommer sans Délai, ce grand et important Ouvrage; A cet Effet, Les Hautes Parties Contractantes ont

---

[1] P.R.O., S.P., E., 122, The original Text; accents have been inserted in the text according to modern usage.

nommé et constitué Leurs Ambassadeurs Extraordinaires, et
Ministres Plénipotentiaires respectifs, savoir, Sa Sacrée
Majesteè Le Roy de la Grande Bretagne, le très Illustre et très
Excellent Seigneur, Jean, Duc, et Comte de Bedford, Marquis
de Tavistock, etc.: Son Ministre d'Etat, Lieutenant Général
de Ses Armées, Garde de Son Sceau Privé, Chevalier, du très
noble Ordre de la Jarretière, et Son Ambassadeur Extra-
ordinaire et Ministre Plénipotentiaire, près de Sa Majesté
Très Chrétienne, Sa sacrée Majesté Le Roy Catholique, Le
Très Illustre et Très Excellent Seigneur Don Jerome Grimaldi,
Marquis de Grimaldi, Chevalier des Ordres du Roy Très
Chrétien, Gentilhomme de la Chambre de Sa Majesté Catholique avec Exercice, et Son Ambassadeur Extraordinaire
auprès de Sa Majesté Très Chrétienne, Sa Sacrée Majesté le
Roy Très Chrétien, Le Très Illustre et Très Excellent Seigneur
Cesar Gabriel de Choiseul, Duc de Praslin, Pair de France,
Chevalier de Ses Ordres, Lieutenant Général de Ses Armées,
et de la Province de Bretagne, Conseiller en tous Ses Conseils,
et Ministre, et Secretaire d'Etat, et de Ses Commandemens,
et Finances; Sa Sacrée Majesté Le Roy Très Fidéle, Le Très
Illustre et Très Excellent Seigneur Martin de Mello et Castro,
Chevalier Profés de l'Ordre de Christ, du Conseil de Sa
Majesté Très Fidéle, et Son Ambassadeur et Ministre Pleni-
potentiaire, auprès de Sa Majesté Très Chrétienne.

LESQUELS après s'être duement communiqué leurs Pleinpouvoirs en bonne Forme, et dont les Copies sont transcrites
à la Fin du présent Traité de Paix, sont convenus des Articles
dont la Teneur s'ensuit.

Article 1er

Il y aura une Paix Chrétienne, universelle, et perpétuelle,
tant par Mer, que par Terre, et une Amitié sincère et con-
stante, sera rétablie entre Leurs Majestés Britannique, Catholique, Très Chrétienne, et Très Fidéle, et entre leurs Heri-
tiers, et Successeurs, Royaumes, Etats, Provinces, Pays,
Sujets, et Vassaux, de quelque Qualité et Condition qu'Ils
soient, sans Exception de Lieux, ni de Personnes; Ensorte que

P

les Hautes Parties Contractantes apporteront la plus grande Attention à maintenir Entre Elles, et leurs dits Etats, et Sujets, cette Amitié et Correspondance réciproque sans permettre dorénavant, que, de Part ni d'autre, on commette aucunes Sortes d'Hostilités, par Mer, ou par Terre, pour quelque Cause, ou sous quelque Prétexte, que ce puisse être, et on évitera soigneusement tout ce qui pourroit altérer à l'Avenir, l'Union heureusement rétablie, s'attachant au contraire, à se procurer réciproquement en toute Occasion, tout ce qui pourroit contribuer à leur Gloire, Intérêts, et Avantages mutuels, sans donner aucun Secours ou Protection, dirèctement, ou indirèctement, à Ceux qui voudroient porter quelque Préjudice, à l'Une, ou à l'autre des dites Hautes Parties Contractantes; Il y aura un Oubli général de tout ce qui a pu être fait ou commis, avant, ou depuis, le Commencement de la Guerre qui vient de finir.

Article 2.

Les Traités de Westphalie de Mil Six Cent Quarante huit, Ceux de Madrid, entre les couronnes de la Grande Bretagne et d'Espagne, de Mil Six Cent Soixante Sept, et de Mil Six Cent Soixante Dix, les Traités de Paix de Nimégue, de Mil Six Cent Soixante Dix huit, et de Mil Six Cent Soixante Dix Neuf; de Ryswick, de Mil Six Cent Quatre Vingt Dix Sept; Ceux de Paix et de Commerce d'Utrecht de Mil Sept Cent Treize; Celui de Bade, de Mil Sept Cent Quatorze, le Traité de la Triple Alliance de la Haye, de Mil Sept Cent Dix Sept, Celui de la Quadruple Alliance de Londres, de Mil Sept Cent Dix huit; Le Traité de Paix de Vienne de Mil Sept Cent Trente huit; le Traité Définitif d'Aix la Chapelle, de Mil Sept Cent Quarante huit; Et Celui de Madrid entre les Couronnes de la Grande Bretagne et d'Espagne, de Mil Sept Cent Cinquante; aussi bien que les Traitée entre les Couronnes d'Espagne et de Portugal, du Treize Février Mil Six Cent Soixante huit; du Six Fevrier, Mil Sept Cent Quinze; et du Douze Fevrier, Mil Sept Cent Soixante Un; Et Celui du Onze Avril, Mil Sept Cent Treize, entre la France et le Portugal, avec les Garanties de la Grande Bretagne, servent de Base, et de Fondement à la Paix, et au présent Traité; Et pour cet Effet, Ils sont tous renouvellés et confirmés dans la meilleure Forme, ainsi que tous les Traités en général, qui subsistoient entre Les Hautes Parties Contractantes avant La Guerre, et comme s'ils étoient insérés ici Mot à Mot; En sorte qu'ils devront être observés exactement à l'Avenir, dans toute leur Teneur, et réligieusement executés, de Part et d'autre, dans tous leurs Points, auxquels il n'est pas dérogé par le présent Traité, nonobstant tout ce qui pourroit avoir été stipulé au contraire par aucune des Hautes Parties Contractantes; Et toutes les dites Parties déclarent, qu'elles ne permettront pas qu'il subsiste aucun Privilége, Grâce, ou Indulgence, contraires aux Traités ci-dessus confirmés, à l'Exception de ce qui aura été accorde et stipulé par le présent Traité.

Article 3.

Tous les Prisonniers faits de Part et d'autre, tant par Terre que par Mer, et les Otages enlevés ou donnés, pendant la Guerre, et jusqu'à ce Jour, seront restitués, sans Rançon, dans Six Semaines au plus tard à compter du Jour de l'Exchange de la Ratification du présent Traité, chaque Couronne soldant respectivement les Avances qui auront été faites pour la Subsistance et l'Entretien de ses Prisonniers, par le Souverain du Pais où ils auront été détenus, conformément aux Reçus et Etats constatés, et autres Titres autentiques qui seront fournis de Part et d'autre. Et il sera donné réciproquement des Suretés pour le Paiement des Dettes, que les Prisonniers aunoint pu contracter dans les Etats, où ils auroient été détenus, jusqu'à leur entière Liberté. Et tous les Vaisseaux tant de Guerre, que Marchands, qui auroient été pris depuis l'Expiration des Termes, convenus pour la Cessation des Hostilités par Mer, seront pareillement rendus de bonne Foy, avec tous leurs Equipages, et Cargaisons, Et on procedera a l'Exécution de cet Article immédiatement après l'Echange des Ratifications de ce Traité.

Article 4.

Sa Majesté Très Chrétienne renonce à toutes les Prétensions qu'Elle a formées autrefois, ou pu former, à la nouvelle Ecosse, ou l'Acadie, en toutes Ses Parties, et la garantit toute entière, et avec toutes Ses Dépendances, au Roy de la Grande Bretagne; De plus Sa Majesté Très Chrétienne cède et garantit à Sa dite Majesté Britannique, en toute Propriété, le Canada, avec toutes Ses Dépendances, ainsi que l'Isle du Cap Breton, et toutes les autres Isles ce qui dépend des dits Païs, Terres, Iles et Côtes, avec la Souveraineté, Propriété, Possession, et tous Droits, acquis par Traité, ou autrement, que le Roy Très Chrétien, et la Couronne de France, ont eus jusqu'à présent, sur les dits Païs, Isles, Terres, Lieux, Côtes, et leurs Habitans, ainsi que le Roy Très Chrétien cède et transporte le tout au dit Roy, et à la Couronne de la Grande Bretagne, et cela de la Manière et Dans la Forme la plus ample, sans Restriction et sans qu'il soit libre de revenir sous aucum Prétexte, contre cette Cession et Garantie, ni de troubler la Grande Bretagne dans les Possessions susmentionnées. De Son Côte, Sa Majesté Britannique convient d'accorder aux Habitans du Canada, la Liberté de la Réligion Catholique; En consequence, Elle donnera les Ordres les plus précis, et les plus effectifs pourque Ses Nouveaux Sujets Catholiques Romains puissent professer le Culte de leur Réligion selon le Rit de l'Eglise Romaine, en tant que le permettent les Loix de la Grande Bretagne. Sa Majesté Britannique convient en outre, que les Habitans François, ou Autres, qui auroient été Sujets du Roy très Chrétien, en Canada, pourront se retirer en toute Sûreté et Liberté, où bon leur semblera, et pourront vendre leurs Biens, pourvu que ce soit à des sujets de Sa Majesté Britannique, et transportés leurs effets, ainsi que leurs Personnes, sans être gênés dans leur Emigration, sous quelque Prétexte que ce puisse être, hors Celui de Dettes, ou de Procès Criminels; Le terme limité pour cette Emigration sera fixé à l'Espace de Dix huit Mois, à compter du Jour de l'Echange des ratifications du présent Traité.

Article 5.

Les Sujets de la France auront la liberté de la Pêche et de la Sêcherie sur une Partie des Côtes de l'Isle de Terre neuve, telle qu'elle est spécifiée par l'Article Treize du Traité d'Utrecht, lequel Article est renouvellé et confirmé par le présent Traité (à l'exception de ce qui regarde l'Isle du Cap-Breton, ainsi que les autres Isles et Côtes dans l'Embouchure et dans le Golphe St. Laurent); et Sa Majesté Britannique consent de laisser aux Sujets du Roy Très Chrétien la Liberté de pêcher dans le Golphe St. Laurent, à Condition que les Sujets de la France n'exercent la dite Pêche qu'à la Distance de Trois Lieues de toutes les Côtes appartenantes à la Grande Bretagne, soit Celles du Continent soit Celles des Isles situées dans le dit Golphe Saint Laurent. Et pour ce qui concerne la Pêche sur les Côtes de l'Isle du Cap-Breton, hors du dit Golphe, il ne sera pas permis aux Sujets du Roy Très Chrétien d'exercer la dite Pêche, qu'à la Distance de Quinze Lieues des Côtes de l'Isle du Cap Breton; et la Pêche sur les Côtes de la nouvelle Ecosse, ou Acadie, et par tout ailleurs, hors du dit Golphe, restera aur le Pied des Traités antérieurs.

Article 6.

Le Roy de la Grande Bretagne cède les Isles de St. Pierre, et de Miquelon, en toute Propriété, à Sa Majesté Très Chrétienne, pour servir d'Abri aux Pêcheurs François. Et Sa dite Majesté Très Chrétienne s'oblige à ne point fortifier les dites Isles, à n'y établir que des Batimens Civils pour la Commodité de la Pêche, et à n'y entretenir qu'une Garde de Cinquante Hommes pour la Police.

Article 7.

Afin de rétablir la Paix sur des Fondemens solides et durables, et écarter pour jamais tout Sujet de Dispute, par rapport aux Limites des Territoires Britanniques et François, sur le Continent de l'Amerique, il est convenu qu'à l'avenir les Confins entre les Etats de Sa Majesté Britannique, et Ceux de Sa Majesté Très Chrétienne, en cette Partie du Monde seront irrevocablement fixés par une Ligne tirée au Milieu du Fleuve Mississippi, depuis Sa Naissance, jusqu'à la Rivière d'Iberville, et de là par une ligne tirée au Milieu de cette Rivière, et des Lacs Maurepas et Pontchartrain, jusqu'à la Mer; Et à cette Fin Le Roy Très Chrétien cède en toute Propriété, et garantit à Sa Majesté Britannique la Rivière, et le Port de la Mobile, et tout ce qu'il Possède, ou a du posseder, du Côté Gauche du Fleuve Mississippi, à l'exception de la Ville de la nouvelle Orléans, et de l'Isle dans laquelle Elle est située, qui demeureront à la France, bien entendu, que la Navigation du Fleuve Mississippi sera également libre, tant aux Sujets de la Grande Bretagne, comme à ceux de la France, dans toute sa Largeur, et toute son Etendue, depuis sa Source jusqu'à la Mer, et nommément cette Partie qui est entre la susdite Isle de la nouvelle Orléans, et la Rive droite de ce Fleuve, aussi bien que l'Entrée, et la Sortie par son Embouchure; Il est, de plus, stipulé, que les Batimens appartenans aux Sujets de l'Une, ou de l'Autre Nation ne pourront être arrêtés, visitées, ni assujettis au Payement d'aucun Droit quelconque. Les Stipulations insérées dans l'Article 4 en Faveur des Habitans du Canada, auront Lieu de même pour les Habitans des Païs cédés par cet Article.

Article 8.

Le Roy de la Grande Bretagne restituera à la France, les Isles de la Guadeloupe, de Mariegalante, de la Désirade, de la Martinique, et de Belleisle, et les Places de ces Isles seront rendues dans le même Etat où Elles étoient, quand la Conquête en a été faite par les Armes Britanniques, bien entendu, que les Sujets de Sa Majesté Britannique qui se seroient établis, ou ceux qui auroient quelques Affaires de Commerce à regler dans les dites Isles et autres Endroits, restitués à la France par le présent Traité, auront la Liberté de vendre leurs Terres, et Leurs Biens, de regler leurs Affaires, de recouvrer leurs Dettes, et de transporter leurs Effets, ainsi que leurs Personnes, à bord des Vaisseaux, qu'il leur sera permis de faire venir aux dites Isles, et autres Endroits, restitués comme dessus, et qui ne serviront qu'à cet Usage seulement, sans être gênés à Cause de leur Religion, ou sous quelque autre Prétexte que ce puisse être, hors Celui de Dettes, ou de Procès Criminels; Et pour cet Effet le Terme de Dix huit Mois est accordé aux Sujets de Sa Majesté Britannique à compter du Jour de l'Echange des Ratifications du présent Traité; Mais, comme la Liberté accordée aux Sujets de Sa Majesté Britannique, de transporter leurs Personnes, et leurs Effets, sur des Vaisseaux de leur Nation, pourroit être sujette à des Abus, si l'On ne Prenoit la Précaution de les prevenir; Il a été convenu expressément entre Sa Majesté Britannique et Sa Majesté Très Chrétienne, que le Nombre des Vaisseaux Anglois qui auront la Liberté d'aller aux dites Isles, et Lieux, restitués, à la France, sera limité, ainsi que le Nombre de Tonneaux de Chacun, Qu'ils iront en Lest, partiront dans un Terme fixé, et ne feront qu'un seul Voyage; Tous les Effets appartenants aux Anglois, devant être embarqués en même tems, il a été convenu en outre, que Sa Majesté Très Chrétienne fera donner les Passeports nécessaires pour les dits Vaisseaux, que pour plus grande sûreté il sera libre de mettre deux Commis ou Gardes françois, sur chacun des dits Vaisseaux qui seront visités dans les Atterages, et Ports des dites Isles, et Lieux restitués, à la France, et que les Marchandises qui s'y pourront trouver seront confisquées.

Article 9.

Le Roy Très Chrétien cède et garantit à Sa Majesté Britannique, en toute Propriété, les Isles de la Grenade, et des Grenadines, avec les mêmes Stipulations en Faveur des Habitans de cette Colonie, insérées dans l'Article Quatre pour Ceux du Canada; Et le Partage des Isles, appellées Neutres, est convenu et fixé de Manière, que Celles de St. Vincent, la Dominique, et Tobago, resteront, en toute Propriété, à la Grande Bretagne, et que Celle de Sainte Lucie sera remise à la France, pour en jouir pareillement en toute Propriété, Et Les Hautes Parties Contractants garantissent le Partage ainsi stipulé.

Article 10.

Sa Majesté Britannique restituera à la France l'Isle de Gorée dans l'Etat où Elle s'est trouvée quand Elle a été conquise; Et Sa Majesté Très Chrétienne cède, en toute Propriété, et garantit au Roy de la Grande Bretagne la Rivière de Senegal, avec les Forts et Comptoirs de St. Louis, de Podor, et de Galam, et avec tous les Droits et Dépendances de la dite Rivière de Senegal.

Article 11.

Dans les Indes Orientales, la Grande Bretagne restituera à la France, dans l'Etat où Ils sont Aujourd'hui, les différens Comptoirs que cette Couronne possedoit, tant sur la Côte de Choromandel, et d'Orixa, que sur celle de Malabar, ainsi que dans le Bénégale, au Commencement de l'Année 1749. Et Sa Majesté Très Chrétienne renonce à toute Pretension aux Acquisitions, qu'Elle avoit faites sur la Côte de Choromandel et d'Orixa, depuis le dit Commencement de l'Année 1749. Sa Majesté Très Chrétienne restituera de son Côté, tout ce qu'Elle pourroit avoir conquis sur la Grande Bretagne dans les Indes Orientales, pendant la présente Guerre, et fera restituer, nommément, Nattal, et Fapanoully, dans l'Isle de Sumatra; Elle s'engage de plus à ne point origer de Fortifications, et à ne point entretenir des Troupes dans aucune Partie des Etats de Subah de Benegale.—Et Afin de conserver la Paix future sur la Côte de Choromandel et d'Orixa, les Anglois et les François reconnoitront Mahomet Ally Khan pour legitime Nabob du Carnate, et Salabat Jing pour lègitime Subah du Décan; et les Deux Parties renonceront à toute Demande, ou Prétension de Satisfaction qu'elles pourroient former à la charge l'une de l'autre, ou à Celle de leurs Alliés Indiens, pour les Déprédations, ou Dégats, commis, soit d'un Côté, soit de l'Autre, pendant la Guerre.

Article 12.

L'Isle de Minorque sera restituée à Sa Majesté Britannique, ainsi que le Fort St. Philippe, dans le même Etat où Ils se sont

trouvés lorsque la Conquête en a été faite par les Armes du
Roy Très Chrétien ; et avec l'Artillerie qui y étoit, lors de
la Prise de la dite Isle, et du dit Fort.

Article 13.

La Ville, et le Port de Dunkerque seront mis dans l'Etat,
fixé par le dernier Traité d'Aix la Chapelle, et par les Traités
antérieurs. La Cunette sera détruite immediatement après
l'Echange des Ratifications du présent Traité, ainsi que les
Forts et Batteries qui défendent l'Entrée, du Côté de la Mer,
et il sera pourvu, en même Tems, à la Salubrité de l'Air, et à
la Santé des Habitans, par quelque autre Moyen, à la Satisfaction du Roy de la Grande Bretagne.

Article 14.

La France restituera tous les Païs appartenans à l'Electorat
d'Hanovre, au Landgrave de Hesse, au Duc de Brunswick, et
au Comte de la Lippe Buckebourg, qui se trouvent, ou se
trouveront, occupés par les Armes de Sa Majesté Très Chrétienne, Les Places de ces differens Païs seront rendues dans
le même Etat où Elles étoient quand la conquête en a été faite
par les Armes Françoises ; Et les Pièces d'Artillerie qui auront
été transportées ailleurs, seront remplacées par le même
Nombre, de même Calibre, Poids, et Metal.

Article 15.

En cas que les Stipulations contenues dans l'Article 13 des
Préliminaires ne fussent pas accomplies lors de la Signature du
présent Traité, tant par rapport aux Evacuations à faire, par
les Armées de la France, des Places de Cleves, de Wesel, de
Gueldres, et de tous les Pays appartenans au Roy de Prusse,
que par rapport aux Evacuations à faire par les Armées Britannique et Françoise des Pays qu'elles occupent en Westphalie,
Basse Saxe, sur le Bas Rhin, Le Haut Rhin, et dans tout l'Empire ; Et à la Retraite des Troupes dans les Etats de leurs

Souverains respectifs, Leurs Majestés Britannique et Très Chrétienne promettent de procéder de bonne Foy, avec toute la Promptitude, que le Cas pourra permettre, aux dites Evacuations dont Ils stipulent l'Accomplissement parfait avant le 15 de Mars prochain, ou plutôt si faire se peut. Et leurs Majestés Britannique et Très Chrétienne s'engagent de plus, et se promettent, de ne fournir aucun Secours, dans aucun Genre, à leurs Alliés respectifs, qui resteront engagés dans la Guerre d'allemagne.

Article 16.

La Division des Prises faites en Tems de Paix, par les Sujets de la Grande Bretagne, sur les Espagnols, sera remise aux Cours de Justice et de l'Amirauté de la Grande Bretagne, conformément aux Règles établies parmi toutes les Nations, de sorte que la Validité des dites Prises entre les Nations Britannique et Espagnole, sera decidée et jugée, selon le Droit des Gens, et selon les Traités dans les Cours de Justice de la Nation qui aura fait la Capture.

Article 17.

Sa Majesté Britannique fera démolir toutes les Fortifications que Les Sujets pourront avoir érigées dans la Baye de Honduras, et autres Lieux du Territoire de l'Espagne, dans cette Partie du Monde, Quatre Mois après la Ratification du présent Traité; Et Sa Majesté Catholique ne permettra point que les Sujets de Sa Majesté Britannique ou leurs Ouvriers, soient inquiétés, ou molestés, sous aucun Prétexte que ce soit, dans les dits Lieux; dans leur Occupation de couper, charger, et transporter, le Bois de Teinture ou de Campêche; Et pour cet Effet, Ils pourront batir sans Empéchement, et occuper sans Interruption, les Maisons et les Magazins qui sont nécessaires pour Eux, pour leurs Familles, et pour leurs Effets; Et sa Majesté Catholique leur assure par cet Article, l'entière Jouissance de ces Avantages, et Facultés, sur les Côtes, et Territoires Espagnols, comme il est stipulé ci-dessus, immédiatement après la Ratification du présent Traité.

Article 18.

Sa Majesté Catholique se désiste, tant pour Elle, que pour Ses Successeurs, de toute Prétension qu'Elle peut avoir formée en Faveur des Guipuscoans, et autres de Ses Sujets, au Droit de pêcher aux Environs de l'Isle de Terre Neuve.

Article 19.

Le Roy de la Grande Bretagne restituera à l'Espagne tout le Térritoire qu'il a conquis dans l'Isle de Cuba, avec la Place de la Havane; Et cette Place, aussi bien que toutes les autres Places de la dite Isle, seront rendues dans le même Etat où Elles étoient quand Elles ont été conquises par les Armes de Sa Majesté Britannique; bien entendu, que les Sujets de Sa Majesté Britannique, qui se seroient etablis, ou ceux qui auroient quelques Affaires de Commerce à régler dans la dite Isle, restituée à l'Espagne, par le présent Traité, auront la Libérté de vendre leurs Terres et leurs Biens, de régler leurs Affaires, de recouvrer leurs Dettes, et de transporter leurs Effets, ainsi que leurs Personnes, à bord des Vaisseaux qu'il leur sera permis de faire venir à la dite Isle, restituée comme dessus, et qui ne serviront qu'a cet Usage seulement, sans être gênés à Cause de leur Religion, ou sous quelque autre Prétexte que ce puisse être, hors Celui de Dettes, ou de Procès Criminels; Et pour cet Effet le terme de Dix huit Mois est accordé aux Sujets de Sa Majesté Britannique à compter de Jour de l'Echange des Ratifications du présent Traité. Mais, comme la Libérté, accordée aux Sujets de Sa Majesté Britannique, de transporter leurs Personnes, et leurs Effets, sur des Vaisseaux de leur Nation, pourroit être sujette à des Abus, si l'on ne prenoit la Précaution de les prévenir; Il a été convenu expressément entre Sa Majesté Britannique, et Sa Majesté Catholique, que le Nombre des Vaisseaux Anglois qui auront la Libérté d'aller à la dite Isle, restituée à l'Espagne, sera limité, ainsi que le Nombre de Tonneaux de Chacun; Qu'ils iront en lest; partiront dans un Terme fixé, et ne feront qu'un seul Voyage; Tous les Effets appartenans aux Anglois, devant être embarqués en même Tems; Il a été

convenu en outre, que Sa Majesté Catholique fera donner les
Passeports nécessaires pour les dits Vaisseaux; Que pour plus
grande Sûreté, il sera libre de mettre Deux Commis ou
Gardes Espagnols, sur chacun des dits Vaisseaux, qui seront
visités dans les Attérages et Ports de la dite Isle restituée à
l'Espagne, et que les Marchandises, qui s'y pourront trouver,
seront confisquées.

Article 20.

En Conséquence de la Restitution stipulée dans l'Article
précédent, Sa Majesté Catholique cède et garantit, en toute
Propriété, à Sa Majesté Britannique, la Floride, avec le Fort
de St. Augustin, et la Baye de Pensacola, ainsi que tout ce que
l'Espagne possède sur le Continent de l'Amerique Septen-
trionale, à l'Est, ou au Sud Est, du Fleuve Mississippi, et
généralement tout ce qui dépend des dits Païs, et Terres, avec
la Souveraineté, Propriété, Possession, et tous Droits acquis
par Traités, ou autrement, que le Roy Catholique, et la Couronne d'Espagne, ont eus jusqu'à présent sur les dits Païs,
Terres, Lieux, et Leurs Habitans, ainsi que le Roy Catholique
cède, et transporte, le tout au dit Roy, et à la Couronne de
la Grande Bretagne, et cela, de la Manière, et de la Forme la
plus ample; Sa Majesté Britannique convient de Son Côté
d'accorder aux Habitans des Pays ci-déssus cédés, la Liberté de
la Réligion Catholique; En conséquence, Elle donnera les
Ordres les plus exprès, et les plus effectifs, pourque ses nouveaux Sujets Catholiques Romains puissent professer le Culte
de leur Réligion, selon le Rit de l'Eglise Romaine, en tant que
le permettent les Lois de la Grande Bretagne; Sa Majesté
Britannique convient en outre, que les Habitans Espagnols,
ou autres, qui auroient été Sujets du Roy Catholique dans les
dits Pays, pourront se retirer en toute Sûreté et Liberté,
où bon leur semblera, et pourront vendre leurs Biens, pourvû
que ce soit à des Sujets de Sa Majesté Britannique, et transporter leurs Effets, ainsi que leurs Personnes, sans être gênés
dans leur Emigration, sous quelque Prétexte que ce puisse être,
hors celui de Dettes, ou de procès criminels; le Terme limité

pour cette Emigration étant fixé à l'Espace de Dix huit Mois,
à compter du Jour de l'Echange des Ratifications du présent
Traité. Il est de plus stipulé que Sa Majesté Catholique aura
la Faculté de faire transporter tous les Effets qui peuvent Lui
appartenir soit Artillerie, ou autres.

Article 21.

Les Troupes Espagnoles, et Françoises, évacueront tous les
térritories, Campagnes, Villes, Places, et Châteaux de Sa
Majesté très Fidéle en Europe, sans reserve aucune qui pour-
ront avoir été conquis par les Armées d'Espagne et de France,
et les rendront dans le même Etat où Ils étoient quand la
Conquête en a été faite, et avec la même Artillerie, et les
Munitions de Guerre qu'on y a trouvées. Et à l'egard des
Colonies Portugaises en Amérique, Afrique, ou dans les Indes
Orientales, s'il étoit arrivé quelque Changement, toutes
Choses seront remises sur le même Pied où Elles étoient, et
en Conformité des Traités précédens qui subsistoient entre
les Cours, d'Espagne, de France, et de Portugal, avant la
présente Guerre.

Article 22.

Tous les Papiers, Lettres, Documens, et Archives, qui se
sont trouvés dans les Pays, Terres, Villes, et Places qui sont
restitués, et ceux appartenans aux Païs cédés, seront délivrés,
ou fournis respectivement, et de bonne Foy, dans le même
Tems, s'il est possible, de la Prise de Possession, ou au plus
tard, Quarte Mois après l'Echange des Ratifications du présent
Traité, en quelques Lieux que les dits Papiers, ou Documens,
puissent se trouver.

Article 23.

Tous les Païs et Territoires qui pourroient avoir été conquis,
dans quelque Partie du Monde que ce soit, par les Armes de
Leurs Majestés Britannique et Très Fidéle, ainsi que par celles
de Leurs Majestés Catholique et Très Chrétienne, qui ne sont
pas compris dans le present Traitée, ni à Titre de Cessions,

ni à Titre de Restitutions, seront rendus sans Difficulté, et
sans éxiger de Compensation.

Article 24.

Comme il est nécessaire de désigner une Epoque fixe pour
les Restitutions, et les Evacuations, à faire par chacune des
Hautes Parties Contractantes; Il est convenu que les troupes
Britanniques et Françoises, completteront avant le 15 de
Mars prochain, tout ce qui restera à éxécuter des articles 12
et 13 des Préliminaires signés le Troisième Jour de Novembre
passé, par rapport à l'Evacuation à faire dans l'Empire ou
ailleurs. L'Isle de Belleisle sera évacuée Six Semaines après
l'Echange des Ratifications du présent Traité, ou plutôt si
faire se peut—La Guadeloupe, La Désirade, Marie Galante, la
Martinique, et Ste. Lucie, trois Mois après l'Echange des
Ratifications du présent Traité, ou plutôt si faire se peut.—
La Grande Bretagne entrera pareillement au bout de Trois Mois
après l'Echange des Ratifications du présent Traité, ou plutôt
si faire se peut, en Possession de la Rivière, et du Port de la
Mobile, et de tout ce qui doit former les Limites du Territoire de la Grande Bretagne, du Côté du Fleuve de Mississippi,
telles qu'Elles sont specifiées dans l'Article 7—L'Isle de Gorée
sera évacuée par la Grande Bretagne, Trois Mois après l'Echange des Ratifications du présent traité, et l'Isle de Minorque,
par la France, à la même Epoque, ou plutôt si faire se peut;
et, selon les Conditions de l'Article 6. La France entrera, de
même, en Possession des Isles de St. Pierre, et de Miquelon,
au Bout de Trois Mois après l'Echange des Ratifications du
présent Traité—Les Comptoirs aux Indes Orientales seront
rendus Six Mois après l'Echange des Ratifications du présent
Traité, ou plutôt si faire se peut.—La Place de la Havane avec
tout ce qui a été conquis dans l'Isle de Cuba, sera restituée
Trois Mois après l'Echange des Ratifications du présent
Traité, ou plutôt si faire se peut; Et, en même tems, la Grande
Bretagne entrera en Possession du Païs cédé par l'Espagne
selon l'Article Vingt.—Toutes les Places et Païs de Sa Majesté
très Fidéle, en Europe, seront restitués immédiatement après

l'Echange des Ratifications du présent Traité; Et les Colonies
Portugaises, qui pourront avoir été conquises, seront resti-
tuées dans l'Espace de Trois Mois dans les Indes Occidentales,
et de Six Mois dans les Indes Orientales, après l'Echange des
Ratifications du présent Traité, ou plutôt si faire se peut.
Toutes les Places dont la Restitution est stipuleé ci-dessus,
seront rendues avec l'Artillerie, et les Munitions qui s'y
sont trouvées lors de la Conquête—En Conséquence, de quoi,
les Ordres nécessaires seront envoyés par chacune des Hautes
Parties Contractantes, avec les Passeports réciproques pour
les Vaisseaux qui les porteront, immédiatement après l'Echange
des Ratifications du présent Traité.

Article 25.

Sa Majesté Britannique, en Sa Qualité d'Electeur de Bruns-
wick, Lunebourg, tant pour Lui, que pour ses Héritiers et
Successeurs, et tous les Etats et possessions, de Sa dite
Majesté en Allemagne, sont compris, et garantis par le présent
Traité de Paix.

Article 26.

Leurs Sacrées Majestés Britannique, Catholique, Très
Chrétienne, et Très Fidéle, promettent d'obsérver sincèrement, et de bonne Foy, tous les Article, contenus et établis,
dans le présent Traité; et Elles ne souffriront pas qu'il y soit
fait de Contravention directe ou indirecte, par Leurs Sujets
respectifs, et les susdites Hautes Parties Contractantes Se
garantissent généralement, et réciproquement, toutes les
Stipulations du présent Traité.

Article 27.

Les Ratifications solemnelles du présent Traité expediées en
bonne et due Forme, seront échangées en cette Ville de Paris,
entre les Hautes Parties Contractantes, dans l'Espace d'un
Mois ou plutôt s'il est possible, à compter du Jour de la
Signature du présent Traité.

En Foy de quoi, Nous Soussignés leurs Ambassadeurs

Extraordinaires et Ministres Plénipotentiaires, avons signés, de Notre Main,—en Leurs Nom, et en Vertu de Nos Plenipouvoirs, le présent Traité Définitif, et y avons fait apposer le Cachet de nos Armes.

Fait à Paris le Dix de Fevrier Mil Sept Cent Soixante-Trois. Bedford, C.P.S.—El Marquis de Grimaldi—Choiseul, Duc de Praslin.

Articles Separés.

I.

Quelques uns des Titres, employés par les Puissances Contractantes, soit dans les Pleinpouvoirs, et autres Actes, pendant le Cours de la Négociation, soit dans le Préambule du présent Traité, n'étant pas généralement reconnus, il a été convenu, qu'il ne pourroit jamais en resulter aucun préjudice pour aucune des dites Parties Contractantes, et que les Titres, pris ou omis, de part et d'autre à l'Occasion de la dite Négociation, et du présent Traité ne pourront être cités, ni tirés à Conséquence.

2.

Il a été convenu et arrêté, que la Langue Françoise, employée dans tous les Exemplaires du présent Traité, ne formera point un Exemple, qui puisse être allégué ni tiré à conséquence, ni porter préjudice, en aucune manière, à aucune des Puissances Contractantes; Et que l'on se conformera à l'avenir, à ce qui à été observé, et doit être observé, à l'égard de la part, des Puissances, qui sont en usage, et en Possession de donner, et de recevoir, des Exemplaires de semblables Traités, en une autre Langue que la Françoise—Le présent Traité ne laissant pas d'avoir la même Force et Vertu, que si le susdit usage y avoit été observé.

3.

Quoique le Roy de Portugal n'ait pas signé le présent Traité définitif, Leurs Majestés Britannique, Catholique et Très

Chrétienne reconnoissent néanmoins, que Sa Majesté Très Fidéle y est formellement comprise comme Partie Contractante, et comme si elle avoit expressément signé le dit Traité; En Conséquence Leurs Majestés Britannique, Catholique et Très Chrétienne s'engagent respectivement et conjointement, avec Sa Majesté Très Fidéle de la façon la plus éxpresse et la plus Obligatoire, à l'éxécution de toutes et de chacune, des clauses, contenues dans le dit Traité, moyennant son Acte d'Accession.

Les présens Articles séparés auront la même Force, que s'ils étoient insérés dans le Traité.

En foy de quoi nous Soussignés Ambassadeurs Extraordinaires et Ministres Plénipotentiaires de Leurs Majestés Britannique, Catholique, et Très Chrétienne, avons signé les présent Articles séparés, et y avons fait apposer le Cachet de Nos Armes.

Fait à Paris ce Dix de Fevrier Mil sept cent soixante et trois. Bedford C.P.S.—El marquis de Grimaldi—Choiseul, Duc de Praslin.

"LE CONSEIL D'ETAT" or
"LE CONSEIL D'EN HAUT"

The attention of the author of this book was drawn to the importance of finding out the position of the French foreign minister with regard to the other French ministers and members of the French Council dealing with foreign affairs by the following considerations (a) The various views of the members of St. James and their differences as regards the policy of peace during the Stanley-Bussy Negotiations in 1761: (b) The opposition with which Pitt was confronted throughout that stage of the negotiations: (c) The secrecy which surrounded the beginning of the negotiations in England in 1762: (d) The fact that even when the negotiations for peace between England and France were officially declared, all members of the English cabinet were not equally acquainted with the different details of the negotiations. For this purpose, it was of great importance to find the minutes of the discussions of the French Council concerned with foreign affairs: "Conseil d'en haut". A search in the "Archives Nationales" for these minutes was fruitless, not a single "procés verbal" could be traced. It seemed that this important Council did not keep any minutes. This supposition is confirmed by a statement made in the *Inventaire Sommaire et Tableau Méthodique des Fonds conservés aux Archives Nationales*, namely that that Council "N'avait point d'archives",[1] and by a declaration made by an archivist at the "Quai d'Orsay" where a further search was made for the same purpose. He said that the French Cabinet even nowadays does not keep any minutes of discussions concerning foreign affairs.

It was only in an indirect way that a research student could find out anything about what happened in some of the important meetings of that "Conseil d'en haut". At the "Quai d'-Orsay" among the letters of the "Correspondance Politique",

[1] p.33.

one could trace some few of these meetings: for instance Duke of Choiseul's memoir of September 6th 1761,[1] which he had presented to the Council in order to defend his policy of alliance with Spain and the rupture of the negotiations of peace with England. Volume 570, "Mémoires et Documents, France et Divers Etats",[2] is also of some help, throwing light on some decisions of "Conseil d'en haut" in regard to the negotiations of 1761. Practically nothing is known about the role played by this Council in the negotiations of 1762. At the end of July, the Count of Choiseul wrote to Count of Chatelet,[3] complaining of the fact that the Court of Vienna, in spite of her promise, had already informed Peter III of Russia about the negotiations between France and England; and informing him that the French government was so so secretive that till then: "le Conseil du Roy n'en a pas eu connoissance".[4] Whether this statement is true one could not tell, for it might have just been stated in order to magnify the wrong of the Court of Vienna.

It is worth noting that the "Conseil d'Etat" which concerns us here, was the most important of the five councils[5] which existed in France at the close of the reign of Louis XV. This council was successively called:

"*grand* conseil", "conseil *secret*", "conseil *étroit*", "conseil *du Roi*", "Conseil *privé*", "conseil de *cabinet*", "conseil *d'en haut*", "conseil *d'Etat*".

The last two terms were the more frequently used at that time.[6]

As to its members G. Dejardins stated that:

"En 1762 les secrétaires d'Etat en font partie mais non le contrôleur général. Les autres ministres d'Etat sont le maréchal prince de Soublise, pair de France; le maréchal Comte d'Estrée et le marquis de Puysieulx".

[1] See Chapter III, p. 98.

[2] A.E., M.D., France et Divers Etats, 570.

[3] The French Ambassador in Vienna at that time.

[4] A.E., C.P., Autriche, 290, f.170r, Count of Choiseul to Chatelet, July 31st 1762.

[5] The other four were: "celle des dépêches ou de l'intérieur, celle des finances, celle du commerce et celle de la justice administrative," Carré, 59.

[6] Boislisle, 64.

Dejardins resumed his description of the council by stating its functions:

> "C'était avec ses sept personnes que le roi délibérait sur les grandes affaires de l'Etat, la politique intérieure et extérieure, la guerre et la paix".[1]

However, the "secrétaires d'Etat" were not, as a rule, allowed to take part in these important meetings unless they had proved their capabilities and discretion.[2]

Explaining in more details the functions of that council, Boislisle quoting Spanheim,[3] made the following statement which indicates its importance:

> "C'est dans ce conseil du Ministère que se traitent toutes les grandes affaires de l'Etat, tant de paix que guerre; que les ministres qui y entrent y font rapport de celles de leur département particulier; qu'on lit les dépêches des ministres du Roi dans les cours étrangères, les réponses qu'on y fait, et les instructions qu'on leur donne, qu'on y délibère sur les traités, les alliances et les intérêts de la couronne avec les puissances étrangères; enfin qu'on y propose et qu'on y resout tout ce qui regarde le gouvernement et qui peut être de quelque importance pour le Roi, pour la Cour, pour l'Etat, en un mot, pour le dedans et pour le dehors du Royaume".[4]

In spite of the importance of the subjects deliberated, it is worth nothing that it had practically no real authority as it was the King who had the last word.

> "Le Conseil d'en haut délibérait sur les affaires politiques, principalement sur les affaires extérieures; il donnait des avis au Roi, qui seul décidait".[5]

During the negotiations for peace it was first the Duke of Choiseul alone, and later on with his cousin, the Count of Choiseul, who directed the foreign policy of France at that time. But, as already indicated in relating the negotiations, the Duke of Choiseul was confronted with a certain opposition holding different views on the foreign policy of France; lack of information on this subject, namely the minutes of the meetings, makes further explanations and definite statements on this subject impossible.

---

[1] Desjardins, 23-24.   [2] Boislisle, 73.

[3] Author of *Relations de la Cour de France en 1690*, 159; see also Carré, 60.

[4] Boislisle, 68-69.

[5] *Inventaire Sommaire et Tableau Methodique des Fonds conservés aux Archives Nationales*, 33.

FERNÀN NÙÑEZ AND CHARLES III

It is of importance to trace the origin of the mistakes which historians, Spanish, English, and French have generally committed in their assessment of the policy of Charles III. The Spanish historians of this reign set the tone. There are three histories: two of which were published in the second half of the 19th century, the third one at the beginning of the 20th. It appears strange that of these the one which most likely misled the other historians, and influenced their judgments, was the last to be published, namely, *La Vida de Carlos III*, by Fernàn Nùñez (edited by A Morel Fatio and A. Paz y Melia in Madrid, 1898). The explanation of this is quite easy. This biography was written by a contemporary, and was finished in 1790. It is also worth noting that this biography in a manuscript form has been in the British Museum since 1835.[1] The title of this manuscript has suffered some alterations, till finally, in 1791 its title was fixed by Nùñez as follows: *Compendio Historico de La Vida de Carlos III, Rey de Espane y de las Indias.*[2] This manuscript or a copy of it must have been seen by Ferrer del Rio, who is very much influenced by Fernàn Nùñez's biography. In his turn, Ferrer del Rio influenced French and English historians by his own conclusions. These historians were therefore indirectly influenced by the *Vida de Carlos III* of Fernàn Nùñez.

Why did Fernàn Nùñez free Charles from all responsibility for what he regarded as a disastrous foreign policy? An outline of his life gives us the answer. Fernàn Nùñez owed much to Charles III and was deeply grateful for the favours he had received. He was educated at the expense of Ferdinand IV in the "Seminario de Nobles" (a college for preparing children of the poor nobility to serve the King). He joined the Royal

[1] B.M., Add. MSS, 9943. This manuscript together with other Spanish documents was acquired from a person called M. O. Rich; see Morel Fatio, *Etudes sur l'Espagne*, 2 ieme Serie, 347.

[2] *Ibid.*, 347.

Guards as a cadet on March 18, 1752, and obtained promotion, crosses and distinctions from King Ferdinand and his Queen during his military career. Later he travelled in Bavaria, but was back in Madrid in 1768. After a short stay at Cordoba, he spent the period from 1769-1771 partly with the Court in Madrid and in Aranjuez, and partly with his unit in Valencia and Carthage. In 1772, he went to Andalusia and soon afterwards started his travels in Italy, France, Germany. In 1775 he had accompanied O'Reilly's expedition against Algiers.[1] In the following year, as a reward for his services in Algeria, Charles III promoted him to the rank of "Mariscal de Campo". A month later, he was appointed Lord of the Bed-Chamber. On December 7th of the same year, Charles gave him the Grand Cross of St. Charles. In 1778, Fernàn Nùñez entered on a diplomatic career, the King of Spain considered him the appropriate person to fill the post of Ambassador to Portugal. Fernàn Nùñez did not seem pleased with this appointment when he referred to it in a letter to his friend the German Prince Salm Salm. After the signature of the treaty of peace of 1783, Charles III conferred on him the Golden Fleece. In 1787 he was appointed ambassador in Paris, where he stayed till 1791. He visited Brussels in the same year. He also stayed for a short period in Switzerland in 1794. In February of the following year he went to Rome in order to receive the benediction of the Pope. On February 23rd, soon after his arrival in Madrid, he died. He was 52 years and seven months old.[2]

From this short survey of the life of Fernàn Nùñez, and if we bear in mind how greatly he was indebted to Charles III for his worldly success, it is not hard to see the reason why he was anxious to represent the nobility of his benefactor's character and why he chose to attribute to his generous impulses his response to the appeals of Louis XV. Whilst he was not blind to the real causes of the disasters which befell Spain in her war against England, he allowed his judgment to be modified by his own personal sense of gratitude.

[1] For more details on this expedition see Rousseau, 11, 86-92.

[2] For more details on the History of Fernàn-Nùñez, see Nùñez, II, 331-309 ("Biografia del Conde de Fernàn-Nùñez", written by A. Morel-Fatio and A. Paz y Mélia).

GRIMALDI'S INSTRUCTIONS IN JANUARY 1761

The accession of Charles III to the throne of Spain in August, 1759, was soon followed by a momentous change in Spanish foreign policy. Under Ferdinand VI Spain had refused to join in the Seven Years War as the ally of either France or England, although her alliance had been desired by France and had also, in the initial stages of the war, been sought by England. Much has been written on the origins of the Family Compact, and Charles III has often been represented as a puppet whose movements were controlled by the Duke of Choiseul. Spanish historians have been especially inclined to adopt this view. In their desire to explain why Charles involved his country in a disastrous war, they have argued that his original policy was to maintain Spain's neutrality, but that his generous nature and loyalty and affection to the head of the House of Bourbon were exploited by Choiseul in order to bring her into the war. As subsidiary causes for Charles's intervention they have assigned his desire to expel the English from their illegal settlements in Honduras and his resentment at the insult offered him by Commodore Martin in 1742.[1] Sentiments such as these, however, seldom play a great part in the formation of foreign policy.

Early in 1760 the English Envoy in Madrid noted that Charles "means solely to pursue the Interests of the Throne on which He is placed".[2]

[1] See Nûñez, 1, 160-161; Ferrer del Rio, 1, 281-288; Collado, 11, 109-111, 166-167. Although the last Spanish historian gives weight to some of the subsidiary causes for the intervention of Charles III, yet he was aware that the alliance with France was to stop the progress of the British in America and in Europe; Jobez, V, 540: this historian goes as far as to accuse Charles III of sacrificing his own country's interests to those of the Duke of Choiseul; Ruville, II, 279, also attached a great deal of importance to Charles's bourbonism and to his resentment of the insult of 1742; See also Soulange-Bodin, 136; Corbett, II, 185-186, was of opinion that Grimaldi was ahead of his Court and that his arguments and dexterity soon brought Charles up to the point of a defensive alliance, though he hesitated about making it offensive.

[2] P.R.O., G.D., 12, Bristol to Pitt, February 11th, 1760.

In fact at this time support of France appeared to be an obvious Spanish interest. England's success in the war seemed to foretell the destruction of the French Colonial empire and to indicate that the Spanish empire might soon be threatened by English aggression.[1] The policy adopted by Charles at this critical moment and the motives that inspired it are largely revealed in the instructions given to the Marquis of Grimaldi on his appointment as ambassador to the Court of Versailles. They show that Charles was desirous of bringing about an offensive and defensive alliance between France and Spain because he held that Spain needed such an alliance.

Grimaldi's instructions are transcribed below from the photostat of a draft thereof at Simancas. The instructions cover 27 folios of almost foolscap size, and are written only on one side or column of the page, generally the one on the right hand side up to folios 20 and 21, where the indicated passage in the transcription was cancelled, and in its place other matter was inserted in the margin of these folios. The writing continues on the left column of the two following folios, *viz.* 22 and 23. On folio 24, both columns are used. The remaining folios revert to the original order of using the right hand column. In my transcript all abbreviations save V.E. (Vuestra Excelencia) and S.M. (Su Majestad) have been expanded.

INSTRUCCIONES 1761

Instruccion que se dió en 14 de Enero
al Marquès de Grimaldi para la Embajada à Paris

Estado. Leg 3457 no. 38
Leg - 19

(f.2)   Los deseos que hà manifestado al Rey Don Jaime Masones de Lima, su Embaxador extraordinario al Rey Christianisimo su Primo, de venir á besar su Real,

---

[1] For the policy of Charles III, see chapter II.

(f.2) mano, y lograr la dicha de conocer personalmente á su Dueño, juntamente con otras miras de S. M. para emplearle en España con no menos utilidad de su servicio que en Francia, le han movido a darle Succesor

(f.3) en aquella Embajada, y ha recaido / su eleccion en V. E. pues sus circunstancias y las experiencias que tiene de sus talentos, actividad y Zelo no le dejan dudar que ningun otro Sujeto sea mas à proposito para ese desempeño.

Conviene al Real servicio tanto que Don Jaime Masones venga luego a esta Corte como que V. E. se traslade sin perdida de tiempo á la de Paris. Insinuo al

(f.4) primero los motivos de lo / que le toca, y explicaré á V. E. los de lo que le pertenece.

Salio V. E. de esta Corte hace nuebe o diez meses bien instruido de nuestro systhema con lo de Francia e Inglaterra, pues devio imponersele perfectamente de el para su govierno en la negociacion de Paz entre dichas dos Potencias que se supuso iba à entablarse, y que no tubo efecto. Aora referiré à V. E. el estado en que despues aca nos hemos puesto con una y otra. /

(f.5) Dejó V. E. á su paso por Paris pendiente aquella Corte de las tales quales esperanzas que le sugeria neustra mision del Conde de Fuentes á Londres de que abrazando qualquier especie de entrar en negociacion que le diesse el Ministerio Ingles, pudiesse entablarse la de la paz, por su mediacion, ō la de algun Emisario frances que se le permitio ofreciesse iria a Londres en caso necessario; y sabe V. E. lo que mando el Rey al

(f.6) Conde de Fuentes en este particular / reducido à que coadyubasse à los deseos de los franceses, pero sin comprometer en nada à S. M. Los Ingleses no han buscado al Conde de Fuentes mas que para discurrir generalmente, y la mayor confianza que le han hecho ha sido la de que huviessen entrado en la negociacion particular con la Francia que empezo à nacer en La Haya sino se lo huviesse estorbado el Rey de Prusia; por lo que, siguiendo sus ordenes de no ofrecerse, mostrando

(f.7) / gana de la mediacion, sino de admitirla en ciertos
terminos si la solicitassen, se hà estado á la capa, y hà
seguido mui bien aunque sin fruto nuestros propios
negocios. Desaparecida para los franceses la luz de
negociacion que creyeron ver en la Haya, y no des-
cubriendo la que esperaban en Londres por medio del
Conde de Fuentes, dejaron de hablarnos de una y otra,
y han dedicado todos sus esfuerzos para persuadir al
(f.8) Rey / que acaba de tomar parte en su Querella, valien-
dose de la razon, (tantas vezes repetida y tantomas
fortificada con la Conquista del Canada que han hecho
los Ingleses en el anterior verano), de que su engrandecimiento en America expone para lo futuro á inmi-
nente riesgo nuestras posessiones. Ha hallado S. M.
por conveniente no zeder á sus activos oficios ni exaspe-
rarles no obstante, antes bien dejandoles entender que
mientras no remediasse el abandono en que ha encon-
trado sus Plazas de la America, Su marina y tropas, les
(f.9) seria inutil / Aliado, y solo serviria de ofrecer nuestros
triunfos al Enemigo con mayor campo para su ambicion.
Havra mes y medio que estrecharon tanto sus oficios
como que tubo orden este Ministro d 'Ossun de decir
á S.M. que se sirviesse explicar positivamente si era su
voluntad entrar en la guerra aora, ô que tiempo necesi-
taba para prevenirse y empezarla en su union y auxilo,
pues si S. M. no les daba alguna prenda, tomarian por
si el partido de buscar á qualquier precio la paz que /
(f.10) solos les era imposible sostener mas tiempo la guerra
sin nuebas razones. S. M. respondio desengañandoles
de que se determinasse desde luego a la guerra y tampoco
empeñando su palabra para tiempo determinado. No
por esso se han mostrado ofendidos, pero si nos han
dicho, que no teniendo que esperar de la España, van à
ver como hacer Su Paz, y salir del Pantano lo menos
maltratados que les sea possible. Pudiera aver exagera-
(f.11) cion en el extremo / conque nos dicen van a entregarse a
este partido; pero convinada la necesidad de la Paz que
tiene la Francia con los resortes que obran en su Minis-

(f.11) terio, es de creer que esta vez nos han hablado con sinceridad. Esta es nuestra situacion politica en el momento con la Corte de Paris, y solo devo añadir á V. E. para que no ignore ni aun nuestras presunciones, que aunque aparece desengañada de embolvernos en su Guerra, no lo esta tanto como demuestra, pues ligera-

(f.12) mente atribuyen / aquellos Ministros á una criminal par-cialidad mia la Resistencia del Rey á sus instancias, y la creen poco durable con tan debiles cimientos, como lo seria realmente si no errassen en el supuesto. Son, al contrario, tan solidos, que estriban en la recta Balanza con que pesa la religion de S. M. y su amor a los vasallos las causas que le deven obligar ō no á meterlos en los orrores de una guerra, y gracias al Altissimo que le ha

(f.13) hecho arvitro / le ha dotado de talentos los mas señala-dos para no dejarse arrastrar de las pasiones de sus Ministros, ni de las persuasiones de los Extranos, y tomar por si el partido mas acertado.

El estado á que hemos llegado con la Corte Londres es mas lastimoso porque su injusticia, è insolencia, precisa casi á que caiga aquella Balanza que tiene el Rey en su mano del lado á que no han podido reducirla

(f.14) las sugestiones de los franceses. / Por la confianza que se merece tan zeloso servidor del Rey como V. E. aun mas que por la necesidad supo V. E. las Instrucciones que llevó Conde de Fuentes à Londres, para solicitar y son-seguir de aquella Corte que satisfaciesse à S. M. prin-cipalmente sobre tres capitales quejas: una, los agravios hechos à la Bandera Española durante la presente Guerra; otra, la libre navegacion de los Españoles a la pesca de vacallao en Terranova, que sin razon le impiden los

(f.15) Ingleses, / y otra (la mas exempcial), La evacuacion de los Establecimientos con Fuertes y sin ellos que han hecho furtibamente en nuestras Costas de Honduras. Pues las resultas han sido responder a las fundadas Memorias que el Conde de Fuentes a dado que los insultos de la Bandera no son consentidos, y que se procuraran evitar; pero en la restitucion de los Navios

(f.15) Españoles injustamente apresados, y en el castigo de los
Delincuentes, han mostrado poco mas de actividad que
(f.16) la anterior en la justicia: que no pueden / permitirnos el
derecho de la pesca por que seria la ruina del principal
ramo de su navegacion y comercio, y que se le tenemos
cedido por lo mismo que no le hemos disfrutado sin
intermission, como argumento aunque tan debil se les
ha rebatido provando lo contrario que supone; y que
no evacuaran los Establecimientos de Honduras, si el
Rey no se oblige primero à subministrarles el Palo de
tinte, que necesitan; proposicion tan insolente como
(f.17) lo fuera que exigiesen / una obligacion de darles para sus
fabricas la Lana de nuestros Carneros que les damos sin
ella como objeto de Comercio reciproco; y tanto mas
intolerable quanto necesitando nosotros mas el vacallao
que no nace en sus Dominios sino en los de todos
que son los mares, ni aun ir á buscarlo permitten.
El Conde de Fuentes ha podido con las razones que el
Rey le ha subministrado convencer al Ministro Ingles de
(f.18) la Justicia clara que le asiste en estos dos / puntos, del
vacallao, y Establecimientos de Honduras sin dejarles
que explicar; y lo que ha sacado por ultimo es, que á
la Memoira que dio por escrito sobre el primero le
respondieran si se quiere, mas con una negativa absoluta,
y que à lo que igualmente presento sobre el ultimo no
respondan formalmente por que no pudiendo hacerlo à
nuestra satisfaccion serviria solo de agriarnos y precipitar
lo que debe, segun ellos, ser assumpto de negociacion
(f.19) sempiterna, pues hace tantos años que subsiste sin / fruto,
como sucedera por mas que alargen, sentando ellos por
Preliminar que pues necesitan el Palo se lo hemos de
dejar tomar ô dar, y sino que no han de soltar la Pesca
de los Establecimientos.

El ultimo Correo del Conde de Fuentes es el que há
trahido al Rey el ultimo desengaño que va explicado, y
es el que sino le ha determinado a una rotura con
(f.20) Inglaterra hasta aora le ha hecho balanzear / con la duda
de si há llegado ô no el caso de la obligacion en que se

(f.20) ha impuesto a si mismo caminar por su honor y el de su Monarquia, y de no consentir usurpaciones de lo que Dios le ha hecho Dueño.[1]

(f.20) in the margin
Siendo para ello buena ocasion (si es que pueda averla buena pars emprender una guerra) la de coger á la Inglaterra cansada, aunque triunfante, de la que sostiene contra la francia, seria fuerte desgracia que llegasse

(f.21) in the margin
nuestra necesidad / de hacersala quando con una paz ventajosa se huviesse libertado de la otra y puede recelarse que succeda sin nuestro conocimiento atendidos los antecedentes que ha referido á V. E. al fin de mi descripcion de nuestro estado politico con la Francia. Persuaden estos y algunos otras indicios con que nos hallamos, que la solicita esta eficazmente antes de

(f.22) left column
empezar / nueba Campaña, y los avisos del Conde de Fuentes nos inclinan à creer que recivira de buena gana al Ministro Ingles sus proposiciones porque no está tan solidamente unido despues de nuestro Reinado como antes, y porque sintiendosse ya demasiado las ruinas que causa la guerra empiezan a ser dificultosos los medios de hellar fondos para consumarla. Acaso Monsieur Sorba, Ministro de Genova en Paris, cuia introduccion familiar con los Ministros de francia conoce V. E. sera un Canal de que se sirvan para propalar las primeras aberturas

(f.23) left column
/ en Londres a donde pasa comisionado de su Republica; y con esta sospecha há mandado el Rey prevenir al Conde de Fuentes que le observe atentissimamente. Pero de V. E. es de quien S. M. con especialidad confia que ha de descubrir qualquier trato de Paz que en Paris se emprenda, ô admita, siendo importantissimo que no

---

[1] At this point the following two short paragraphs were cancelled:—

(f.20) Pero si se resuelve à este tremendo partido convendria sin duda establecer un Plazo de union con la Francia, enemiga actual de la Inglaterra, y para establecerle con mas ventajas nuestras convendria, no

(f.21) menos, disimular que son nuestros negocios los que nos / han movide à tomarle, y aparentar que son los Syuos, aviendo por fin dejadonos arrastrar de sus clamores.

Viene nui à protosito à este intento la ida de V. E. a Paris, pues podra atribuirse à su persona el vencimiento de la resistencia que han experimentado hasta aora.

(f.23)
left
column
(f.24)
left
column
la negocien sin que lo sepamos; mucho mas cara que antes, por el critico punto á que han llegado nuestros particulares negocios con / los Ingleses. Este es el primer servicio que ha de procurar V. E. hacer al Rey luego que llegue a Paris, y para proporcionarle si es posible el modo de conseguirlo le da S. M. permiso de introducirse en conversacion de union suya con el Christianisimo para continuar la guerra, aunque sin empeñar mas que su propria persona, y no la de S. M. hasta tener expressa orden. Parece podria V. E. hacerlo de esta manera.

(f.24)
right
column
Si no es en la primera, à pocas conversaciones se quejara naturalmente con V.E. el / Duque de Choiseul de que los hemos abandonado en la guerra actual y repetirá su sermon acostumbrado del riesgo que nos ofrece el engrandecimiento de los Ingleses. Bagasse V. E. el desentendido (que no lo extrañara viendole recien llegado) de todas nuestras repulsas, y procure inspirarle nuebas esperanzas, metiendole, si es posible en la idea

(f.25)
de que ofrezca à V. E. un Plazo de union / sobre el supuesto de que si este nos fuesse lisongero y tiene V. E. otras amañas que Don Jaime Masones para prometerse que no se desprecien entrando V. E. tan en lo interior es tambien natural que le descubra algun paso si tubiessen dado para la su negociacion particular con Ingleses, ô à lo menos que lo traluzca la penetracion de V. E. por el efecto que le haga una abertura tan clara de parte de

(f.26)
V. E. que le sorprendiera / como mas pesada. Ve aqui uno de dos objetos que lleba el encargo à V. E. de hacer este paso. Otro es, que si despues de pensarlo con la madurez que merece, se resolviesse el Rey à emplear sus fuerzas para tomar satisfaccion de las injusticias de los Ingleses, convendria sin duda establecer antes un Plan de union con la francia su Enemiga actual, y sacar en eso las posibles ventajas, dissimulando à este fin que Son nuestros

(f.27)
negocios / los que nos mueben, y aparentando que no son sino los suyos, aviendo por fin dejadonos arrastrar de sus razones, y clamores. Suelte pues V. E. como pensamiento suyo que si nos ofreciessen à Menorca

(f.27) en deposito para adquirirla en caso de tener favorable
exito la alianza seria fuerte tentacion para que no la
Ressistiessemos, pues el Rey estaria mui seguro de que
con este principio abrazarian gustosos la guerra sus vas-
(f.28) allos y se animarian à los mayores esfuerzos. /

Con lo dicho dá el Rey á V. E. campo para emplear
desde luego en Paris su activo zelo, y abrirse acaso
camino para las grandes Empresas de la Politica,
qual fuera, en caso de la necesidad que tenemos immediata,
un Pacto de union con la Francia ofensivo y defensivo.[1] S. M.
espera de V. E. los mayores aciertos y yo descole que
Dios le guarde.

---

[1] The words in italic were added between the lines in order to unfold the
ambiguity of "las grandes Empresas de la politica". The following words were
written in the margin beside this addition:—

O sino, asegurada en la una Prenda que nos pussiesse al abrigo de
ser por ella abandonados como otras vezes, ô cuia adquisicion nos
sirviesse à lo meons de consuelo.

APPENDIX 5

BIBLIOGRAPHY

Notes on Abbreviations

Shortened versions of the titles of the main works of reference have been used. Full details for the identification of them are only found in the bibliography, pp. 244-254.

The following abbreviations have also been used:

A.E., C.P.	Affaires Etrangères (Archives du ministère des), Correspondence Politique (Paris).
A.E., M.D.	Affaires Etrangères (Archives du ministère des), Mémoires et Documents (Paris).
A.H.R.	American Historical Review.
B.M., Add. MSS.	British Museum, Additional Manuscripts.
E.H.R.	English Historical Review.
H.A.H.R.	Hispanic American Historical Review.
J.M.H.	Journal of Modern History.
L.H. MSS.	Lansdowne House Manuscripts.
Pol. Corr.	Politische Correspondenz Friedrich's des Grossen.
P.R.O., S.P., F.	Public Record Office, State Papers, Foreign.
R.H.	Revue Historique.
R.H.D.	Revue d'Histoire Diplomatique.
R.H.S.T.	Royal Historical Society Transactions.

1. Manuscript Sources

I. Public Record Office:

State Papers, Foreign, France (S.P. 78), vols. 253-255.
State Papers, Foreign, Holland (S.P. 84), vols. 486, 487.
State Papers, Foreign, Portugal (S.P. 89), vols. 57, 58.
State Papers, Foreign, Spain (S.P. 94), vols. 159, 162, 166.
State Papers, Foreign, Treaties (S.P. 108), vol. 122.

Egremont Papers (G.D. 47), vols. 1, 3, 12, 21. This collection was deposited in the Public Record Office by Lord Leconfield of Petworth House, Sussex, as late as January 1947. It has never hitherto been used by any historians.

Vol. 1, contains some of the correspondence, mainly in copies, of Count of Viry, the Bailly de Solar, the Sardinian Envoys at the Courts of London and Paris respectively. Besides these there are letters from the Duke of Choiseul, the Count of Choiseul, relative to the Secret peace negotiations between England, France and Spain in 1762.

This volume contains only three original letters relative to these negotiations. By comparing that of April 16th from the Count of Choiseul to Egremont with a copy of the same letter in the Lansdowne House Manuscripts, 9, ff. 128-134 (now at the Clements Library at Ann Arbor, Michigan), only a few insignificant differences in the spelling, and the use of capital letters could be noticed. Copies of the same letters in this volume could also be found (apart from the L.H. MSS.), in the Newcastle Papers: Add. MSS. 32934-32942.

Vol. 3, contains some of Egremont's drafts, intended to be sent to Viry or to the two Choiseuls. These drafts are very interesting to compare with the final form of the letters in the Newcastle Papers, or in the Lansdowne House Manuscripts (in the Clements Library, at Ann Arbor in Michigan). Two drafts of the letter intended to be sent to Viry on March 21st are in this volume, a copy of the letter is in the Newcastle Papers, Add. MSS. 32936, ff. 1-8.

Vol. 21, of great value for it contains minutes of the secret first meetings on the peace negotiations in March 1762: e.g. that of March 9th, the very first known to have been held on the secret negotiations of 1762 between the "King's Ministers", before the peace question had ever been discussed in an open meeting. This minute is not in the Newcastle's Memoranda: Add. MSS. 32999-33000 where the rest of the minutes of the Cabinet Meetings on these negotiations can be found, other valuable information was drawn from the minutes of the two secret meetings of March 9th, and March 18th in this

R

volume: i.e. the names of the English Ministers in the secret of the negotiations.

II. British Museum:

Newcastle Manuscripts: Add. MSS: vols. 32866, 32901, 32902, 32918, 32921, 32923-32926, 32928, 32934-32941, 32944, 32999 (Memoranda vol. VII, April 1760-March 1762), 33000 (Memoranda vol. VIII, April 1762-June 1765).

III. Lansdowne House Manuscripts: (now in the Clements Library at Ann Arbor, Michigan) vols. 9-12.

Vols. 9-11, or according to another cataloguing vols. 1-3. These three volumes contain copies of the secret correspondence which passed at the end of 1761, in 1762 and 1763, relative to the peace between France, England and Spain. Most of these letters are those of Viry and Solar, the two Sardinian Envoys in London and Paris. In addition to these there are letters from the Duke of Choiseul, the Count of Choiseul; Lord Egremont, Lord Bute, some memoirs on proposals of the terms of peace etc. . . . The Viry-Solar correspondence, which constitutes the greater part of these volumes, contains all the correspondence which took place between the two Sardinian Envoys during the peace negotiations. Though a few of these letters are in the Egremont Papers, or in the Newcastle Manuscripts, yet the history of the peace negotiations of 1762 would have been incomplete if the Lansdowne House MSS. had not been consulted.

IV. Archives des Affaires Etrangères, Paris.

Correspondence Politique: Angleterre, 443, 444, 446-449. Autriche, 274, 275, 281, 286-288, 290. Espagne, 530-534, 536, 537. Hollande, 503. Portugal, 93, 94.

Mémoires et Documents: Angleterre, 41. Espagne, 574, 97, 189.

Espagne 189: is a very valuable memoir written by Sautreau de Marsy, an official of the French Ministry of Foreign Affairs, also a literary man (see Chapter III, p. 110, footnote 1). In this "Analyses des negocations entre la France et les Autres Puissances de l'Europe, 1748-1797", Sautreau particularly treats the relations between France and Spain from an impartial point of view. Many of his assessments on the policy of the Duke of Choiseul are sound and very true. Whereas the "Correspondance Politique" (at Quai d'Orsay, Paris) is well known to historians and often consulted by them, the "mémoires et Documents", in the same Library, are hardly consulted. The only work consulted in connection with this book, in which this memoir was used is L. Blart's *Les Rapports de la France et de l'Espagne après le Pacte de Famille.*

FRANCE et DIVERS ETATS, vol. 570, "Tableau Historique de la guerre de 1756 et des Négociations de la France, avec les differentes Cours de l'Europe depuis le Traité d'Aix la Chapelle jusqu'à la paix générale de 1763". This volume is of great value for explaining what had taken place in some of the French Cabinet meetings. Besides it is a valuable source on relations between France and England and Spain. This volume is not used at all by any of the books relevant to the subject.

V. Simancas, Madrid.

Estado. Leg. 3457, n.38: Instructions of January 14th 1761, to Grimaldi for his embassy in Paris. A very valuable document in defining the policy of Charles III towards France.

2. PRINTED BOOKS

ADOLPHUS, JOHN. *The History of England from the Accession to the Decease of King George The Third*, 7 vols., London 1840-1845.

AITON, ARTHUR S. "The Diplomacy of the Louisiana Cession", *American Historical Review*, vol. XXXVI, pp.701-720, 1931. Valuable article based on original authorities.

ALBEMARLE, (G. T. Keppel) Sixth Earl of. *Memoirs of the Marquis of Rockingham and his Contemporaries*, 2 volumes, London, 1852.

ALVORD, CLARENCE W. *The Mississippi Valley in British Politics*, 2 vols. Cleveland, U.S.A., 1917.

BECCATINI, FRANCESCO. *Vida de Carlos III de Bourbon, Rey Católico de España y de Las Indias*, 2 vols. Madrid, 1790.

BEDFORD, (John Russell) Fourth Duke of. *Correspondence of*, Ed. Lord John Russell, 3 vols. London 1842-1846. Important original documents.

BEER, G. L. *British Colonial Policy, 1754-1765*, New York 1907.

BLART, L. *Les Rapports de la France et de l'Espagne après le Pacte de Famille*, Paris 1913. Useful bibliography; MSS. authorities.

BOISLISLE, A DE. *Les Conseils du Roi sous Louis XIV*, Paris 1884.

BOURGUET, ALFRED. "Le Duc de Choiseul et L'Angleterre, La Mission de Monsieur de Bussy à Londres", *Revue Historique*, vol. LXXI, 1-32, 1899. Based on official documents.

———"Le Duc de Choiseul et l'Angleterre, Les Pourparlers de La Haye", *Revue d'Histoire Diplomatique*, vol. XVII, pp. 456-468, 541-556, 1903. Based on official documents.

———*Le Duc de Choiseul et l'Alliance Espagnole*, Paris 1906. Based on official documents.

———"Le Duc de Choiseul et l'Alliance Espagnole, après le Pacte de Famille", *Revue Historique*, vol. XCIV. pp. 1-27, 1907. Based on original sources: French Manuscripts authorities.

———*Etudes sur la Politique Etrangère du Duc de Choiseul*, Paris 1907. Based on official documents.

BOUTARIC, E. *Correspondence Secrete de Louis XV*, 2 vols., Paris 1866.

BROWN, VERA LEE. *Studies in The History of Spain in the second half of the Eighteenth Century* (Smith College Studies in History, vol. XV, Nos. 1, 2, 1929-1930). 1st Study: "The Spanish Court and Its Diplomatic Outlook after The Treaty of Paris 1763", especially useful in explaining the policy of Charles III. 2nd Study: "Anglo-French Rivalry for the Trade of the Spanish Peninsula, 1763-1783". Very useful survey of the commercial relations between England and Spain from 1667-1764.

BUCKINGHAMSHIRE, (John Hobart) 2nd Earl of. *Despatches and Correspondence of*, ed. A. D. Collyer, 2 vols., London 1900-1902. Useful for Frederic's views of Bute's desertion. Dorn, W. L. used it in defending Bute's policy towards Frederic II in his article "Frederic the Great and Lord Bute".

CAMBRIDGE HISTORY of British Foreign Policy, vol. 1, Cambridge 1922. Useful introduction by A. W. Ward.

CAMBRIDGE HISTORY of the British Empire, vol. 1, Cambridge 1929. Useful bibliography on "The Peace of Paris" by H. W. TEMPERLEY.

CARRÉ, HENRI. *Le Règne de Louis XV, 1715-1774* (Histoire de la France depuis les Origines jusqu'à la Révolution, vol. VIII, 2) Paris 1909. Useful for inside information on Government administration in France at that time.

CHATHAM (William Pitt), First Earl of. *Correspondence of*, ed. W. S. Taylor and T. H. Pringle, 4 vols. London 1838-1840.

CHOISEUL. *Correspondence entre Bernstorff et, 1758-1766*, Copenhagen, 1871. The Duke of Choiseul unfolds his policy and views to his Danish friend.

CHOISEUL, DUC DE. *Mémoires du, 1719-1785*, ed. F. Calmettes, Paris 1904. Especially Choiseul's "Mémoire Justificatif" of 1765, explaining his policy.

CHRISTELOW, ALLAN. "French Interest in the Spanish Empire During the Ministry of The Duc de Choiseul, 1759-1771", *Hispanic American Historical Review*, vol. XXI, pp. 515-537, 1941. Based on original authorities; especially on Beliardi's (French Consul General in Spain at the time) Papers in the Bibliothèque Nationale, Paris.

——"Economic Background of The Anglo-Spanish War of 1762", *Journal of Modern History*, vol. XVIII, pp. 22-36, 1946.

——"Great Britain and The Trades from Cadiz and Lisbon to Spanish America and Brazil, 1759-1783", *Hispanic American Historical Review*, vol. XXVII, pp. 2-29, 1947.

COLLADO (Manuel), DANVILA Y. *Reinado de Carlos III*, 6 vols. Madrid 1893-1896.

CONN, STETSON. *Gibraltar in British Diplomacy in the Eighteenth Century* (Yale Historical Publications Miscellany, vol. XLI), London 1942.

CORBETT, JULIAN S. *England in the Seven Years' War*, 2 vols., London 1907.

COXE, W. *Memoirs of the Kings of Spain of the House of Bourbon from 1700-1788*, 4 vols., London 1813.

DESJARDINS, G. *Fonds du Conseil d'Etat, Extrait de la Bibliothèque de l'Ecole de Chartes*, Paris 1898.

DORN, WALTER L. "Frederic the Great and Lord Bute", *Journal of Modern History*, vol. 1, pp. 529-560, 1929. Valuable article for acquitting Bute on charges of treachery towards Frederic. Based on official documents.

ENTICK, JOHN. *The General History of the Late War*, 5 vols., London 1763-1764.

FITZMAURICE, Lord EDMOND C. *Life of William Earl of Shelburne*, 3 vols., London 1875-1876.

FLASSAN, GAETAN DE RAXIS DE. *Histoire Générale et Raisonnée de la Diplomatic Française . . . depuis la fondation de la Monarchie jusqu'à la fin du Règne de Louis XV*, 7 vols., Paris 1811. Valuable assessments on French diplomacy towards Spain and England. Often uses passages from A.E., M.D., Espagne, 189; and A.E., M.D., France et Divers Etats, 570 without referring to them.

FRIEDRICHS DES GROSSEN. *Politische Correspondenz*, ed. by J. C. Droysen, M. D. Duncker, H. C. L. Von Sybel, 30 vols., Berlin 1879-1885.

GENTLEMAN'S MAGAZINE, vol. XXVI, 1756. (England's and France's declarations of war against each other in 1756).

GEORGE III. *Letters from, to Lord Bute, 1756-1766*, ed. Sedgwick Romney, London 1939.

GRANT, M. W. LAWSON. *La Mission de M. de Bussy à Londres en 1761*, Paris 1906.

GRENVILLE PAPERS. Ed. W. J. Smith, 4 vols., London 1852.

GUILLON, E. *Port Mahon, La France à Minorque sous Louis XV*, Paris 1893.

HOTBLACK, KATE. "The Peace of Paris, 1763", *Royal Historical Society Transactions*, Third Series, vol. 11, pp. 235-267 1908.

——*Chatham's Colonial Policy*, London 1917.

HUNT, WILLIAM. *Political History of England from the Accession of George III to the Close of Pitt's First Administration, 1760-1801*, London 1905.

——"Pitt's retirement from office, 5 October 1761", *E.H.R.*, XXI, pp. 119-132, 1906.

ILCHESTER (G. S. H. Strangways), Sixth Earl of. *Henry Fox, First Lord Holland*, 2 vols., London 1920.

INNIS, HAROLD ADAMS. *The Cod Fisheries*, New Haven 1940.

JENKINSON PAPERS, 1760-1766. Ed. Ninetta S. Tucker, London 1949.

JOBEZ, M. ALPHONSE. *La France sous Louis XV, 1715-1774*, 6 vols., Paris 1864-1873.

JOHNSON, SAMUEL. *Works of*, new edition, 12 vols., London 1806 (vol. 11).

LECKY, W. E. H. *A History of England in the Eighteenth Century*, 7 vols. New edition, London 1895.

LENNOX, Lady SARAH. *Life and Letters of, 1745-1826*, ed. Countess of Ilchester and Lord Stavordale, 2 vols., London 1902. A useful introductory memoir by Henry Fox on the policy of the period in England.

LODGE, RICHARD. *Great Britain and Prussia in the Eighteenth Century*, Oxford 1929.

LUYNES (Albert), DUC DE. *Mémoires du, sur La Cour de Louis XV, 1735-1758*. Published by L. Dussieux, and E. Soulie, 17 vols., Paris 1864. Useful contemporary reports and accounts.

Mauduit, Israel. *Considerations on The Present German War*, 4th ed., London 1761 (Pamphlet).

Mémoire Historique *sur La Négociation de la France et de l'Angleterre, depuis le 26 mars 1761 jusqu'au 20 Septembre de la même Année, avec les pièces justificatives*, Paris 1761 (see chapter III, p. 112, footnote 4).

Mitchell, Sir Andrew. *Memoirs and Papers of*, ed. A. Bisset, 2 vols., London 1850.

Morel-Fatio, A. *Etudes sur l'Espagne*, 2ième Serie, Paris 1890.

Muret, Pierre. *La Prépondérance Anglaise, 1715-1763* (Peuples et Civilisations, vol. XI), 2nd edition, Paris 1942.

McLachlan, Jean O. "The Seven Years' Peace and the West Indian Policy of Carvajal and Wall", *English Historical Review*, LIII, pp.457-477, 1938.

——*Trade and Peace with Old Spain, 1667-1750*, Cambridge 1940.

Namier, L. B. *England in the Age of the American Revolution*, London 1930.

Nuñez, Fernan. *la Vida de Carlos III*, published by Morel-Fatio and A. Paz y Melia, 2 vols., Madrid 1898.

Pares, R. *War and Trade in the West Indies 1739-1763*, Oxford 1936.

——*Colonial Blockade and Neutral Rights, 1739-1763*, Oxford 1938.

Parliamentary History of England. Ed. W. Cobbett and T. Wright, 36 vols., 1806-1820.

Perey, Lucien. *Un Petit neveu de Mazarin*, 3rd ed., Paris 1891. (The Duke of Nivernais, French plenipotentiary in London during the negotiations of peace between France and England in 1762-1763.)

——*le President Hénault et Madame du Deffand, La Cour du Régent, La Cour de Louis XV et de Marie Leczinska*, Paris 1893.

Pol. Corr. See *Friedrichs des Grossen Pol. Corr.*

RAMSEY, JOHN F. *Anglo-French Relations, 1763-1770*, (University of California Publications in History, vol. XVII, No. 3) 1939.

RECUEIL DES INSTRUCTIONS *données aux ambassadeurs et Ministres de France depuis les Traités de Westphalie jusqu'à la Revolution Française.*

——*Russie 11*, vol. IX, Paris 1890.

——*Espagne III*, vol. XII, bis, Paris 1899, of great value for the French Foreign policy of that period.

RENAULT, FRANCIS P. *Le Pacte de Famille et l'Amerique, La Politique Coloniale Franco-Espagnole 1760-1792*, Paris 1922.

RIKER, THAD W. *Henry Fox, first Lord Holland*, 2 vols., Oxford 1911. Very useful for the policy of that period in England.

RIO, D. ANTONIO FERRER DEL. *Historia de Renado de Carlos III in España*, 4 vols., Madrid 1856.

ROBERTSON, CHARLES G. *Chatham and the British Empire*, London 1946.

ROPES, ARTHUR R. "The Causes of the Seven Years' War", *Royal Historical Society Transactions*, New Series, vol. IV, pp.143-170, London 1889.

ROUSSEAU, FRANÇOIS. *Règne de Charles III d'Espagne, 1759-1788* 2 vols., Paris 1907.

RUVILLE, A. VON. *William Pitt, Earl of Chatham*, translated by H. J. Chaytor and Mary Morison, 3 vols., London and New York 1907.

SOULANGE-BODIN, A. *La Diplomatie de Louis XV et Le Pacte de Famille*, Paris 1894.

SAINT-LÉGER, ALEXANDRE DE. *La Flandre Maritime et Dunkerque sous la domination Française (1659-1789)*, Paris 1900.

SUTHERLAND, L. S. "The East India Company and the Peace of Paris", *English Historical Review*, vol LXII, pp. 179-190, 1947.

TEMPERLEY, H. W. See *The Cambridge History of the British Empire*.

THACKERAY, FRANCIS. *A History of the Right Honourable William Pitt, Earl of Chatham*, 2 vols., London 1827. Very useful for its documents especially with regard to France and England during the negotiations of 1761, and to Spain and England in 1759-1761.

WADDINGTON, RICHARD. "Le Renversement des Alliances en 1756", *Revue Historique*, LVIII, pp. 1-43, 241-275, Paris 1895.

——*Louis XV et le Renversement des Alliances*, Paris 1896.

——*La Guerre de Sept Ans*, 5 vols., Paris 1899-1914. Very valuable work based on different Manuscript Sources.

WALPOLE (Horace), Fourth Earl of Orford. *Letters of*, ed. Peter Cunningham, 9 vols., London 1857-1859.

——*Memoirs of The Reign of George II*. Ed. Lord Holland, 2nd edition, 3 vols., London 1846.

——*Memoirs of The Reign of George III*. Ed. by Denis le Marchant Bart, 4 vols., London 1894.

WILLIAMS, BASIL. *The Life of William Pitt, Earl of Chatham*, 2 vols., London 1913.

WINSTANLEY, D. A. *Personal and Party Government, 1706-1766*, Cambridge 1910.

YORKE, PHILIP C. *The Life and Correspondence of Philip Yorke, Lord of Hardwicke*, 3 vols., Cambridge 1913.

INDEX

255

S₁